Dying to Tell

Dying to Tell

ANGOLA
Crime, Consequence, Conclusion
at Louisiana State Penitentiary

by
Anne Butler
and
C. Murray Henderson

Published by The Center for Louisiana Studies
University of Southwestern Louisiana
Lafayette, Louisiana

ABOUT THE AUTHOR

Anne Butler has been a working photojournalist since 1964 when she graduated from Sweet Briar College in Virginia with a BA in English. She received an MA in English from Humboldt State in California, and began her first job in Washington, D. C., writing tour books for AAA. She worked on the West Coast for several years, then moved back to her native Louisiana, where she and her two children live near rural St. Francisville on a family plantation dating from the 1790s.

She is a regular contributor of feature articles for such regional publications as the *Baton Rouge State Times-Morning Advocate* newspaper, *Louisiana Life*, and *Mississippi Magazine*. She has also written for national magazines like *Country Woman* and *Victorian Accents*, and has done video scripts and promotional copy. She is the author of nine published books.

Other Books by Anne Butler (Hamilton)

James M. Imahara: Son of Immigrants

Little Chase and Big Fat Aunt May

Little Chase and Big Fat Aunt May Ride Again

*The Little Chase and Big Fat Aunt May Recipe Book:
A Cook's Tour of Hog Heaven*

*A Tourist's Guide to West Feliciana Parish:
A Little Bit of Heaven Right Here on Earth*

The Herman and Little Leon Stories

The Travels of Baby Stewart

*More Than a Cookbook:
An Eclectic Collection*

*Angola: Louisiana State Penitentiary,
A Half-Century of Rage and Reform*

Library of Congress Catalog Number: 91-77530
ISBN Number: 978-1-935754-56-5

University of Louisiana at Lafayette Press
P.O. Box 40831
Lafayette, LA 70504-0831
http://ulpress.org

CONTENTS

Acknowledgments

Photographs provided by *The Angolite*, Michael Burge, Nell Holmes, Capitol City Press, Vernon and Elizabeth Harvey, The Shreveport Times, Kay Smith.

We are grateful to past and present Angola administrators for professional courtesies extended.

We are also grateful to those who had the courage to share their stories with our readers.

Introduction

Severe neglect and abuse during the formative childhood years, institutionalization in our "schools for crime" for delinquent youth, racial prejudice and mistreatment, the trauma of savage combat and the commission of terrible atrocities in a questionable and unappreciated war, greed and a hunger for power, maybe even bad blood . . . all of these are factors contributing to the killings and dyings we cover in depth in this book.

Are these factors and others like them to be blamed for the wasted lives, the suffering and pain, perhaps making of the criminal as much of a victim as the object of his lawless acts? Or are they mere excuses, cop-outs for crime? Are criminals born, or are they made by an environment insensitive to their early cries for help, one which forces them to fight viciously for survival and goads them until they lose any sense of compassion for their fellow man?

No one wants to be the victim of a crime, especially not a violent one, and this book is not intended as an *apologia* for criminal actions. But we must understand that, however easy it is to condemn crime on the face of it, issues are never quite so clear-cut black and white once we delve beneath the surface and recognize all of the participants, both criminal and victim, as flesh-and-blood people who come in all shades of gray.

Given that they all started out as equals, how did one happen to take the crooked path to a life of crime, preying upon those trodding the straight-and-narrow? And more importantly, how can we keep the children of the future from becoming criminals in their time? For it is at that earliest end of the spectrum, the beginning of life and the origin of experience, that we must concentrate our preventive efforts; what we do at the other end, in particular the imposition of the death penalty, seems to have proven futile. It has been said, and rightfully, that the best crime-prevention tool we have is Operation Head Start. It's no use, the old folks have always admonished, closing the barn door once the cow's gotten out.

Our examination of the fascinating details of these criminal cases and the people involved may shed some light on the age-old dilemma of what to do about crime and make it possible to draw some conclusions as to causes and solutions.

We will be guided in our search for answers by one of the country's most highly respected professional penologists, C. Murray Henderson, former warden at the state penitentiaries of Iowa, Louisiana and Tennessee, which state he also served as Commissioner of Correction. In the Louisiana correctional system, where these stories take place (though there are similar cases in every prison population), Henderson was the longest tenured warden of the sprawling 18,000-acre state pen at Angola and later chief executive officer of the state's forensic facility for the criminally insane, from which he recently retired.

His extensive experience in corrections, combined with his law degree and training in psychiatric social work, rendered him uniquely qualified to fill those demanding positions, and also allows him to help us make some sense of crime and criminals.

For, after all, it is only in understanding the problem that we may reasonably expect to come up with some solutions.

Dying to Tell

I

"Racist Pigs Who Hold Us Captive":
Death of a Correctional Officer

The hottest new trends and latest fashions might surface first in Los Angeles or New York, but it never takes long for each movement to make its way inland from the coasts, sweeping across the entire country, seeping into even the most isolated nooks and crannies. This was especially so during the turbulent decade of the seventies, uneasy years scarred by well-televised anti-war activism and racial militancy, punctuated by catch words like Angela Davis and the Soledad Brothers, *Hair* and Ravi Shankar's sitar music, McGovern and Muskie and Humphrey, the wounding of George Wallace and death of longtime FBI head J. Edgar Hoover, folk hero-hijacker D. B. Cooper parachuting into the wilderness with his ransom money and Jane Fonda winning an Academy Award, astronauts walking on the moon and on earth the far-reaching tragedies of the Vietnam involvement. "Power to the People" and "Hell No, We Won't Go." "Come Together" and "Up Against the Wall, Motherfucker."

Into the South spread this same unrest, threading tendrils of tension throughout the crowded cities, unfurling fog-like fingers of unease along rural backroads ripe for upheaval. At a regional seminar on the Baton Rouge campus of Southern University, U.S. Congressman Charles C. Diggs of Michigan, one-time head of the congressional black caucus, denounced Louisiana's representative John R. Rarick as a bigot, calling Rarick on his own home turf the laughing-stock of Congress because of his vicious and outdated racial prejudice.

It was also in Baton Rouge that a bloody street battle would take place on January 10, 1972, near the Temple Theater on North Boulevard, a blighted black section downtown. Pitting Black Muslims against police, the violent confrontation would leave two sheriff's deputies and three black militants dead, a local television newsman beaten so badly as to cause permanent paralysis and brain-damage, 700 national guardsmen and 100 state police activated to enforce nightly curfews, and persistent rumors of assassination plots targeting the local mayor, district attorney and police chief in the aftermath of the struggle. The riot was said to have been incited by out-of-state militants who arrived in Louisiana's capital city late in December promising to "deliver the city back to black people," according to newspaper accounts.

Not far north of Baton Rouge, in the isolated reaches of West Feliciana Parish, a struggle of a different sort was going on at the immense Louisiana State Penitentiary known as Angola, the familiar fight for improved race relations and human rights somehow becoming inextricably intermingled with an entirely separate struggle for power and political clout, an inappropriate combination that turned an already chaotic situation into an explosive and deadly one.

Some 18,000 acres combining several plantations whose antebellum slaves had come from the African country giving the prison its name, Angola was purchased by the state of Louisiana around the turn of the century, the initial idea being to profit from the backbreaking labor of its convicts, whom the state had formerly leased to private planters to till the same rich farmlands.

Surrounded on three sides by the Mississippi River whose raging floodwaters often engulfed its low-lying fields and on the fourth side by the rugged Tunica Hills wilderness area, Angola was still not so isolated as to remain untouched by the tensions of the times, particularly in light of the deplorable conditions perpetuated by pathetically inadequate funding, political patronage and public unconcern.   Governor John J. McKeithen had in 1968 reached out of state to enlist the aid of professional penologists C. Murray Henderson and Lloyd W. Hoyle, Jr. Challenged to clean up the penitentiary as warden and deputy warden, the two men, one from Tennessee and the other from Iowa, found Angola in a shocking state and, during the time they were there, longer than any other administration, would make drastic and far-reaching changes.

To supervise some 4000 inmates, they found less than 300 paid employees, some of whom, illiterate and untrained, could hardly be called professionals. To supplement the meager paid staff, convict trusties were armed for guard duty, a situation rife with abuse and all too often punctuated by shotgun blasts as opposing inmate-guards blazed away at each other from watchtowers or "accidentally" settled old scores with bullets.   Inmate canteens, where prisoners were supposed to purchase necessities with coupons torn from individual books at the cash register, were mismanaged to the extent that correctional officers rather than inmates were spending "wads of coupons as big as your fist," none of which should have been in their possession. This abuse was made possible by the lack of a reliable identification system for the prison; inmates were identified solely by the name and number stencilled on their clothing, with no allowance made for the ability of clever inmates to switch outfits.

At least two of the farflung inmate camps on prison grounds had repeatedly been condemned, with makeshift stoves and filthy wooden tables in unsanitary kitchens full of roaches and rats, cratered concrete floors where stagnant water stood for weeks at a time, malfunctioning sewers, electrical panels filled with pennies in place of fuses and exposed wires from which laundry was hung. If prisoners wanted decent clothing or toilet articles, they pretty well had to get them from home, for the prison had no funds to furnish even these basic necessities. Inmates were triple and quadruple-bunked, dangerously jammed into crowded dormitories lacking window screens or ventilation, filled during the interminable hot summer nights with armies of bloodthirsty mosquitoes and heated in

Colonel Mike Gunnells.
Photo courtesy of *The Angolite.*

Right: Deputy Warden Lloyd Hoyle.
Photo courtesy of *The Angolite.*

winter by a single small stove. In Camp H, one of the worst, just two working showers and four toilets, rarely all functional at once, served the needs of some 600 prisoners.

Inmates from predominantly urban areas were put to work in agricultural pursuits, rather than given any vocational training which might prove useful upon release, and the agribusiness section owed almost $300,000 for unpaid convict incentive wages. Said Lloyd Hoyle, "There wasn't anything up there that met any acceptable standards, and you've got to take care of the standard of living before you can do anything with rehabilitation. If an inmate doesn't have a decent place to sleep or adequate bedding or showers or clothing, you can't do anything with him, because all he's going to be doing is complaining about the facilities and the support. What we wanted to do was start academic and vocational programs to give the inmates avenues to do something other than cut sugar cane and pull Johnson grass out of the vegetables."

On top of deplorable living conditions, the prison in the early seventies remained totally segregated, a situation bound to bring trouble given the large majority of black inmates. This served to attract the attention of Dorothy Taylor of New Orleans, a black member of the state legislature who campaigned for office on a platform promising prison reform and who made several well-publicized fact-finding trips to the state penitentiary. While welcoming any assistance in upgrading conditions at the prison, which they heartily agreed were substandard and unacceptable, penitentiary administrators soon realized that tension noticeably increased following Mrs. Taylor's visits and eventually barred her from the grounds after members of her retinue organized a sit-down strike among inmates.

It was impossible, however, to shut out the racial unrest sweeping the country, and soon a small Black Panther group organized behind prison walls. In early April the fourth anniversary of the slaying of Dr. Martin Luther King was marked by memorial services in Baton Rouge, where area black leaders called for renewed vigor in the push for minority rights. By the middle of the month, black militants within Angola would choose a more violent method to leave their own bloody mark on history.

Sunday, April 16, 1972, was correctional officer Mike Gunnells' first day working at Hickory dormitory. Only 18 when he had first applied for a job at the prison the year before, Gunnells lived in Lettsworth, across the Mississippi River from Angola where many of the penitentiary's most dedicated employees came from. His own father worked at Angola until retirement, as did an older brother. So it was only natural that Mike consider a career in corrections as well, once he graduated from Innis High School, married and became an expectant father.

But Sunday, April 16, was very nearly Mike Gunnell's *last* day working at Hickory dorm as well as his first. This was the era of understaffing, remember, when dorm units consisting of four buildings, each holding up to 75 inmates, were of necessity supervised by only one or two employees. One officer had to escort inmates to the dining hall to eat, leaving a single guard alone on the dormitories during mealtimes. Outside the dorms was a little wooden shack, maybe 5 x 5-feet square, with a window on each side and a telephone on the wall. There the overworked officer operated keys for opening and closing doors, oversaw the constant inmate roaming from dorm to dorm, performed head counts of all four dormitories, used the phone as his only outside contact with superiors, and checked dorm interiors as well as busy walkways.

Unarmed, unequipped with beepers or radios or other modern-day means of alerting authorities to trouble or calling for help, the dorm officer could have as many as 300 inmates to supervise, a near impossibility, and some of those inmates just might be coming back from work in the industrial and vocational areas carrying concealed contraband items like handmade knives or combustibles. In the metal shops where prison furniture was made, in the tag plant where license plates were produced, in any of the shops inmates could steal a bit of metal and hone it into a dangerous weapon. Shakedown crews searched the inmates as often as possible and came up with washtubs full of knives from surprise dormitory raids, but with limited manpower, it was a matter of robbing Peter to pay Paul, leaving another area uncovered in order to man a shakedown team. This was thus a period at Angola marred by unnecessary violence, like the firebombings when the little wooden guard shacks were set afire, sometimes with lightbulbs which had been drilled, filled with combustible liquid and replaced to await the flip of the light switch, when the unwary guard would be showered with a sheet of flame.

Mike Gunnells was sitting in just such a guard shack outside all-black Hickory dorm the afternoon of Sunday, April 16, working on his rosters, when he happened to notice some suspicious inmate movement on the walk. "It was right after the other officer left me to go to the kitchen to feed, and I knew something was wrong, because there was a lot of movement on the walk and it was like people were moving not so much to go somewhere and do something but more to get out of the way of what was possibly going to happen. I felt something was wrong, but because of my lack of experience, I didn't really know what it was."

He continues, "I remember looking back, and I saw two inmates coming toward the shack, and one of them had one of these big cans like we ordered peanut butter in, about a five-gallon can, gold in color. The other one, he was a real tall black guy with a bandana over his face, and he was lighting a piece of paper, and it just kind of flared up. I hadn't been there long, but I knew that something serious was happening."

Trapped in the guard house, Gunnells decided that if he made a run for safety, he'd surely be drenched by the flammable liquid he figured was in the can and turned into a human torch. His alternative was not much more attractive, but he decided to remain inside the shack. "It was all happening pretty fast," he recalls, "but I decided the best thing for me to do was just wait and when it came in, to just do what I could. So they came on up the walk and when they got to the door, the guy with the can threw it into the shack. When he threw it, I ducked and got real low. It smelled like gasoline or diesel, and hit the desk and the wall. The other guy threw in the paper, right away, and it burst into flames."

The inmates didn't wait to see the results, heading immediately up the walk toward the dorm called Walnut. "When they did," Gunnells says, "I busted out of the shack." Hair singed, ear badly burned, shirt on fire, the young correctional officer hurried into the lavatory of Hickory I, where he threw water on his flaming shoulders and rinsed his eyes, then reported the incident to the guard captain working on the next unit.

Twenty-one-year-old black inmate Rory Mason, in Angola on a fifteen-year sentence from New Orleans for attempted aggravated rape, would be identified by Gunnells as one of the inmates who set the guard shack afire; his accomplice would never be officially identified. Mason denied involvement as well, but would later be tried and convicted of aggravated arson. A letter, addressed to the editor of the *Sunday Advocate* newspaper in Baton Rouge and intercepted by prison authorities immediately after the crime, took credit for the burning of Gunnells and promised other unspecified acts of violence aimed at bringing Angola to the attention of a public which had "turned away," making the public as guilty as "the racist pigs who hold us captive." Signed by "The VanGuard Army, Long Live the Angola Prison Involvement," the letter added that a "people's court" held Sunday had convicted prison authorities of "extreme racism."

The shaken young officer, who asked to be taken off the walk and assigned to a patrol job for awhile before returning to work in close contact with inmates, even then had the insight to realize that there was nothing personal in the attack. "There was this Black Panther movement at the time among some of the inmate population," Gunnells relates, "and I think their motive or objective was to seriously hurt an officer. I hadn't been there very long, I'd never had any kind of problem with the inmates, and I don't think it was personal. It was just something that they had to do, and it didn't matter if I'd been John Doe, it was going to happen. It was just a movement that was going on and a part of the times, and it just happened."

Futhermore, Gunnells continues, "Looking back, I can see that it was all related. They wanted to seriously hurt an officer, and the first one would have been me. And when they didn't succeed with that, well, then, the next day it was Brent."

Brent Miller, like Mike Gunnells, came by his correctional career naturally, having grown up on Angola, where an older brother worked and his father, Huey, sometimes known to other employees as "Hoglot" Miller, supervised the swine farm, riding herd on up to 5,000 hogs until declining health forced his retirement after 19 years. The seven Miller children were exceptionally close, part of a loving and respected Angola family. Says Jewel Miller, the mother, "We didn't have very much money, but we had a lot of love in our family, I mean a *lot* of love. We were all very, very close."

Brent, to whom his mother refers as "a little blond-headed boy, blue-eyed and very, very sweet," was a middle child, born after Huey Jr. and Nix, born before Hardy, Stan, Wanda and John. All of the children were musically talented and formed a popular family band to play at school dances and other entertainments, and most of the boys played football, with Nix winning an athletic scholarship to Northeast and Brent hoping to follow in his footsteps until an early marriage tied him to Angola for good.

Brent Miller in high school.
Photo courtesy of Mrs. Huey Miller.

The 1968 *Felicianian*, yearbook of St. Francisville High, pictures Brent Miller as an outstanding junior wingback on the Saints' football team, returning punts, making touchdowns and escorting one of the maids in the homecoming court. Interestingly, the only autographs in the back of this yearbook are inscriptions to Brent from loving younger siblings, a pencil-drawn heart labeled "Sisterly Love," an inscription "To a brother that is so nice and considerant (*sic*) and so true, I think you are so sweet because I take after you" from Wanda, another "To a sweet, smart and nice brother that I love" from John. And in a childish scrawl, the inevitable "Brent the Rat!"

As the year 1972 began, Huey Sr. was supervising the pig farm at Angola, Huey Jr. was working on the front gate at the prison, Nix was away at college in Monroe studying to become a history professor, and Brent, having graduated from high school and travelled to Oklahoma to work, had returned to Angola with plans of working there only temporarily before returning to an anticipated job opening in the midwest or enrolling in college. Then on February 5 he married Leontine Rogers, daughter of an engineer in the penitentiary sugar mill who had her own roots at Angola, and the young couple settled down to life there; ironically, the call for Brent to return to work in Oklahoma would come, but several weeks too late.

The night of April 16, 1972, Huey Jr. had worked at the front gate, and when he got off duty, Jewel Miller recalls that he stopped to tell her of trouble in the main prison. The two went next door to a neighbor's home where they could use one of the special Angola telephones to call Brent, who'd just gone on duty at 6 a.m. in the medium-security section of the prison. "Huey Jr. went and called, and he talked to Brent," Mrs. Miller remembers. "I went with him over there. And he said 'Brent, you'd better be careful.' That was around 7 o'clock in the morning. And Brent said, 'Oh, I am.' He said, 'They're spitting on my cage right now.' The inmates were spitting on the guard cage that he was in. And it wasn't but I guess just a few minutes later that that happened."

What happened was that Brent Miller, sometime between 7:30 and 7:45 on the morning of Monday, April 17, 1972, the day after the burning of correctional officer Mike Gunnells in the same medium-security area made up of four dormitory complexes called Pine, Hickory, Oak and Walnut, apparently left the guard shack and entered Pine I dormitory to have coffee with an elderly inmate named Hezekiah Brown. The other correctional officer on duty in the same area, Lemuel Hunter, had been summoned to the prison kitchen to help quell a disturbance caused by inmate workers refusing to serve breakfast and demanding to be put on a two-shift workday, leaving Miller alone in an area which should ideally have been staffed by at least five professionals. The disturbance, called in Angola's peculiar parlance a "buck," would later prove to have been a planned distraction to draw security officers off the walk.

In his sixties, gregarious Hezekiah Brown was at Angola with a sentence of natural life for aggravated rape in New Orleans, where he had a family and worked as a longshoreman. Brown had served short sentences in institutions in Oklahoma,

Mississippi and Arkansas, but only for relatively minor crimes. An old ankle injury put him on "light duty" status at Angola, where he made coffee every morning in Pine I.

He was bending over the coffee pot on the morning of April 17, as officer Brent Miller sat on his bunk conversing and awaiting a cup, when Hezekiah Brown heard a scuffle and looked up to see an inmate grab Miller around the neck from behind and stab him. Other inmates joined in, dragging the officer from the bunk as they too savagely stabbed him. Hezekiah Brown backed up against the dormitory wall, frozen with fear, as the assailants left the young officer in a widening pool of blood and ran out of the dormitory door.

Brent Miller's mother recalled his telling her that once during a disturbance at Angola, other officers had given him a chain to use in subduing unruly inmates. "He said that the inmates were begging him not to hit them, and he said to me, 'Mama, I wouldn't hit one of them for nothing in the world, I just couldn't do that.'" Now this fair-haired laughing baby boy who loved everybody, this high school football hero, this new bridegroom, lay dead on the floor, stabbed thirty-two times with at least two knives, his hands in death rigidly clenched into fists from trying to grab and fend off the sharpened blades.

Death came quickly, within four minutes, according to West Feliciana Coroner Dr. Alfred Gould, and resulted primarily from a five-inch-deep cut through the front chest into the upper lobe of the left lung and another six-inch-deep wound through the left shoulder into the chest cavity which cut the left side of the trachea, causing aspiration of blood into both lungs and subsequent asphixiation. The blows were so brutal as to collapse the chest cavity completely; during the mandatory autopsy, small medical sticks inserted into each wound for the purpose of photographic evidence gave the body a porcupine appearance, according to a lab assistant, and afterward, a #10 tin can was inserted into the caved-in chest to return some contour to the body.

Correctional officer Brent Miller, age twenty-three at the time of the attack, had had time to mouth only one last word. That word was an anguished "Why?"

Hezekiah Brown ran wildly from the dormitory, realized he was still dressed in his pajamas, returned to throw on some clothes and rushed off to the blood plasma unit of the prison to establish an alibi. When prison authorities, along with interrogators from the parish sheriff's department and state police, questioned him along with the 800 other inmates assigned to the medium-security area, he denied any knowledge of the incident for several days, until the warden confronted him with the testimony of a second inmate called "Specs," who had also been in the back of the dormitory that day and, while not in a position to see the killing, knew that Hezekiah Brown had been present and *had* seen it.

Brown identified three inmates as the killers: "Fox, Hooks and Noxema Black." These were the prison nicknames of three convicts from the New Orleans area. "Fox," whom Brown named as the one who had first grabbed Miller, was Albert Woodfox, age twenty-five and with a mottled skin condition making him easily identifiable. Known as a hardcore militant, Woodfox was in Angola with a term of fifty years for the armed

Right: Angola inmate Rory Mason.
Photo courtesy of *The Angolite*.

Below: Confiscated inmate weapons.
Photo courtesy of *The Angolite*.

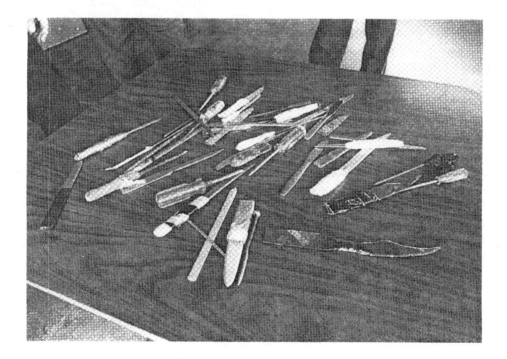

Right: Inmate Albert Woodfox.
Photo courtesy of *The Angolite*.

Above: Inmate Chester Jackson.
Photo courtesy of *The Angolite*.

Right: Inmate Herman Wallace.
Photo courtesy of *The Angolite*.

robbery of a New Orleans bar and ensuing gunbattle with police. He had also been convicted of aggravated rape and theft. Aggravated escape charges added another fourteen months to his sentence, Woodfox having staged a spectacular escape in October 1969 when taken to court on another armed robbery charge, pulling a pistol slipped to him by someone in the courthouse on two parish prison guards, whom he left in the prison elevator handcuffed together with the elevator operator, two retired policemen and five other prisoners. Woodfox had been returned to Louisiana from New York after doing time in that state.

A second inmate named by Brown was Herman "Hooks" Wallace, thirty, serving two fifty-year sentences for armed robbery in Orleans Parish, where he too staged a daring escape as one of a group of seven prisoners who cut their way out of the parish prison in 1971 and climbed from the roof of the three-story building on a rope made of blankets. Wallace's past record dated back to 1959 and included armed robbery, possession of a stolen car, theft and bank robbery.

Chester Jackson, called "Noxema Black," age thirty-three, was the third inmate named by Hezekiah Brown, and his record included sentences for several armed robberies and attempted murder. A tall, slight man at 5'9" and 135 pounds, Jackson had a reputation as a follower and as a "gal-boy," a weaker inmate winning protection from stronger ones in return for sexual favors.

These were the three suspects named by Hezekiah Brown in front of numerous investigators, including Warden C. Murray Henderson, Deputy Warden Lloyd W. Hoyle, Jr., and Field Security Captain Hilton Butler. Unfortunately, a fourth inmate would soon be inserted into the case as a suspect for reasons considered questionable at best.

Young Brent Miller was buried on Wednesday, April 19, in Pine Ridge Cemetery west of Tangipahoa, following funeral services at the Pine Ridge Methodist Church which his mother described as packed with mourners. "A lot of Angola people came to the funeral," she says, "a real outpouring. Brent had a lot of friends and was very popular, and there were flowers, flowers, flowers. It was an awfully sad funeral, it really was. It was just a bad time all around. When the prison chaplain, Reverend Wilson who was our neighbor, came and told us the morning Brent was killed, it was terrible. You know when something like that happens, you don't think, and I remember walking around in a pair of highheel shoes with my nightgown and housecoat on. I guess that's the first thing I saw and I just stuck my feet in them, a pair of highheel shoes. The whole day seemed like it lasted just a few minutes to me, and it was a bad time afterwards for a long long time."

On Tuesday, the day before the funeral, authorities announced that they had found a large homemade knife under Pine I, the dormitory where Miller had been stabbed; a smaller knife had apparently also been used. Warden Henderson released a statement calling the killing "the most senseless thing I've ever seen happen in a prison," and placed part of the blame on lack of funding. "The man was supervising four dormitories by himself in an area where the original plans call for it to be manned by five," he said in reference to the situation whereby inmate guards were being phased out under a federal court ruling but adequate funding had not been provided for their replacement by trained professional employees. "We've had a chronic problem in leaving a man by himself in an area like that. We've constantly asked for money for adequate supervision but we haven't been able to get it."

On Wednesday, the Angola warden informed the press that a number of suspects had been confined, but that the investigators were proceeding carefully in order to ferret out all evidence. This was not an easy task when "the brothers stick together and it's hard to get them to talk," Henderson said. "We have some people that are doing long sentences and they want to think of themselves as political prisoners, but they're serving time for rape, murder and armed robbery, and I can't see those as political crimes." He insisted that Miller's killing was not personal. "They would have killed anybody who was in there."

It would not be until the beginning of May that the names of the suspects in the killing of Brent Miller would be released to the public. By then, the case would have been complicated considerably by the highly questionable insertion of a fourth suspect, as well as the involvement of a district judge and a parish grand jury, plus the appearance of a new secretary of the state department of corrections and a new state governor, making this far more than a simple murder case. As awful as that murder was, the subsequent maneuverings took on an aspect that was even more despicable.

On Friday, April 21, the Miller family returned to Angola from their hometown near Amite, where they had buried Brent and remained to spend some quiet time with Mrs. Miller's brother. As they drove onto prison grounds, a meeting of correctional officers was just beginning in the Administration Building, and some unnamed party telephoned the Miller house to inform them of the assemblage. Mrs. Miller recalls that Huey and the older boys left the home immediately.

The phone was simultaneously ringing in the residence of Deputy Warden Lloyd Hoyle, who was at home recuperating from surgery. He had been told just that morning, returning with the warden from an appearance before the grand jury called into session by Twentieth Judicial District Judge William Bennett to investigate the slaying, that his presence at the meeting would not be required and that he should spend the afternoon resting at home. When his wife answered the telephone, a male voice told her to inform Hoyle that the warden needed him at the A Building. Dressing hurriedly, the deputy warden left his house to attend the meeting.

The stage had just been set for a near-fatal confrontation. Threats of a strike from the officers brought administration calls for state police and national guard assistance in maintaining security at the prison, which would not after all be required when most of the officers did in fact man their duty posts after the heated meeting, supplemented by Hilton Butler's field crew, classification officers and other administrative staff. But that was not until after the deputy warden had nearly been killed when the older brother of Brent Miller, college student Nix Miller, struck Hoyle and pushed him through a plate-glass door, injuring him severely.

The meeting had been called by correctional officers from the second and third shifts, who were demanding tighter security, a separate camp for black militants, three men assigned to each dormitory, and the firing of Deputy Warden Hoyle. To explain their demands and the desperate actions of Nix Miller, it is necessary to backtrack sufficiently to set the scene for this stage-managed confrontation.

One of the major problems at Angola during this era was the lack of individual cells for disciplinary confinement. The infamous Hole, the dark airless sweatbox which had been used (and abused) for isolation of the worst problem cases, had been ordered demolished following the heel-cutting scandals of the late fifties, when a group of inmates slashed their heel tendons to attract the attention of the press and public to deplorable conditions in the prison. Now there were only 341 single cells and all of the rest of the prisoner space was open dormitory, a situation Warden Henderson was quoted in newspapers as calling "a chronic problem. There's no way we can lock up all our problem cases. We have to release some."

Recalls Deputy Warden Hoyle, "The lack of cells to handle disciplinary problems caused a real management problem. The whole Brent Miller tragedy probably never would have happened had we had sufficient cells at Angola to take care of these severe, hardcore problem-makers. We had so many of them that there weren't enough cells. Subsequently, you had to take the worst ones and the current problem-makers and keep shuffling them in and out of those cells."

This checker-playing with dangerous inmates was exacerbated by two factors: one, the situation was being inhumanely abused by some staff members; and two, the federal courts were keeping an eye on whether due process was being afforded these lockdown prisoners. Certain staff members defied explicit orders not to double up prisoners in the 8 x 12-foot lockdown cells, which had no bunk or other furniture, and one unfortunate incident in July or August, when the weather was brutally hot, ended in tragedy when five inmates were confined in a single cell and denied access to any water except that in the commode.

Four of the prisoners in the hot crowded cell apparently survived by getting water out of the commode to cool off, but one refused to do that, and after being confined all one day and part of the night, he informed the officer in charge that he was sick. The officer let him out of the cell for awhile, even let him sit in front of a fan in his office, but it was too late. The prisoner said, 'I'm gonna die, this is gonna kill me,' and the officer reportedly retorted, 'Well, die and prove it,' returning him to the stifling cell. By the time the prisoner was sent to the hospital early the following morning, after guards had hosed him off, he was in a coma and soon died. The autopsy revealed the cause of death as heat stroke. The officer in charge was fired and the incident referred to the parish grand jury.

Staff abuse of the situation was not confined to cell over-population, however. Desperately needed cell space was being occupied by inmate informants or prisoners from whom these informants felt they needed protection, and some staff members resisted administration orders to document the need for confining these men. Recalls Lloyd

Hoyle, "The federal courts had indicated that any time you changed the housing status of an inmate and removed him from a lesser degree of security to a higher degree, you had to accord him an appropriate hearing. And a lot of these people who were locked up in these cells had never been afforded that process. In the CCR (Close Custody Restricted) cells at the reception center, we had a lot of hardcore prisoners locked up and they had been there for a considerable length of time, and this was primarily where the problems were. These were the people that the courts were concerned about."

In CCR cells, prisoners were in what is called solid lockdown; they didn't go to meals, they didn't go to work, they didn't go to school, they remained locked in their cell with only one hour of exercise time daily. As problem cases and threats to security, they needed to be placed in disciplinary confinement, but they still had to be accorded certain rights, having already legally established their rights to file writs, to be accorded due process, to face their accusers and to have someone defend them before a disciplinary committee. As Warden Henderson said, "The constitution doesn't wait outside the prison gate for inmates, after all; it follows them in, and they're due their rights." Federal Judge E. Gordon West, called by the warden "one of the most honorable men I've ever worked with," was trying to work with prison administration to avoid putting the penitentiary under federal court order, nudging the state to make changes in response to prisoner lawsuits and precedents which had already been set across the country.

Just before the killing of correctional officer Brent Miller, it became apparent that far too many prisoners in lockdown cells had not in fact been accorded their due process rights, a situation which had to be rectified right away in the face of lawsuits and court orders. Recalls Hoyle, "The warden had said that all these cases had to be reviewed, and if the reasons for confinement weren't documented, these reasons had to be put in the record, which was rather simple. If you found that a guy hadn't been properly documented, you got your staff together and you decided whether or not this guy needed to be in that cell, and then you would take appropriate action and document whether this guy was a threat to security, whether you had certain information from reliable sources or just whatever it took to get his record documented, so he had the hearing. The administration wasn't necessarily concerned about these guys being *released;* they just wanted to make sure the records were documented so that they could assure the inmates their legal hearings. Basically, it was the responsibility of whoever locked the inmates up to document the records at that time. All they had to do was bring these guys back before the disciplinary board."

Explaining that the U.S. Justice Department had been involved in setting up a mediation process supervised by the federal government, Hoyle continues, "We had procedures set up whereby these inmates could have been afforded hearings, and there wasn't any real problem except that someone had to go in and physically review the records to determine whether or not the inmates were locked up properly. And this was assigned to Hayden Dees, the associate warden for security. He was assigned to go up and go through all these records on CCR. But apparently he wasn't doing it on schedule and wasn't interested in it. His attitude seemed to be that all these men were locked up appropriately and if the federal government wanted them released, then the government could release them."

Struggling to keep abreast of federal court rulings across the country, the warden knew that the prisoners had to be accorded their rights in timely fashion, and consequently asked the deputy warden to take over the job of reviewing the cases for proper documentation. "The warden says, 'There seems to be a little footdragging, would you mind going up and checking through these records and seeing if these men are all appropriately handled,'" recalls Hoyle. "So this I did. I went up, reviewed every record of every inmate there. A lot of them had been documented; it was not a case of *nobody* doing his job. But there was a group of inmates, it must have been about fifteen of them, with no documentation in their record at all.

"So I took a list of these men to Dees, and I told him he had two alternatives, to document the records or release the men. I said, 'Now I want some documentation in these records, and all you have to do is just jot down that you got this from a reliable source or whatever. And if you don't, we've got no alternative but to put them back where they came from. And if you don't want these guys back where they came from, you're going to have to do a little homework and get your staff together and get these people documented. I don't care what you do, you can leave them in there, but you've got to have something in those records so that when the reviews are made or the guy files suit, we've got something administratively so that we can say he was locked up and had a rehearing and was put back in because he was a threat to security.'"

Associate Warden Dees, who'd come from a dairy farm to Angola as a guard in 1953 and worked his way up through the ranks (until a brother-in-law, a dietician by training, was temporarily made acting warden, at which point Dees' rise would reportedly accelerate considerably), would insist in open court hearings that what he called "a certain type of militant or revolutionary inmate, maybe even a *Communist* type" needed to be kept in lockdown at all times. He resisted Hoyle's order, primarily, Hoyle says, "because he was eventually going to have to disclose who the informants were who told him whatever he made his decisions on to lock these men up. You couldn't convince him that this wasn't going to be public record. Basically it didn't matter to him who had access to the information; in his mind, somebody was gonna come in and make him tell who his informants were, and he said as long as he was working in this prison he would never disclose them. I said he didn't have to disclose them, just put something in the record. It wasn't that big a deal. And I said, 'If you don't, then it indicates to me that you had them locked up inappropriately in the first place, because if they're that hardcore and you don't want them in the population, then you ought to do your job and go ahead and rehear the case and record it. No big deal.'"

Hoyle said he told Dees, "Here's the list, and you got a week to do it or I'm gonna put them back in the population. He said, 'You're gonna get somebody killed.' And I said, 'Hayden, this is not the first time you've told me that. Every time a decision is

Right: Hayden Dees,
shown in 1979 as warden of
Dixon Correctional Institute.
Photo courtesy of *The Angolite.*

Above: Former Angola warden
Hilton Butler.
Photo courtesy of *The Angolite.*

Right: Inmate
Gilbert Montegut.
Photo courtesy of
The Angolite.

made in here, you say somebody's gonna get killed.' And I said, 'The only reason you have problems in these prisons is because your staff causes the majority of them.' I said, 'If you talk it long enough that somebody is gonna get hurt in this prison, eventually they're gonna get hurt. That's all it takes, because when it comes from people in authority, eventually it's gonna cause problems.'"

Continued Hoyle, "But I said, 'That's not the problem. The problem is we've got inmates up here that have been locked up inappropriately, they have not been afforded their due process, and you need to document their records and hear them or put them back in the population.' And then I said, "If you can't get this done, then work up the transfers and we'll handle it.' He wouldn't do it. He didn't *want* to do it, apparently. And I said, 'Well, if he doesn't want to do it, apparently these people are not a threat to anybody, because here's our chief of security, associate warden for security, who apparently doesn't have enough on them to lock them up or doesn't want to do it or whatever, it's immaterial; we're still violating their rights and we've got to do something with them.' So Dees worked up the transfers transferring them back to the main prison population and he put *my* name on them; he wouldn't even put his own name on them."

One of these prisoners transferred from CCR lockdown was named Gilbert Montegut. Only twenty-one, Montegut listed his occupation as "revolutionary" on prison intake records and had sat through his 1971 trial for the robbery of a New Orleans theater cashier with his mouth taped shut after shouting militant slogans in the courtroom. At the time of that trial, he had already been charged with truancy, creating a disturbance at school, rape, theft, malicious mischief, simple robbery, armed robbery, attempted murder, attempted kidnapping and aggravated battery in a criminal career which began at the tender age of fourteen, progressed through several terms at Louisiana Training Institute as an incorrigible juvenile delinquent, and escalated to an escape by crashing through a window in the Fourth District Police Station in New Orleans. Angola workups would subsequently mention antisocial behavior, paranoia, unconventional and revolutionary thinking, and anticipated adjustment problems due to feelings of persecution because of his race and affiliation with the Black Panther Party. Montegut's name would figure prominently in the under-the-table machinations as a tragic but simple murder case took a bizarre twist.

The only eyewitness to the Miller slaying, Hezekiah Brown, had initially named just three assailants: Albert Woodfox, Chester Jackson and Herman Wallace. None of these men had been released from maximum-security lockdown by orders of the deputy warden. Chester Jackson had been assigned to Hickory 4 on the medium-security yard by the classification committee in January of 1972 and was still there until locked up in connection with Miller's death; Herman Wallace had been assigned by the classification committee first to Camp A, then to Pine I and later to Pine 3 on the medium-security yard, where he remained except for brief periods of disciplinary confinement until locked up in connection with Miller's death; and Albert Woodfox had been assigned to Hickory 4 on the medium-security yard by the classification committee in 1971 and remained there until locked up in connection with Miller's death. Montegut, on the other hand, *had* been released from CCR by Hoyle, and someone seemed to be working awfully hard to add Montegut's name to the list of suspects. Someone who knew better, it would seem.

Recalls Hoyle, "When Gunnells got burned, no one knew who did it at first, but they went down and picked up all these guys that I had turned out of CCR, and they locked them up again. It was pretty evident that none of them could have done it, because they weren't even assigned in those areas where it happened. But they got blamed for that at first, these particular men. I think Montegut was in that bunch picked up for administrative lockdown. They only had them in for a short time before they released them, because they began to find out they'd locked up the wrong ones. I think that was kind of the catalyst that started the whole problem, really. When Brent Miller was killed, right quick they had all these men that had been released from CCR picked up again, Montegut included."

In the midst of the extensive interrogation process which involved all 800 inmates from the medium-security area of the prison where Miller was slain, Hoyle recalls that he and the warden were sitting in on the interview of "an inmate by the name of Chester Jackson. Right away quick, when he came in, Dees made the statement that with this inmate you could believe anything he said, that he had always given him reliable information. They were asking him their usual questions and of course he said he didn't know too much about it. I don't know whether it was myself or Murray who asked the guy exactly what his involvement had been in the killing. And right there in front of the whole bunch of interrogators, he ran the whole thing down exactly, saying, 'I didn't stab him, I didn't stab him, I just held him while they killed him.'

"And Dees could have fallen out of his chair. Jackson didn't name Montegut. He named the rest and was willing to testify and the whole ball of wax. He said Montegut had nothing to do with it. The District Attorney and everybody else there knew they couldn't get anything on Montegut because they had a state's eyewitness. Of the ones he named, not any of them had been released from CCR by me. Matter of fact, Jackson was an informant for Dees. So anyway, it was common knowledge to Dees before the meeting with the correctional officers that none of the people I'd interviewed or released had done the killing. But apparently he didn't communicate it very properly."

Hilton Butler, head of security in the field and a dedicated, capable officer upon whom the warden often called in times of crisis, recalls the events leading up to the killing, which he helped to investigate, going several days without sleep. "The warden knew we were fixing to have to start following some federal guidelines, so he told us to go and review the records and for anybody who needed to be kept locked up, to put some type of documentation of the reason in the records, and if there was no reason to lock them up, to release them from CCR. There's always been a shortage of space, and I reckon there always will be. And Dees had two or three opportunities to keep anybody he wanted locked up by just documenting it, but he never did do it. And so finally something had to be done, and the warden told Hoyle to go ahead and take care of it. And he did. We had all kinds of people locked up with no documentation showing why they were locked up. If Hayden would have gone on and done that himself, Hoyle wouldn't even have had to get involved. Hoyle did it because somebody had to do it."

Montegut, one of the group of inmates released from CCR due to lack of documentation, was, according to Butler, a real agitator and "probably involved in organizing some of the problems, but he wasn't actually one of the ones who killed Miller. And some of them wanted to convict him so bad that I was afraid at one time we would get the whole prosecution messed up, with them trying to convict Montegut when he wasn't actually there. What they were trying to say, a little group of officers, was that Hoyle was the cause of Miller's death by releasing those people from CCR, but none of the people that Hoyle released was actually involved in the murder."

At the meeting of the correctional officers, Butler recalls, "One of these officers got up and demanded Hoyle's resignation. He said Hoyle was the cause of Brent Miller's death. And I got up and told him that we had the people locked up, I knew who had killed Miller but didn't want to mess up the case by telling them exactly who. But I would tell them that not one person that Hoyle released from CCR was involved in the killing. I told them that at that time, before it ever went to court. The witnesses that I talked to said it was Woodfox, Jackson and Wallace, the ones who were actually convicted, and nobody else."

Butler refers to a daily diary he kept through the many years of his employment at Angola, where he would one day be warden himself. On Monday, April 17, 1972, he records the inmates "bucking for two shifts," refusing to work during breakfast to draw security personnel away from the area where Brent Miller was being killed; going on duty at 5 a.m. Monday, Butler would not go off until 8:30 the next morning, working inexhaustively on the investigation all night and returning to work early the next afternoon. By Tuesday he records the locking up of several suspects and members of the Black Panther group, and by Wednesday, he states in his diary, "We have enough evidence on three men to get a conviction."

On Friday, April 21, the day of the correctional officers' threatened strike and meeting, Butler records in his diary that he attended the 1 p.m. meeting with 150 to 200 officers from the 2-to-10 shift and the 10-to-6 shift. "Their first request," he recorded in his diary on that date, "was that Mr. Hoyle be fired as he was responsible for the murder of Brent Miller by releasing five inmates out of CCR. I got up and explained to these men that they had the wrong information, that I had set in on the investigation of the murder and knew who killed Brent, and we had enough evidence to send three men to the electric chair, but I could not reveal the information until the men went to court, but that I could tell them that Mr. Miller was *not* killed by any of the inmates that Mr. Hoyle released from CCR. Nix and Hardy Miller were standing outside the door listening when these stupid people made the statement that Mr. Hoyle was the cause of Brent's death."

It was unfortunately not the first time that Brent Miller's brothers had heard Hoyle accused of responsibility in the death. Brent's mother remembers that shortly after the killing, "Everybody was saying that Hoyle was responsible, that the inmates had killed him but that Hoyle was responsible. Even then they were putting that in our minds. Some people came and told us that it wasn't intended for Brent, that it was intended for Hunter, who was working with him. And others told us that the militants had intended to kill ten that morning when they went back there, and a lot of them said that Dorothy Taylor had started that riot and that she had talked to Hoyle."

More specifically, she continues, "Now Dees told us that Hoyle was the one that had turned him out into the main prison population. I know Dees told us about it afterward, that it was Hoyle, that Hoyle had been told not to release him by Dees and that he went ahead and released him anyway after Dorothy Taylor had been up there. A lot of the people had come and they were all talking it all over the house, and that's what got Nix riled up and why he went and did what he did. He had come home from college soon as he heard about Brent; he and Brent, being closest in age, kind of ran together, and Brent just idolized Nix. When they had that meeting, we had just driven back into Angola, and someone must have called Huey and the boys and asked them to come, 'cause they didn't know a thing about it. Huey, Huey Jr. and all of them went, all of them that were big enough."

Tension built at the meeting, with strike threatened. The warden prepared to maintain security with state police and national guardsmen if necessary. Tempers flared. Recalls Hoyle, "All it would have taken was for Dees to stand up there and make an announcement or have a roll call or anything to relieve the tension, which is what I would have done if I'd been associate warden for security and one of my officers had been killed. The first thing I would have done would be to communicate to everybody, 'Hey, we got these worthless things locked up, now let's get back to the business at hand of running the prison.'" But Dees never got up.

"Hilton Butler got up," Hoyle continues, "and told them about the situation, and you could see tension kind of easing a little bit. I wasn't feeling so sharp anyway after surgery, so I walked outside the building when it seemed like the meeting was about over and the warden said, 'Let's get back to work now.' So I walked outside and the minute I opened the door, it felt like somebody hit me across the back of my head with a piece of pipe or something. I had turned my head to address somebody over on the right, so I didn't see anybody coming at me."

Knocked backward through the plate glass entrance doors to the Administration Building, Deputy Warden Lloyd Hoyle suffered a deep laceration of the left face and ear so severe it would require nearly 400 stitches to close it, extending from two inches in front of the ear through the ear and into the scalp, loss of a large portion of his left ear lobe, loss of a number of teeth, severance of his facial nerve resulting in a permanently drooping eyelid, partial paralysis of the left side of the face and persistently recurring headaches which would plague him for the rest of his life. Blood gushed across the concrete sidewalk.

All Hoyle could hear was talk: "My God, looks like he's dead." "Somebody killed him." Never totally unconscious, he also heard, "Well, that worthless son of a bitch got what he deserved, let him die." And he vividly recalls that nobody wanted to drive the ambulance which Henderson had swiftly summoned. Finally career officer Ray Dixon took the wheel to transport Hoyle to the hospital; an inmate hospital orderly rode in the back with the patient, holding his bleeding severed face pressed together with slippery hands.

In spite of a rushed diagnosis at the hospital in St. Francisville where they had stopped to stabilize the patient that "this guy's not gonna make it to Baton Rouge," and a surgeon at the Baton Rouge General Hospital emergency room who brusquely yelled, "Get a bucket over here, this guy's bleeding all over the floor," Lloyd Hoyle pulled through and discovered that it had been Nix Miller, older brother of Brent, who had accosted him. When he saw the boy years later at a ballgame, Hoyle said Nix told him he regretted the action and "kinda implied that if I'd had the same information that he'd had, I might have done the same thing. I could have ruined that boy, basically, but I felt the family had been through enough. He had already lost his brother, and what do you accomplish by ruining someone else's life? We grieved for the family and for the situation. No one was any more upset about Brent's death than we were and still are today."

Continues Hoyle, "But to blame someone personally and individually for a tragedy of that type in such a huge institution is almost incomprehensible. Montegut was the only one they had any grounds to associate with me, so Dees' attempts to keep Montegut involved in the crime were designed to keep me involved directly and C. Murray indirectly. I think what they really were attempting to do was to have a confrontation. Maybe they weren't even thinking, but knowing what they were dealing with, they should have assumed that that boy was capable of doing almost anything. Somebody should have corrected the family's impression. As a matter of fact, the boy's wife filed a million-dollar suit against me as being totally responsible and even quoted in there that Associate Warden Dees had said these men had been released by me from CCR and committed the murder."

Unlike Brent Miller, Deputy Warden Lloyd Hoyle did not have to ask, "Why?" He pretty well knew. "Nix Miller is the key to the whole thing," he explains. "Nix I didn't even know, though the Miller family I had a lot of respect for. The death of Brent was just one of those things that happens in prison work that people have to understand; it's a very volatile, explosive situation, and anything can happen at any time. If you're looking for somebody to blame and you're gonna get involved in second-guessing what can happen in prisons, you're gonna have problems. It's inherent to prison management. Anytime you have a riot, it's usually stirred up by the staff talking in front of the inmates, degrading the administration or the governor or whoever it could be. It's commonplace. Until the political involvement in the Louisiana prison system gets out of the picture totally, you're always gonna have problems."

Governor Edwin W. Edwards was in the process of taking over the reins of state government from John J. McKeithen, and had just appointed as first female secretary of the Department of Corrections Elayn Hunt, longtime prison reform advocate, attorney and in private life wife of John Eicher, whose name would years later figure prominently in the Champion Insurance scandals. Hunt was requesting a $5 million budget increase to provide several hundred additional correctional officers at Angola and a fifty percent increase in pay for those already working there, increased daily feeding budgets (prisoners were then being fed for a shocking 82 cents per day) and other improvements, but those would not come soon enough.   With the state administration changing, some of the employees at Angola were unsettled and vying for position, trying to solidify or improve their positions and creating considerable anxiety inside the penitentiary.

And one of those jockeying for position was undeniably the associate warden for security, the very man who should have been doing his utmost to calm the situation rather than stirring it up. Said Hilton Butler, "Dees said there ought to be people in Louisiana smart enough to be warden. He resented C. Murray and Hoyle, both from out of state, because they were his superiors. Hoyle was probably the one that he was fighting, though he had animosity for Henderson too. It was one of those deals where if he had gone on and done his job, there would have been no problem. But Dees resented Hoyle and Henderson from the day they came in there."

Hoyle had borne the brunt of resentment a number of times before the Miller slaying. Arriving at Angola after nineteen years in corrections in his home state of Iowa, only to be shocked by outdated prison practices other states had long since abandoned, Hoyle was confronted with "the convict-guard problems, prison enterprise problems, deteriorated facilities, convicts carrying weapons, no types of rehabilitative problems, the black and white issue, these were things you couldn't imagine were still going on in this country, really." Henderson had requested his aid at Angola, though, even creating the job of deputy warden just for him, and Hoyle's reasons for taking a cut in pay to move to Louisiana were primarily humanitarian. "'Course no one in Louisiana ever really understood that people could come down and try to do something for humanitarian reasons. They always thought I was a Yankee coming down here and taking all the good jobs."

When General David Wade, head of the state Department of Corrections, suggested that the two new top men at Angola replace present prison administrative staff with their own congenial team of progress-minded professionals, Hoyle demurred. "In my benevolent way," he remembers, "I suggested that we should get to know these people and make every attempt to change their philosophies, since they had been under the supervision of several political appointees before we came in. But there was never the real concept of input from them, never any enthusiasm, even though what we were doing benefitted the employees, raised their standard of living and improved their working conditions. As long as the institution functioned and they were following procedure and doing the job, though, idle gossip and complaints never bothered me.

"But there was a terrific amount of resentment toward me," Hoyle continues, "and not only toward me, but toward the warden also. Hayden Dees had felt he should have been warden, there wasn't any question about it, and I think the general feeling was that the way to get rid of the warden was to get rid of me, because if they got rid of me, then the warden would have to assume all my duties and responsibilities in addition to his, which would have been practically impossible. I think it's more or less inherent in the Louisiana prison system, that everybody who has got a boss either wants his job or wants to see him ousted to be replaced with somebody who's not going to put on any pressure. That was just the way it was, and it's still that way. The same thing would have transpired regardless of who had been in those positions."

Hoyle's wife and three children suffered repercussions just as cruel, if not more so. "Every time we would make a change at the prison," Hoyle says, "not only was I persecuted but my family was persecuted as well. We lived right down there on B Line in the free housing section, and out in the back yard my kids had some pet mallard ducks that they were really attached to. Well, the decision had to be made that free staff could no longer use the prison doctors. They'd been going to the doctor there for free and would get medication from the pharmacy, in spite of having hospitalization and access to private physicians in town. We told the employees they could only use prison doctors for emergency medical attention, since there weren't enough medical personnel to see even part of the convicts. And the day after this decision was made...I didn't make all of these decisions, but I got blamed for them...here was one of the pet mallards, dead, hanging on the front doorknob of the house."

Also unpopular with staff was a decision not to tie up the only prison bus ferrying free-family football players who lived on Angola to and from practice at the high school in St. Francisville. The Hoyles' son found himself double and triple-teamed on nearly every practice play, even after his parents began using their personal station wagon to provide transportation for the boys. Garbage was dumped all over the front yard of the Hoyle home, and the backyard toolshed was set ablaze in the middle of the night; the state fire marshall ruled it arson after finding a gasoline can, which had been in the middle of the shed, some 20 yards away and untouched by the flames.

"The kids took it in school, too," Hoyle relates with regret. "Many's the time they'd come home crying that somebody had picked on them and said, 'Your dad's a nigger-lover' and all this type thing. It was a real difficult decision when all the staff pulled their kids out of public school and sent them to private school, and here we were trying to integrate the prison. I could have probably afforded to send my kids to private school, but what would that do for the institution? You can't integrate the prison and talk it up if the convicts can say, 'Hey, your kids are going to private school, what the hell you doing up here preaching?' So consequently my kids were part of this thing as far as the prison was concerned, and it was a very difficult situation."

Perhaps the worst time was when Hoyle's daughter Lee, then sixteen, came screaming into his bedroom about three o'clock one morning. "I went in and looked, and here was a hole in her bedroom window. So I got ahold of Dees, and I said, 'Somebody fired a damn shot through this window.' You know what his response was? He said, 'Oh, somebody was probably mowing his grass and a rock got thrown.' And I said, 'At three o'clock in the damn morning? You got to be kidding.'"

Dees may have had his own political ambitions and his own agenda, but he had willing accomplices on and off the penitentiary grounds, not the least formidable of whom was Twentieth Judicial District Judge William Bennett. The week Brent Miller was killed on Monday, Bennett announced on Wednesday that he was convening a special session of the West Feliciana Parish Grand Jury for 9 a.m. Friday, initially announcing the jury's purpose as being to investigate the slaying of the security officer, then later amending that charge to "specifically *not* investigate the killing of Miller, but to investigate security measures being taken at the penitentiary." The judge indicated the district court just might intervene in prison operations if the jury found security was not sufficiently tight, and designated a committee from the grand jury to inspect prison records.

Pointedly announcing that not only inmates but also officers and employees of the state penitentiary came under the purview of the court's jurisdiction, Bennett stated for the record, "I want it known that we expect the full cooperation, unqualified cooperation of those in control, management at the penitentiary, to do everything in their power that they legitimately can to maintain proper security at Angola. We expect them to do this. We expect the director of corrections to see that this is done and to support the warden and his associate and deputy wardens in the maintenance of security and peace and order at the penitentiary. Now when I say I expect as judge for this to be done, it means simply this: if it is not done, then the court would feel it incumbent on the court under the constitution to hold responsible those who are responsible for it not being done. Do I make myself clear?"

The judge continued, "If this is not done, if all possible security measures are not taken, gentlemen, you will be called back and I will charge you as to the law under those circumstances. We will cooperate in every way with whoever is in charge of the department of corrections at Angola to the end that there will be security for those who live and work at Angola so that they will not fear they will be killed, so they will know they are going to be protected and so that the convicts who violate the law will find out they cannot get away with it."

Proclaiming himself "not without considerable experience in this field," Judge Bennett further charged that the jurors had been called into session because "there is a general feeling of unrest and a feeling of fear among employees at Angola resulting from recent disturbances and troubles up there. This feeling is also among the people outside of Angola. In the parish, there is that same feeling of insecurity, the fear of a break or escape and that sort of thing, and we have concluded that the fact that a grand jury of this parish is in session will have a very salutory effect upon our people for whom and to whom we owe a duty to see that they are secure in their persons and property from anything that might take place as far as any escapes from Angola or trouble arising up there."

When correctional officers threatened to walk out during the meeting at the end of the week Miller was killed, Judge Bennett sent word through associate warden Hayden Dees that the grand jury was investigating prison security and would hear from several guards the following week; he would later take credit for the officers' returning to work, for the most part, though a dozen or so would resign in the wake of the slaying. Bennett's heavy-handed guidance of the investigation of the grand jury, its foreman the son of a longtime parish sheriff and numbering among its members several Angola employees, seemed especially designed to strengthen Dees' position in the administration of the penitentiary.

Indeed, the grand jury's recommendations for security changes at the penitentiary were admittedly proposed by Dees, including such regressive measures as the installation of steel mesh screens in visiting areas and the ordering of special coveralls to be worn during inmate visits with family. The jury report specifically noted that some inmates had been released from custodial detention "without clearance of the Associate Warden in charge of security *Hayden Dees*," that other inmates had been discharged from maximum-security quarters "over the objection of *Dees*," that communication problems between the administration and the correctional officers existed "but no such complaints were found against *Dees*," though "it is believed that *Hayden Dees* has not been given the proper backing so that he can make their jobs more safe."

The report recommended that *Dees* be given authority to approve or disapprove all changes in living quarter assignments and that *Dees* be given proper authority and backing, that the medium-yard dormitories be separated by security fencing, that better training for officers in self defense and inmate control be provided, that security staff be beefed up and that a penal facility near New Orleans be constructed, since "approximately fifty percent of all inmates at Angola are from the metropolitan area of New Orleans."

Though he would soon insert himself into the Death Row dilemma at Angola and file injunctions and restraining orders to delay the release of Death Row inmates into the general prison population after the U.S. Supreme Court did away with the existent death penalty as cruel and unusual punishment and hence unconstitutional, Judge Bennett told reporters as he read the grand jury report, "You are going to be reading that this court is trying to take over and run the penitentiary, and nothing could be further from the truth. The only thing we are going to do is that we are not going to sit here and let those tough eggs as revolutionaries take over. Somebody might say I am trying to take over Angola. What in the hell would I want to run Angola for?"

Yet it wouldn't be long before parish district attorney Richard Kilbourne, called by Henderson "a decent and honorable man with a sense of fair play," would take out a paid advertisement in the Baton Rouge *Morning Advocate* distancing himself from all the maneuverings. Answering "certain derogatory reports which are being circulated in the Parish of West Feliciana relative to my alleged opposition to the recent and continuing

Grand Jury session which was called shortly after the murder of Correctional Officer Brent Miller at Angola on April 17," Kilbourne noted that he would indeed have opposed calling a grand jury at that particular time, but that such was not a function of the district attorney's office, the grand jury instead being under the control of the district judge. To call the jury into session at the time a murder case was under intensive investigation, Kilbourne continued, was not only surprising but surely not helpful, perhaps even harmful to the investigation.

The diversion of the grand jury investigation from the murder to a concentration on security problems at Angola, Kilbourne stated, "although the same Grand Jury had visited the prison only five weeks before and had rendered a report on some aspects of prison security then," was taking on "the aspect of a vendetta against some of the prison officials. I have no part in this and do not want any. During all the years that I have been District Attorney and, doubtless, for many years before that, there have been repeated instances when there was public clamor for West Feliciana Parish Grand Juries to take over the supervision of some segment or another of the operations at Angola."

Not only is Angola, a state-owned and operated institution, not the responsibility of the parish of West Feliciana, but grand juries, Kilbourne insisted, have no more jurisdiction over the prison than over any other portion of the parish, where they are limited by law to finding indictments or no true bills as to crimes committed there. Moreover, he continued, "In past instances of public agitation for interference by Grand Juries in Angola affairs, it has been my observation that those complaining the loudest about conditions at Angola usually had some private axe to grind."

That the grand jury was distracted from its foremost duty of considering the murder evidence and indicting those implicated, to concentrate instead on investigations "of extraneous complaints of a nature that have been chronic at Angola for many years," was a matter of sincere regret to Kilbourne, who insisted that he would continue to oppose as he always had "the involvement of a Grand Jury in any matter which is clearly outside the scope of the legal authority of Grand Juries, particularly matters having political overtones such as power struggles between those who are running Angola and those who want to run it. I can think of nothing more calculated to undermine public confidence in the Grand Jury system than any such involvement. If ever that confidence was needed, it is now."

The necessity for prosecution, conviction and punishment of the murderers of Brent Miller, Kilbourne closed his heartfelt message by saying, would still be waiting after "the hullabaloo and hot air" subsided. And so they were. The mandamus suit filed in Judge Bennett's courtroom seeking the installation of tighter security measures at Angola like security fencing, visiting coveralls and electronic weapon scanners, was assigned to another judge, District Judge Richard P. Boyd, Jr., of Harrisonburg, assigned to the Twentieth District for a six-month period by the Louisiana Supreme Court to replace an ailing Judge Bennett.

With the backing of the state corrections office, Angola's administration resisted such regressive orders as the installation of heavy intrusive screens to separate inmates from visitors, having previously upgraded its visiting room to permit the far more humane practice of "contact visiting," allowing a father to hold his visiting child, for example. Insisting this method of visiting wasn't a security problem as long as prisoners were searched thoroughly before and after visiting under the watchful eyes of security officers, the state took its protests to court, successfully represented by able attorney Camille Gravel, and the whole thing gradually faded away so staff could finally get back to the matter of running the prison. A new grand jury impaneled in September reported, in sharp contrast to the earlier one, that security at the prison had been greatly improved.

Also in September, the trial of those charged with the murder of Brent Miller was shifted from West Feliciana, where four black militant inmates had been indicted by the parish grand jury in May. Four? Instead of the three initially named by Hezekiah Brown, state's eyewitness, now there were four: Albert Woodfox, Chester Jackson, Herman Wallace, and Gilbert Montegut, whom Associate Warden Dees had finally been successful in officially inserting into the picture. Recalls Hilton Butler, "Hezekiah was one you could put words in his mouth. Hezekiah eventually said that Montegut was involved, but not in the beginning. Hayden kind of put those words in his mouth, because he hadn't told that to me and C. Murray. And then Dees got himself another witness who was blind, and took them down to the state police barracks where we couldn't interrogate them. But I remember writing down that I did not believe that Montegut would ever be convicted, because I did not believe he was involved in the actual killing, even though he may have been in on the planning of it."

Butler continues, "Montegut was at the hospital at the time of the killing, went over there for sick call or something 'cause I think he knew it was coming down. I believe it was Montegut who told me later he had a zip gun on him that morning in the dining room, a zip gun loaded with a .22 bullet, and he almost killed Captain Louie Bunch. Louie Bunch shook him down and didn't find the gun, and he went from there, in the dining room, to the hospital." Longtime hospital employee Bob Colle also remembers Montegut being at the hospital at the time of the killing, sitting in the bullpen awaiting medical examination, as a number of inmates and security officers testified when the case finally came to trial.

First moved to East Feliciana, the trial was later shifted in a change of venue to the court of Eighteenth Judicial District judge Edward N. Engolio in Plaquemine, Louisiana, not getting underway until March of 1973, when Albert Woodfox became the first of the suspects to be tried individually before an all-white jury of nine men and three women. Tight security was in effect, with sheriff's deputies and a penitentiary matron frisking prospective jurors and others entering the courtroom, shotgun-toting guards at the entrance and armed officers outside on the lawn. At one point, nine law enforcement officers sat inside the courtroom railing separating the audience from trial participants, with at least four others scattered throughout the audience.

Twentieth Judicial District DA Leon Picou, Jr., led the prosecution, calling Hezekiah Brown to testify to seeing Woodfox grab Brent Miller around the neck and begin stabbing him with a knife before the other defendants joined in and dragged the guard eight or ten feet away to the entrance of the dorm, stabbing him continually. When John W. Sinquefield, special counsel for the state attorney general's office who assisted Picou in the prosecution, asked Brown to demonstrate on him how Woodfox held Miller, the inmate complied "quite forcibly."

Said Brown, "I looked up and there was Fox, Hooks, Montegut and Noxzema Black. Fox grabbed the man and he couldn't say a word before he hit him with that knife. . . . They didn't say a mumbling word. I just heard the shuffling of their feet when they started jugging (stabbing) the man. They jugged and jugged, jugged, jugged, jugged." The handkerchief over Woodfox's face hardly hampered identification, testified Brown, because the inmate had an easily recognizable mottled complexion and "kind of looks like a leopard. I'm as sure that was Fox as I am black. Now, how black am I?"

Asked to explain the delay in admitting to having seen the murder, Hezekiah Brown confessed his dilemma. "I knew those boys. I liked them. But they fixed me up so I had no way out. I know we was black and that a white man was killed. They are black, I'm black. I felt pretty bad going against my own race. But look, man, I'm an old man and tired and I can't take no more. They left me where I had to tell."

Inmate Joe Richey testified to looking out of the bathroom of Pine Dormitory No. 4, across the walk from the scene of the slaying, and seeing the four defendants leave Pine I. Paul Joseph Favre, another inmate witness, related that Woodfox had a grudge against Miller because the guard had earlier removed him from Pine 4 when he refused to obey orders to leave, and said he had heard Woodfox inform a colleague that the "plot to pull that buck in the kitchen to get the prisoners off the walk so it would give him a chance to get the guard" was still in effect. (Prison personnel recall that it was customary for Hunter, not Miller, to wait on the dorm while Miller took the inmates to the dining room, however, and many thought Hunter was meant to be the object of the violence.)

To conclude the prosecution, West Feliciana Coroner Dr. Alfred Gould testified that all thirty-two stab wounds contributed to Miller's death; Correctional Officer Gerald Joseph Rheams described finding a knife, 7 1/4-inches long, 1 1/4-inches wide, sharpened on both sides and still wet with blood, behind a vent block under the dormitory where Miller's body was found; officer Lemuel B. Hunter told of finding the blood-soaked body; state police photographers and sketch artists introduced evidence of the scene, and West Feliciana sheriff's deputies gave additional details. Paul L. Cobb, Jr., supervisor of the state police crime laboratory, testified that the bloodstains on Woodfox's shoes could not be identified as human, and that the spot on his jacket, while human blood, could not be identified as to type.

Defense attorney Charles Garretson of New Orleans put Woodfox on the stand, where he denied any part in the slaying, insisted he was having breakfast at the time, and testified he and other members of the Black Panthers drew a lot of abuse from guards and other inmates because of what he described as attempts to better prison conditions. "We were trying to organize against old prisoners raping young inmates," Woodfox testified, and "would arm ourselves with any kind of weapon we could" to do so. He described Hezekiah Brown as "part of a lot we were trying to stop" and prosecution witness Richey as someone he'd had a disagreement with over Richey's "wanting to try out a young inmate." The prosecution's third witness was the object of testimony from defense witness Clarence Franklin, who testified he worked in the kitchen with Paul Joseph Favre and that Favre was always stumbling over things because his eyes were so bad.

On cross examination by District Attorney Picou, Woodfox admitted writing letters "encouraging the killing of white racist pigs." But, Woodfox added, "Usually, this is referred to as political rhetoric." Woodfox then admitted tearing a commode from his prison cell because, he said oddly, a correctional officer "was firing an M-37 missile launcher directly at me."

After fifty minutes of deliberation at the close of the three-day trial, Albert Woodfox was convicted on Wednesday, March 7, 1973, of the murder of Correctional Officer Brent Miller at the Louisiana State Penitentiary on April 17, 1972. Because District Judge Edward Engolio imposed a life sentence the same day Woodfox's motion for a new trial was denied, however, the Louisiana Supreme Court, while affirming the conviction, would in early 1974 send the case back for resentencing, noting the absence of a waiver of the mandatory delay provided between conviction and sentencing. Two of Woodfox's defense witnesses, John Ford and Clarence Jones, were among four inmates who would file suit against Angola over being sent to lockdown after the Miller slaying without being given any notice of charges against them or any chance to rebut said charges, thus claiming denial of due process under the law.

By the time the rest of the suspects in Miller's death came to trial in the Baton Rouge courtroom of District Judge Elmo Lear in January of 1974, after initial charges were quashed by Judge Engolio because of defense allegations of racial discrimination in the selection of the grand jury which indicted them, Chester Jackson had turned state's evidence, strengthening the prosecution's case against Herman Wallace particularly. The trial began Tuesday, January 8, 1974, and by the second day, to supplement repeat testimony of inmate Hezekiah Brown as well as coroner Gould and law enforcement investigators, Chester Jackson took the stand to confess that he, Albert Woodfox and Herman Wallace had repeatedly stabbed Miller, who had been chosen at random when Woodfox decided it was time to act on plans to kill a free man. Gilbert Montegut, on the other hand, Jackson claimed he "didn't remember seeing" at the murder scene.

One Howard Baker, an inmate witness produced by West Feliciana District Attorney Leon Picou and Assistant East Baton Rouge District Attorney Ralph Roy, testified to seeing "Hooks" Wallace leaving Pine I Dormitory the morning of April 17, 1972, with blood on his clothing and accompanied by another inmate he identified as one of the defense witnesses named Abraham Thomas. Admitting that he was a runner in prison gambling operations and had gone out early to pick up money at the prison hospital and sew it into the lining of his coat, Baker testified that later that morning, after reporting to his job at the tag plant, he again saw Wallace in the act of burning bloody clothing in a furnace used in the process of making license plates.

DA Picou, in closing arguments, told the jury the state penitentiary was "a jungle" where convicts lived by the law of the jungle. Calling the killing of an unarmed law-enforcement officer "most heinous, most brutal," the prosecutor lamented, "In this country we are far more civilized in the slaughter of our cattle." Defense attorneys Charles C. Garretson and Norbert A. Simmons produced alibi witnesses who testified that Wallace ate breakfast with them before moving directly to his tag plant job and that Montegut had been at the hospital on sick call at the time of the killing. Raising questions of contradictory testimony and the uncertain credibility of inmate witnesses, the defense team told the jury that the state had failed to prove its case beyond a reasonable doubt, particularly in regard to Montegut.

Found guilty and sentenced to a life term in the penitentiary because the killing took place before Lousiana murder law was changed the following year to mandate the death penalty for the killing of a prison guard, Herman Wallace complained bitterly about the makeup of the all-white jury which condemned him after deliberating two hours. Turning to walk away from Judge Elmo Lear accompanied by jailers after sentencing, Wallace shouted, "Fascism," raising his hand in a Black Power salute to the courtroom audience. He then shouted, "Power to the people," and was answered by clenched fists and shouts of "Power" from supporters in the audience, causing tension in the heavily guarded courtroom.

Wallace had waived his right to a three-day delay before sentence was pronounced, telling the judge, "You can sentence me now," and then making his statement on the unfairness of his trial and the makeup of the all-white jury which convicted him. Judge Lear pointed out, however, that the same jury had found co-defendant Gilbert Montegut innocent of the murder charges.

Chester Jackson would die in Angola in 1988, cause of death being cardiopulmonary arrest and terminal cancer. As of late 1991, Albert Woodfox and Herman Wallace are still there, among the 5200 prisoners who are now supervised by a more adequate guard complement numbering about 1535. Rory Mason and Gilbert Montegut were released from the penitentiary, Mason in 1982, Montegut in 1980. Hezekiah Brown's sentence was commuted in 1986.

Dorothy Taylor would form an alliance with corrections secretary Elayn Hunt to work for penal reform in the legislature, then turn her attentions to city politics, but not before she disclaimed responsibility for any unrest at Angola in the seventies, saying she would not be "anybody's scapegoat" and suggesting that General David Wade, state adjutant general and former head of the state corrections department who had called her a publicity-seeking phony who was stirring up trouble, himself needed psychiatric examination. Both Wade and Elayn Hunt have died, Hunt before the end of her initial term as state corrections head. Governor John J. McKeithen left office in 1972 after eight years in the governor's mansion, still supporting Warden C. Murray Henderson of Angola, whom he listed among the "really top-notch people" in his administration.

Mike Gunnells made a career in corrections after all, after a shaky start, and is now assistant warden for custody at Angola. Hilton Butler, who began his career at Angola in 1952, the year before Hayden Dees arrived at the penitentiary, would work his way up in the Angola administration to the warden's position, garnering the respect of professionals along the way, until forced into retirement at least in part by federal court-mandated investigations in which Dees played a role.

Lloyd Hoyle would transfer from Angola to corrections headquarters and head up the statewide inmate construction program which saved Louisiana millions of dollars by using convict labor resources for prison renovation and construction. A $250,000 civil damage suit he filed against the Department of Corrections was dismissed by District Judge Melvin A. Shortess, who ruled that the plaintiff's exclusive remedy was through workmen's compensation. Many of the improvements he and Henderson implemented at Angola during their tenure remain in evidence today, but their great regret remains that the period was marked by unnecessary violence due to a shortage of funding to hire sufficient security officers.

Brent Miller's parents moved from Angola and now operate a restaurant south of St. Francisville with their youngest son, John, but at least one of their other sons remains employed at the prison. Mr. Miller's health is poor and has declined since the killing, which his wife says "really affected the whole family. There's something missing that cannot be replaced, but you just learn to live with it. Vengeance is His, and God will take care of whoever did this. I really don't hold any grudges. I knew at the time that Mr. Hoyle didn't intend for that to happen, but it had been put in us so strong. If he did turn the guilty inmates back into the population, I feel like he didn't intend for this to happen. Jeff Smith, who was the business manager at Angola, came back from that meeting and told me what had happened, and he said Nix probably saved Hoyle's life, because if the rest of the officers would have got hold of him, they would have killed him, so knocking him through that plate glass probably saved his life. We went to the trials, and when the juries came out to pronounce the inmates guilty, they had us stand behind bulletproof glass and then gave us an escort out of town. I just wanted to hear if there was a reason. But they said Brent was killed for his white blood and his uniform."

Nix Miller is a professor in Alabama, returning to visit his parents and siblings whenever possible. A practice firing range for correctional officers on the Angola prison grounds has been made a memorial to Brent Miller. Brent's widow would remarry after nothing came of the $1,010,000 lawsuit she filed in April of 1973 against prison officials and the state Department of Corrections, in which even a year after the death she was still charging that Deputy Warden Lloyd Hoyle, Jr., on or about April 17, 1972,

Employee pistol range at Angola, dedicated to the memory
of slain correctional officer Brent Miller.
Photo courtesy of Mrs. Huey Miller.

"ordered that the four prisoner defendants (Woodfox, Jackson, Wallace and Montegut) be transferred from the maximum security portion of the penitentiary . . . against the advice of Deputy Warden Hayden Dees," which act caused the death of her husband. Depositions answering her petition asserted that none of the inmates found guilty of the murder had been released by Hoyle from maximum security, that Montegut was released from lockdown following the filing of a suit alleging violation of his constitutional rights in the absence of any documentation in his record as to the reasons for his confinement, that there was no record of Associate Warden Dees objecting to Montegut's transfer, and that Brent Miller was violating standing orders by being in the dormitory during the feeding period for inmates instead of on the more highly visible walkway outside the dorm.

Judge William Bennett is dead, and Richard Kilbourne stepped down as district attorney before the protagonists in this case were brought to trial. After serving as Angola's warden for security during the early seventies, at a time when there were so many escapes that one narrow side street leading to the New Orleans Charity Hospital where inmates with major medical needs were sent for treatment carried a makeshift sign reading *"Careful, Escapee Crossing,"* Hayden Dees transferred to headquarters as assistant work release administrator, then became warden of the East Baton Rouge Parish Prison after a stint as warden at Dixon Correctional Institute in Jackson at the insistence of Judge William Bennett, who convinced correctional administrators that the townspeople would never support a prison in that locale unless Dees was its head. The only principal to this story who declined to be interviewed, Dees was temporarily appointed, in the most ironic twist of fate, a well-paid prison expert for the federal court under the auspices of District Judge Frank Polozola, working with former Angola warden Ross Maggio in a continuation of the original federal prison suit filed during the McKeithen administration. Lloyd Hoyle muses over this wry turn of affairs, "Basically, what they're trying to do through the federal courts, Dees has been all of his career diametrically opposed to, and yet there he was, telling people to do what he never would do himself and getting paid for it."

In keeping with the unfortunate national image of Louisiana politics, the situation in state corrections continues to resemble nothing so much as a trip down Alice's rabbit hole, where up is down and big becomes small and nothing is quite what it seems. Only here, a more apt title might be *Malice in Blunderland,* for there is a mean-spiritedness blessedly lacking in Alice's wonderland adventures. Here, the hilarious fun of make-believe has been perverted into a twisted and hurtful reality whereby an already tragic situation can be manipulated and magnified to further a despicable personal vendetta, and where the major obstacle to court-mandated progress in prisons in the past can become the highly paid court expert interpreting federal policy for the future for institutions across the state. Only in Louisiana is the truth that much stranger than fiction.

2009 Update:

After two trials and 36 years in solitary confinement, in 2008 Albert Woodfox's latest murder conviction was overturned on the grounds of deficient counsel; ironically, when the case was previously presented for re-indictment, author Anne Butler was among the jury pool and sat on the grand jury that heard the final eyewitness testimony of Hezekiah Brown, who has since died. The state attorney general has appealed. Both of Brent Miller's parents have died; Hilton Butler and Lloyd Hoyle have retired, although former warden Butler still guides visitors through the Angola museum periodically.

II

"Have It on Your Mind, White Boy": Death in the Check-Out Dorm

It is next to impossible for anyone not intimately connected with prisons and prison life to understand the complex way in which life behind bars is forcibly manipulated into a microcosm of real life on the outside, sometimes to preserve some semblance of normality, other times to gratify strange, strong appetites and desires. In the absence of the real thing, substitutions are made, some more twisted than others.

Take weapons, for example. Only in rare instances are there actual manufacturer-model guns or store-bought knives in the hands of Angola inmates, smuggled in as contraband by friends, relatives or even, unbelievably, correctional officers on the take. Instead, inmates make do with what's at hand, hoarding razorblades and spare bits of metal, honing files or farm tools to sharp points, attaching nails to sturdy carved sticks, breaking the bowls off spoons and sharpening the handles.

By the same token, personal relationships undergo forced changes in the deprived world behind bars. Intimate outside peer groups or gangs on the streets may remain relatively unchanged in prison, becoming cliques or posses or so-called *families* of like-minded inmates, often from the same hometowns and hence known as *homeboys* or *homies*. Even in these family groups, weaker or less aggressive inmates are sometimes viewed by the stronger in less than paternalistic ways, but in disturbances or disagreements with outsiders, clique members stick together and look out for each other, a slight to one being taken as an affront to all.

And in the absence of accessible women, an even greater perversion comes into play. Younger, more easily intimidated, physically attractive inmates are made to assume these submissive roles as well, playing maid, waitress, care-giver and yes, even sexual partner, to stronger and more macho male prisoners. Called in prison parlance *whores, punks, gal-boys* or *kids*, these female-substitutes are nonchalantly referred to by other inmates with feminine pronouns, and often enhance their images by growing long hair on their heads and shaving their legs and underarms, wearing makeup and provocative clothing.

Pushed into assuming the role of *catcher* (for in prison sexual activity, he who assumes the male role *pitches* and adamantly considers himself no homosexual, while he who plays the accepting female role *catches* and *is* considered homosexual), these gal-boys have been the victims of physical force or psychological persuasion in some instances. In others, they may simply have assumed the feminine role for protection against rougher predatory inmates or for personal gain, since the protector can often be generous, as in the real world outside, with attention, money, luxuries or drugs.

35

Whatever the reason for their assumption of the feminine role, these gal-boys mean trouble, directly or indirectly causing a disproportionately high percentage of the violence which erupts so frequently, so unexpectedly, so fatally in a prison population crowded with lusting young men at the peak of their sexuality.

In the warped world behind bars, sex assumes a bloated importance out of touch with reality, involving far more than mere physical gratification. Racial strife, power struggles, the importance of image in prison, all these factors come into play, involving not just the inmates but some correctional officers and other employees as well. There have been well-documented instances of sexual abuse of inmates by guards in defiance of strong regulations to the contrary (one officer, recently dismissed, found himself in the awkward position of attempting to explain exactly how he came to have his penis nearly bitten off between the bars). Before federal court orders of the mid-seventies increased the guard complement at Angola, such abuses were undeniably even more widespread because of greater opportunity, with homosexual abuse between guard and prisoner a frequent occurrence, heterosexual activity between female nurses or social workers and male inmates not unheard of, and even a few amazing instances where higher-up employees living in free housing areas of the prison involved inmate house servants or other available prisoners with both husband and wife. The sexual situation can also at times be exploited by security officers, rewarding informers with access to sex, withholding access from less cooperative offenders.

All of these factors would come into play during a hot night in August of 1983, when the still darkness of one crowded dormitory at Angola would be shattered by muffled bumps and stifled groans. Some inmates feigned sleep, seeking the protection of non-involvement; others took shelter beneath their beds; and at least one was literally scared almost to death, suffering a heart attack in the bathroom. When the dorm security officer finally heard the commotion and flooded the sleeping area with light while simultaneously calling frantically for aid, three black inmates lay bleeding to death, a fourth was seriously wounded, and a white homosexual couple waited quietly by their beds to surrender the lethal weapon, a file which had been sharpened, reportedly by a free guard in return for sexual favors, to a razor-sharp point.

At the center of the storm was Michael Ward Burge, called Iron Mike, a nickname he insists was given him by friends because he was always pumping iron, pumping up at the same time his treasured image as a strong inmate not to be trifled with. Product of a broken Baton Rouge home and a childhood scarred by violent rejection, abuse and parental neglect, Burge seems proof of the old corrections criticism that constant institutionalization only breeds better criminals. In and out of juvenile detention facilities, group homes for wayward or delinquent youth, reform schools, jails and prisons where he undoubtedly found the atmosphere more hospitable than at home, he first ran away at age ten, was a ward of the state welfare department by fourteen, and chalked up a string of escapes from every detention facility to which he was sentenced.

His initial petty thefts, truancy and runaway charges escalated to drug heists, robberies and auto theft, and Burge was eventually sentenced to Angola while still a teenager, already a product of his institutional environment to the extent that he had the old-time inmate's attitude concerning the absolutely vital necessity of maintaining an appearance of strength in a prison population where, in the old days, giving a stronger inmate an inch one day meant he would take a mile (plus your money, manhood, possessions, and whatever else he could get) the next day. Both inmates and correctional officers insist this is no longer quite the case, but for Michael Burge, being considered strong was everything. "I want to be respected," he said at his subsequent trial for three counts of second-degree murder. "I think sometimes the only way to acquire peace is to be strong. Like we sent troops to Libya. To show strength. I don't think you can acquire peace without strength. That don't mean you go around exerting it."

Or perhaps it was just that Michael Burge had taken all the abuse he could stand as a child, and was determined to take no more. An innocent incident from his early childhood, which Mike recalled recently in a letter to a longtime family friend, paints a poignant picture of sensitivity and longing for love, a small boy's sympathy for motherless baby possums starkly contrasted with the terrifying unexpected appearance of his own abusive mother, a woman who, according to the same family friend, cursed and beat Mike and "hated him all his life."

In his letter Mike would write of spending most of his days roaming the woods with his faithful dog Snowball, returning home only late at night when he was hopeful of escaping abuse. "I and Snowball would go in the woods all the time and hunt. I had a BB gun. Snowball was a all around hunter. He loved the woods. I remember once Snowball killed a Mother opossum. She was in a hold with her babies and Snowball stuck his head in the hold and killed it before I could stop him. So, there was about five (5) of these little babies. And I couldn't just leave them there. I felt so sorry for them, I knew they couldn't last without their Mother. So I brought them home. At that time I was living in Houston with my parents. My mother was in the hospital at the time due to a fight she and my dad had. But she came home unsuspected. I had the babies in her bed. (LAUGH!) She must had known I put them there for I was in the back yard playing with Snowball and didn't even know she was in the house, I thought she was still in the hospital. I heard her screaming my name and I thought I was going to die of fear. *My mother was something to be scared of whenever she got mad.* She came to the back door holding the babies by their long tails and threw them in the back yard. All the time looking at me like she wanted to kill me. She had a bandage around her head. And that really scared me all the more. You know how kids are with their imaginary monsters and horror movies, etc. Anyway, she looked like one of those mummies you see in one of those old horror movies. (LAUGH!)"

In spite of his bravely inserted *LAUGH*, there is nothing the least amusing in the picture presented there. Unfortunately, it is typical of the childhood Michael Burge endured, for the sympathy he felt for the baby possums facing life without a mother's

Left: Michael Burge, shown at his grandmother's house in 1954 at age four. Photo courtesy of Michael Burge.

Left: Burge as an elementary school student. Photo courtesy of Michael Burge.

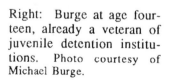

Right: Burge at age fourteen, already a veteran of juvenile detention institutions. Photo courtesy of Michael Burge.

love and support was something he knew far too well. Perhaps it was the ever-present excess of alcohol, or the prescription drugs his mother Floramye abused. Perhaps it was a spill-over of the incessant violence in her marriage, for she and her husband Alfred Louis Burge, a used car salesman and sometime Exxon employee who was himself an two-time alum of Angola, fought violently, beating and stabbing and at one point, according to a family friend, even cutting off each other's ears. Perhaps Flo simply didn't know *how* to care for her children, leaving one to be found crawling alone in diapers along dangerous Plank Road in the wee hours of the morning and reportedly never removing baby Mike from his crib until he literally crawled out himself. Perhaps it was resentment, for Flo Burge was carrying Mike at the time her oldest son Bruce, then aged seven, drowned unattended in Monte Sano Bayou.

Whatever the reason, Michael Burge had an unspeakably awful childhood, receiving what love and guidance he got from his mother's elderly parents, the dearly beloved Willie Ward Sanders and Albert T. Sanders, with whom he lived off and on throughout his troubled youth, going back and forth between the households, he recalls, "like a yo-yo." Even his father would often take Mike to the home of other relatives to get him away from the constant beatings he endured at the hands of his mother, who packed a pistol, shot one subsequent husband, poured boiling water down another's throat as he slept open-mouthed, and would eventually be murdered herself by yet another.

Michael Burge's background is sadly consistent with the picture of the typical juvenile offender painted by Don Wydra, assistant secretary of Louisiana's Office of Juvenile Services in the Department of Public Safety and Corrections. Wydra quotes statistics showing that seventy-three percent of juvenile offenders come from what is described as "a chaotic lifestyle in the family with no sense of order at all;" forty-six percent suffer from drug and/or alcohol abuse at home; and thirty-five percent have suffered sexual abuse. If ever there was a chaotic lifestyle at home, it was the Burge family during Mike's childhood; the alcoholism and infidelities of both parents assured constant violent battles. As for sexual abuse, Mike says he'd rather not talk about that after all these years, that parts of his life are just too painful to re-examine.

Says longtime family friend Nell Holmes, who worked with Flo Burge before Mike was even born and remains closer to Mike today than any surviving blood relatives, "That child was abused in every way there is to abuse someone. Physically, emotionally, mentally, and in whatever area abuse comes under. He used to go out in the woods and just stay by himself rather than go home. He had a horrible, horrible homelife. His mother and father were always drunk, they beat each other up, they stabbed each other. Now that must be terrifying for a child. The father was involved with someone else, the mother was involved; I cannot understand why they stayed in a marriage where five other lives were involved, living like animals, because all of that rubbed off on all of those children. It was nothing for Flo to hit the children in the mouth, and his sister told me that Mike was the one who was most abused. That child has been abused since the day he was born, and he is still being abused."

Born in Baton Rouge on October 16, 1950, Mike views his background with typical ambivalence, describing his commitment to the Brown School in Austin, Texas, when he had just turned fourteen, as stemming from his "not getting along with my mother," besides frequently running away from home and committing home burglaries. "They had a hearing before they sent me to that school in front of a judge, and my grandparents showed up, and my mama was supposed to be there but she never showed up. I guess my grandparents handled the responsibility better."

And yet there was still that undying hope, that love a small child feels for a parent regardless of circumstances, that touching willingness to shoulder the neglected responsibility. Mike recalled in a letter that "once we were going across this long bridge and my Mother always drove fast, lucky she was such a good driver, ha! Anyway, a back tire blew out with no warning whatsoever. Here we were traveling around 85 m.p.h. and she is now losing control of the car, it is swaying all over this four lane bridge. With her avoiding hitting cars in our next lane. It was really terrible and scary. And it went on for a good while too. I then asked her if she could swim? I was only seven at the time. She said, 'No.' And I said, 'Don't worry Momma, I save you!' Said it matter-of-fact too, like it wouldn't be no problem. (LAUGH!)"

At fourteen, Mike says he "kept messing up" at the Brown School; informed by his social worker of an impending transfer to the Louisiana Training Institute, he escaped once again. "They had girls at the school, and there was a girl I got involved with and we had kept running away. I been going with this girl Alice for about the whole time I been there. She was from Atlanta, Georgia. Me and her talked about it and we decided to leave the night before me and the social worker were supposed to catch a plane back to Baton Rouge. We left that night and stole a car in Austin, and we went to Houston and stole another car. And we went to Lake Charles and stole another car, and then we got arrested in Jennings, Louisiana, and they got me in an airplane and put me in Ryan Airport (juvenile detention center) and then I went back in front of the judge and he sentenced me to LTI."

Mike had attended Dufrocq Elementary, Baton Rouge Junior High, Istrouma and Baton Rouge High schools off and on while living at home; now he would attend classes in the reformatory at LTI-Monroe, later earning his GED at the state's maximum-security prison. But the pattern of escapes continued, with at least four from LTI, in spite of a brief period of release to an uncle, a respected state legislator, while his mother remarried and moved to Texas and his father spent some time behind bars in Angola.

It would ironically be the father, Louis Burge, who engineered at least one of the escapes. Mike recalls that the elder Burge "hitchhiked up to LTI, and when he got there he got a pass to take me out for the day. They got a zoo there at Monroe, this was on a Sunday, and he got a pass and was supposed to bring me back at four o'clock. But he never brought me back. He was on the run, too, because he was wanted in Baton Rouge, I think for hot checks. We did a lot of travelling through New Mexico and Texas, and times got kind of hard for me and him financially. My mother and my stepfather were living in Victoria, Texas, so we come back to Texas and my daddy called my mama and they met us at a motel and picked me up and took me back to Victoria with them. I was about fifteen then, and I ran away and hitchhiked all the way to Baton Rouge, going to my grandparents' house. I got apprehended in Baton Rouge, and they sent me back to LTI. They caught my daddy too. He wasn't the first one to ever do that with a child at LTI; I don't know if they wanted to use him as an example or what, but he went to trial for it and got two and a half years. I testified at his trial. He did ten months and parolled out." Comments Nell Holmes on this scenario, "Mike was never ever taught right from wrong; now when Louis carried Mike off with him from reform school, all that was teaching him was to run from the law."

Released to his uncle, sixteen-year-old Mike visited his father at Angola and soon took up residence with his mother, who had returned to Baton Rouge after divorcing her second husband. He would find himself back at LTI before long, however, thanks at least in part to her drinking problem. "My mama's an alcoholic," he explains. "One night I borrowed her car to go out. Well, she had a .25 Baretta in the glove compartment. I didn't know it was there. And while I was out, she called her brother, the one who got me out of LTI, and she told him I took the car and I had a pistol and I was going to break my daddy out of Angola. That wasn't true; it would have been kind of hard! So when I got back to the house, they had all kind of police in there, and they arrested me. I don't know why she told them that; she done things sometimes looking for attention. I don't know, maybe she really thought that, or maybe she'd forgotten she'd loaned me the car, because a lot of times she'd drink so much to where she'd forget things and she would just pass out."

After about a year at LTI, Mike was released a little past his seventeenth birthday. Taking a Greyhound bus back to Baton Rouge, he moved in with his father, who had served his sentence at Angola and been released. With little guidance, young Mike resumed his former habits, frequenting bars and carrying a pistol with the same nonchalance other teenagers carry their schoolbooks. He recounts in one letter being in a Port Allen nightspot called the Riviera at a time when his brother Butch, "a real lady's man," was dating Grace, the feminine half of the popular singing team *Dale and Grace* of the hit song *I'm Leaving It All Up To You*. Recalls Mike, "First a argument started between Butch and Dale in regards to Grace. See, Grace left Dale for Butch, and Dale was loving Grace hard and he got to drinking and all, and he wanted her back! So the next thing you know, Dale pulls out a pistol. Butch never carried a pistol, and I was aware of this. Dale raised the pistol up at Butch, and I pulled out a pistol, too. Everyone was screaming and diving for the floor. The band stopped playing, cause we were right in front of the band, where the dancehall starts and the bar ends. Then it got very quiet. There were about five bouncers in the club, and they usually needed that many, too. They all knew me and Butch. So, when it got quiet, Dale was pointing his pistol at Butch, and I was pointing my pistol at Dale's head.

"I attempted to scare him and make him put his pistol down by telling him, 'You pull that trigger and I promise you, Dale, you won't have to ever worry about Grace anymore. Now just put the pistol down slowly on the table, and I, Butch and Grace are going to walk out of here.' He put the pistol on the table and the lounge owner picked it up. Then I told Butch and Grace to go outside and start the car. A bouncer named 'Big Mike' was behind the bar with a shotgun cradled in his arms, but he didn't point it at me. I knew these people. The owner told me, 'Mike you come back any time you please, ain't no one here going to mess with you behind this. I think you handled it mighty good.' He even offered me a job later, but I didn't think I was old enough or big enough to be a bouncer. I was only seventeen at the time and I didn't weigh 145 pounds and was around six feet tall. Slightly on the skinny side!"

Besides carrying a pistol, Mike resumed another habit from his earlier teen years, one which would send him to Angola for the first time right after he turned eighteen. "When I was a youngster," Mike recalls, "a lot of us kids would go downtown and hang out at the Greyhound bus station and like pick up homosexuals and make money off of them. And then sometimes rob them and stuff. This was something that I had done before for money. We would just go there and stand on the street corner and sometimes guys would come by and start talking to you. At that time that area was real dark, right across the street from the old state capitol. A lot of kids had certain places that would be their area and would even fight for turf. I didn't consider myself homosexual, because I never did commit no homosexual act. Very seldom I would rob one of them. What they would do, like they'd give me and these other kids $10, $20, sometimes you'd find one give you $50, and all they would want to do would be to go down on you. We didn't look at it like we were doing anything, you know, wrong. All we wanted out of it was the money."

It was New Year's Eve the year Mike turned eighteen, and he says he'd been drinking. In a downtown bar not far from the bus station, Bruce's on Third Street, he was approached by a man who asked him to go across the Mississippi River where the bars stayed open all night. "So when we went across the bridge, he pulled off in a canefield and started fondling me. I hit him a couple of times and then I robbed him. He had a pistol that I took from him. I told him to drop me off at the Carousel Club, which he did, and he told me, 'Mike, give me that pistol and I won't say nothing, but it's registered in my name.' But I wouldn't give him the pistol. So he went and called the police and they picked me up at the Carousel and arrested me for simple robbery. I got three years for that."

In Angola for the first time, still a teenager, Michael Burge put his high-school typing instruction to good use as a clerk for a classification officer, then he got into a fight and was sent to the Big Yard in a first-offender dormitory, where he would begin the lifelong struggle to preserve his independence and image. "I went to Pine I Dormitory, and I had some trouble there. They had guys wanting to *turn me out* (prison slang for forcing the acceptance of homosexual advances). I got in some fights. Eventually they just left me alone. I never did belong to nobody. In the first-offender dormitory I'd say about half the guys in there had what they called an *old man,* and if the old man wasn't in that dormitory, then he was in one of the other dormitories where they had second offenders. At that time, Angola was wide open, there wasn't really no discipline, and they (other inmates) would just come in the dormitory whenever they wanted to, or go in other people's dormitories. And they had like one free man for four dormitories, but he sat outside and he'd come and count every hour, but you'd know when he would count. So really, you know, you had to make it on your own. It wasn't because I was tough or anything, 'cause I was a skinny kid; it was just using my mind. They had a couple of the older dudes liked me after they seen me fight a couple of times, and sometimes it don't take but one person to put the word out if he's got a reputation, to leave you alone, and that's about all it takes, really."

Homosexual rape, the forcible *turning out* of one unwilling inmate by another stronger one, is called a violent subculture's definition of masculinity through conquest and subjugation in an *Angolite* article called *Prison: The Sexual Jungle* by knowledgeable prison journalist Wilbert Rideau. "Rape in prison is rarely a sexual act," Rideau explains, "but one of violence, politics and an acting out of power roles," the ultimate humiliation visited upon a male by forcing him to assume the role of a woman. Rideau quotes former Angola chief of security Walter Pence, "It's basically one guy saying to another: 'I'm a better man than you and I'm gonna turn you out to prove it.'" While most will return to normal heterosexual relationships once released, Pence estimates that at Angola a staggering seven out of ten inmates become involved at some point during their institutionalization in homosexual activities. The tone is set early in an inmate's confinement, when the arrival of good-looking inexperienced youngsters, *fresh fish,* has been likened by hardened corrections officials to the parading of a bitch in heat through a kennel of lusty male dogs; the ensuing violence establishes the pecking order for the youngsters' entire prison stays.

Nell Holmes says that within the first few weeks of Mike's arrival at Angola on April 3, 1969, "he was approached by a great big black man who said, 'Hey boy, who you belong to?' And Mike said, 'I don't belong to anybody.' And he said, 'Yes you do too.' Mike said, 'We'll see.' And I understand that one heck of a fight went on behind one of the buildings. But Mike didn't lose the fight. That child is solid gold and his heart is as big as Texas, but he had so much abuse as a child that he takes nobody else's abuse. Mike does not pick fights, and he has a strong tendency to try to protect other inmates, but he does not back down."

He would serve two and a half years on his three-year sentence for simple robbery from West Baton Rouge Parish. While in Angola, Mike scored high enough on placement tests to be referred for vocational training, but apparently the security staff refused to allow him to attend the welding school he was interested in, instead restricting him to field work. He consequently learned no viable skills that could be of any assistance to him when he was released and returned to Baton Rouge to live with his father.

It wouldn't be six weeks before Mike was arrested again, this time for robbing a Plank Road service station of less than $50 and being recognized in a nearby lounge by the station owner later that same night. After serving about four years in the parish prison, he was released and, again, would stay out only a short period. "That was about 1975, I think," he says. "I was about twenty-four years old. I was doing a lot of drugs, mostly just speed. I was into what they call desoxyns and preludes. We had many different ways of getting them; a lot of times we'd take women to different doctors and they would get diet pills, thirty at a time. We'd travel all over Baton Rouge, Lafayette, Donaldsonville, going to different doctors. Desoxyns are those little yellow pills. Sometimes people let them soak in water; they take a bottle of thirty of them and put water in them and let them soak about two or three days. See, the outside of them's the only part that's any good. The water turns yellow, and some people inject that into their arms; some people swallow it. I done both. Preludes, you had to cook them up, wash the outer coating off of them and mash them up, cook them up on a burner and inject them."

It would be the drug robbery of a pharmacy on Veterans Highway in Kenner which would return Mike to Angola. "I wasn't known in Kenner," he says, "and I guess that's why I was doing that around that area. I robbed the drugstore to get drugs, not money. I walked into the drugstore and there were four older people in there, two couples. Two of them owned the drugstore, and the other two were just friends visiting, sitting behind the counter in chairs. The woman was up front, kind of by herself, and I showed her my pistol and I asked her to walk to the back with me. When we got to the back, I told the man to give me all his preludes and all his desoxyns, which he put in a bag for me. So when I got ready to leave, he come up with a shotgun. I was running out of the store and I hit a display case in the center aisle when I seen him coming with the shotgun. I turned around and pointed the pistol at him, and I told him to put it down. Then his wife stuck her hand out on the barrel and pushed it down and told him 'No,' and I ran out in the street."

Despite the fact that he was armed while committing this and other robberies, Mike insists he had no intention of hurting anybody, citing an odd kind of pride among thieves back then. "I'm the kind of person," he says, "I don't mess with nobody unless they mess with me. I never hurt anybody. I come to the penitentiary when I was eighteen, and the kind of people I came into contact with at that time were mostly guys older than me. Back at that time in the sixties, they weren't giving out the kind of sentences they are now, and I think the reason for that is you got these kids nowadays who go out and kill just to be killing. But back then, even though there was armed robbery and whatever, they took pride in the fact that they did everything so professionally that there never was any thought of anybody getting hurt. That's what I felt. I always would case the place before I robbed it, and knew who would be in there. My main worry was who might walk in unexpectedly, so I just tried to get out of there as fast as I could. Now when I robbed that drugstore and took them drugs, I never even took their money; they had money in the cash register, but they were insured for them drugs, so they didn't lose nothing. I just wanted the drugs."

Michael Burge returned to Baton Rouge and thought he had gotten away with the Kenner drugstore robbery. He hadn't. The drugstore was located close to where his married sister lived, and her brother-in-law just happened to work for the local police department. "I found out later that thirty minutes earlier, my sister's brother-in-law was in that same drugstore. I guess she got to thinking about what would have happened if I had robbed that store thirty minutes earlier when he was in there. The one thing they remembered about the robber was that he was wearing a pair of white patent leather shoes, which let my sister know it was me. She was the one told them I did it."

Recognized by undercover narcotics agents in a tiny Port Allen bar called Nick's, Mike grabbed his pistol and ran into some nearby woods, hoping to jump a passing train in the dark. As the freight neared, he could see it was filled with policemen, and a state police dog named Champ soon rousted the suspect from his hiding place. Three escapes from three different Jefferson Parish lock-ups, one lasting more than two months and leading all the way to California, added a year for simple escape charges to the thirty-five-year sentence Mike received on the armed robbery charge.

He returned to Angola in June of 1977, and has been there ever since, most of the time in one kind of trouble or another, which he initially attributed to his reputation as an escape artist. "When I first came up here," he says from Angola today, "I had some armed escapes and stuff. Some of these jails I was in and escaped from, the Baton Rouge authorities would knock them, saying 'They ain't got nothing but tin cans down in Jefferson Parish,' and all, so I put a lot of heat on them. My opinion was that some people from Jefferson Parish contacted people in Angola, I don't want to say to give me a hard time, but to let them know they considered me an escape risk and dangerous."

First classified to CCR, Close Custody Restricted, Burge applied for a work tier at the urging of C. Paul Phelps, who had been a concerned and interested probation officer while Mike was in juvenile detention and had worked his way up in the Department of Public Safety and Corrections to serve as DOC secretary Elayn Hunt's first assistant, eventually replacing Hunt upon her death. Sent to Camp J, Angola's infamous maximum-security lockdown facility, for allegedly assisting in another inmate's escape attempt and then joining a *buck* or strike, Burge, with some assistance from headquarters, worked his way back to a field workline and then into a dormitory on the Walk.

This was his best period at Angola. He was in his late twenties, working in the field all day, playing sports, and at night working out with weights in the gym. He recalls, "I got a nickname from always pumping iron, because sometimes I would pump iron six, seven hours a day if I could. So they started calling me Iron Mike. Then I won the boxing title. So I was getting a lot of respect on the Yard because of it." And that respect, to Mike, was all-important, making it all the more devastating when he was sentenced to the cellblock, away from the dormitory and the weights.

Playing football, he broke his leg in five places, was put in a cast up to his hip and told he could no longer work out with weights. But Mike was determined to try, his stubborn insistence setting off a long string of confrontations with the security staff, beginning before Mike was even out of the hospital ward, where at pill call he was given crushed librium in a clear plastic cup. "So you'd take that crushed-up pill and you'd drink your cup of water behind it, and there ain't no way to save it," Mike explains. "But this guard, I guess I let him get to me, because he would tell me real smart, 'Open your mouth,' and I would say 'For what,' and he would say, 'I want to look in your mouth.' So I told him, 'No.' And every pill call, it would be the same thing over again. I wouldn't open my mouth, so I got about nine aggravated disobedience charges and they locked me in a room. Warden Peabody, whose wife was over the hospital then, came and started shouting at me, telling me I was gonna open my mouth, so I just started refusing the medication. They took me to court in a wheelchair in the pouring-down rain, and Warden Peabody, he sends me to Camp J. They put me back in the room, and I tore my cast off. When I tore my cast off my leg, it was all shrivelled up. I messed up, see?"

As the prison doctor replaced the cast, the phone rang. It was C. Paul Phelps, calling with some badly needed advice. As Mike recalls the conversation, "He said, 'Mike, who's running the department of corrections?' And I said, 'You are.' And he said, 'Who's running the prison?' And I gave the warden's name. And he said, 'Who's running the hospital?' And I said Dr. Barnes was. And he said, 'Mike, you let us run all that, and you run Mike Burge.'" Phelps also saw to it that the petty charges against Mike were dropped, and later, according to Mike, raised cain when he discovered that security staff harassed Mike by making it difficult for him to work out, insisting on long unnecessary walks with his crutches and placing the weights in the blazing sun.

"I don't know what Phelps saw in me," Mike muses today. "I think what it is, is that at Ryan Airport they got a detention center for boys and girls, and right across from it but really connected to it by this little walkway, is where the probation officers got their offices, and I was in that detention center one time and he got the parole board to meet and let me go. I think it was just sympathy and understanding, and I think he realizes what I went through when I was young. That's basically all I can see. I have written him letters and all, and I think he knows what kind of home I come from."

If Mike had rotated between the homes of his parents and grandparents as a child, he continued the yo-yo existence at Angola, bouncing from yard to cellblock to dormitory to Camp J lockdown, struggling to maintain his image of strength, accumulating hard-earned scars like the notches on the grip of a gunfighter's trusty revolver. In the cellblock, a fistfight sent one notorious black inmate to the hospital for stitches. "He had a reputation for being a bad guy," Mike says, "and everybody seen me knock him out. We did five days in the hole and they put us back together, and he told me it was over with, but I didn't think it was. Then I was sitting on the cellblock yard playing cards and he attacked me with a knife, half of a scissors. He come up behind me and hit me in the neck, and when he did, I got up and took out after him, chasing him around the yard trying to take the knife away from him. Then he stopped and made a stand, and I should have kept charging him, but I stopped and was trying to hit him with my fist. I got stabbed everywhere, chest, arm, stomach, back, head. I got stabbed about ten times altogether. I got stabbed in the hand and got a knuckle broke."

Mike's attacker was sent to Camp J, an in-house handling of a potentially deadly stabbing attack which would later figure prominently in Mike's own thought processes and actions. With a cast on his arm up to the wrist, Mike wanted to stay where he was, but again there were administrative objections. "The security man over the block," he says, "wanted to move me to another block, and I told him I was all right there. He was thinking some of this guy's friends might want to do me something. All of a sudden, he comes up with a letter saying my life was in danger if I stayed there, signed by the Black Muslims or something like that. So I went to court and they sent me to CCR for protection. After being up there a couple of months, my people called the warden and asked what I was doing locked down when I was the one got stabbed. So they sent me to Camp H Dormitory."

There, a fistfight with a bully called Sportyman sent Mike to the cellblock, a punishment he considered excessive for the charge when no action was taken against the other participant in the fight. "I'm mad," Mike recalls of that time, "because I know I'm not supposed to be in no cellblock. A fistfight don't carry but five days. So as soon as I get transferred, I told them a lie, I said, 'I can't live here, I got stabbed and this guy's got friends over here.' I was just trying to finagle my way. I figured if they were going to do this to me, I would return the favor. They sent me back to Camp J and put me in the hole. I was due to go to the *check-out* board, protection court, which I ain't never done before, I mean like check out of a place or nothing *(checking out* is requesting a move for protection). So I go to court before Major Carmichael, and he sends me to Mag, Magnolia 3 Dormitory. Magnolia was protection. The people in there needed to be protected. They had like four dormitories in Mag, and out of those four, they had one, two, three, maybe four or five guys wouldn't have had any problems living anywhere, but maybe security had their reasons for putting them in there, or maybe they did what I did and tried to finagle their way in there. I wasn't actually trying to finagle my way to Mag, but I felt like I got messed over, which I did."

Michael Burge, by his own admission, had in the summer of 1988 unwittingly *finagled* his way into the worst possible place at the worst possible time. Says career correctional officer Hilton Butler, who was temporarily at another state facility during this period but would later return to serve as warden of Angola, "Michael Burge should have never been in that dormitory. That was a protection dormitory. And Michael Burge has never needed protection from anybody. He wasn't scared of nobody, and he should have never been in that dormitory at all. You see, there's different times with different convicts, and Mike is one that tries to live thirty years ago, in other words, 'If I'm a man,

I'm gonna *be* a man, and nobody's gonna fool with nothing belongs to me,' and stuff like that. That's the way of life with all the convicts thirty years ago. You had to earn their respect, and then they didn't fool with what was yours."

Ross Maggio, warden of Angola at the time, testified that Michael Burge was in Magnolia "because one of the disciplinary boards there headed up by some of our staff placed him there because they felt he should be put there for his own protection." But Mike Burge would be at Magnolia, referred to as a check-out dormitory, only for a fateful six weeks, and while he was in there, he stood out like a sore thumb among the weaker inmates and misfits and homosexuals who had been classified as unable to make it in the general prison population. "I felt like a duck out of water in Mag," he remembers, "because there wasn't really nobody for me to associate with. I felt out of place there. I felt stronger than most of those people, you know. I just felt different. I felt like I didn't belong there."

He also felt lonely. On the Walk, Burge had had a close relationship with an inmate named Danny. "At first," he relates, "we were just good friends and I kind of took him under my wing. He was just like a young hippie, long hair, good family, and he'd robbed a Pak-A-Sak, first time he'd ever been in trouble. They gave him twenty years for robbery and he came to Angola and got by awhile on his personality, made people like him, 'cause he wasn't physical in no way, shape or form. We never had sex, but anybody knew if they bothered him, I would take care of it."

After awhile, Mike says, the relationship deepened. "He became my *kid,* you know, sexually, and I was his *old man.* In penitentiary terminology, one is not considered a homosexual when they play the role of old man, being he is the one always doing the pitching and the kid is the one catching. Danny only had one old man. The terminology within Angola was that Danny *turned himself out* for me. Turning oneself out means the giving of oneself to another sexually."

Other inmates called Danny Mike's shadow, for the two became inseparable. "We usually got beds next to each other, by paying somebody," Mike recalls. "I was playing football and boxing and stuff, and Danny would go down to the gym with me. He liked being around me. A lot of gal-boys will cause you trouble and stuff, but Danny was the kind of kid where he'd go out of his way to make sure I wouldn't have no problems behind him. Or somebody would say something to him, and he wouldn't come running to tell me, he'd let it go. I had strong feelings for Danny, and I'm not gonna lie to you, it was lust too, sexual attraction. I didn't feel like it was a *marriage;* I looked at it as a friendship, I mean, somebody sometime that you can confide in, when you wake up and your head ain't feeling too good, or you get a bad letter from home or something. Some of these gal-boys play the role to the extreme, shaving their legs and armpits, wearing bikini underwear and tight jeans with the back pockets removed from the buttocks area, wearing makeup, and if you were to view them on the streets there is no way humanly possible you could tell you were looking at a man. Danny never done any of this; he was just himself. I consider myself bi-sexual and have very strong feelings for women, but there's a strong possibility that Danny and I would have maintained a relationship outside."

After several years together on the Walk, Mike and Danny were caught with seven or eight joints of marijuana. Because of an earlier marijuana charge for which the sentence was suspended, Danny went to Line 35, where he had trouble with stronger inmates approaching him sexually, and requested a transfer to Magnolia. Once released from Camp J to Line 35, Mike could surreptitiously send him money and mail through the blood bank. "You ain't supposed to," Mike explains, "but they got workers working there at the plasma unit, and you can leave letters or messages, and when Mag comes over, they'll give Danny the letter, or vice versa. I was sending Danny stuff and long-distance looking out for him, trying to get him to come where I was at. But he done fell in love with another homosexual that he was living in Mag with, so he wouldn't come."

Finally finagling his own way to another dorm in the Magnolia complex, Mike talked to Danny on the yard. "Technically, the way the penitentiary was, he belonged to me, like he was my kid," Mike says. "But Danny told me, 'Mike, I know you've still got strong feelings for me and all, but I want to let you know something, they've got somebody in the dormitory I've been with for about the last two years named Candy, and I really love him and everything, and I want to be with him, and I'd appreciate it if you'd back off.' So I told him, 'All right.' So I backed off."

And backed right into a relationship with Bobby Schriver, not long transferred to Magnolia 3 himself. "I felt out of place there," Mike recalls, "and Bobby was kind of hip, in the sense that I could relate to him. Just from working in the field all day with him, and he'd be bringing me coffee and stuff while I'd be working. See, Bobby had some black guy kind of messing with him, and I went in the dorm, and me and Bobby talked, and this black guy come and talked to me and told me to leave Bobby alone. I said, 'I ain't got no interest in him, you ain't got to worry about that.' So he got me a little angry, because he come back to me an hour later with the same story, and I said, 'I done told you one time.' So the following day, this black guy, he don't work in the field, but me and Bobby go in the field. Bobby had a job like on the headland. For some reason, some of these *linepushers* (mounted field guards), they take these pretty whores that wear makeup and stuff, and put them on the headland and let them work for them, make coffee for them, while the rest of the line works. Bobby wore makeup sometime. And in the field I told Bobby, 'That black guy come up to me two times last night in regards to you, what's happening?' So we got to talking, and I just kinda liked his personality. So that's when I entered the relationship with Bobby."

Bobby, or as he preferred *Bobbie*, was Robert James Schriver, born in September 1955, a personable young multiple offender from Metairie with an admitted past addiction to quaaludes, preludin, cocaine, marijuana and dilaudid from the age of sixteen. Small and slight, with dark hair and eyes, he was a previously married Catholic, trained as an electrician though often employed as a used car salesman, released from the Navy on a medical discharge, with a prior drug arrest stemming from an automobile accident in which he was injured and carelessly asked the deputy questioning him at the East Jefferson Hospital to bring him his pills from his car. Along with the medication, the deputy discovered two quaalude capsules and a box of yellow powder with a small spoon. It was also discovered that Schriver was wanted for probation violation, having left the state after receiving a suspended sentence for simple battery and simple assault in a domestic argument. He also had been charged in the past with illegal weapons use, illegal carrying of weapons, aggravated assault, simple battery, misdemeanor theft and forgery.

In Angola on a thirty-year sentence for armed robbery from Jefferson Parish, where he and an accomplice, both "loaded," robbed a Martinizing store to get money for drugs, Bobby Schriver became behind bars what Mike Burge calls "a gal-boy. She's weak. Anytime she's confronted with a situation where she might have to defend herself, she never has. She's small and unaggressive. I don't think Bobby was like that on the street, because he has a wife. But ninety-nine percent of them are gonna claim they were, because it makes them look better to say they were always like this, nobody forced them. I don't think Bobby was forced. He might have been getting pressure from somewhere and just picked somebody he liked. But Bobby liked to get loaded, and the guy he picked to turn himself out for first was a major marijuana distributor in Camp C."

Burge explains the sexual scenario behind bars. "There are some people who are forced. I see a lot of things that go on in this penitentiary that I don't like at all. Say some young guy gets sentenced to Jaguar or Tiger, which is all lockdown, thirteen men to a tier, and they each get an hour on the hall, and there ain't no free people around, you just open the door and walk right out. So if this guy has an hour in the hall, he can go and do anything he wants to. And they put some little kid on this hallway, and these blacks will go messing with him and try to get to him psychologically. Like they play games, like one of them will play the protector and the other three or four will be acting real agressive toward the kid. They're all in cahoots, but he don't know this, and the one guy will say, 'Y'all leave him alone,' but it's all a game. The kid will come in to this guy that's kind of helping him out, but he's putting himself in a spider web and don't know it.

"But I heard Bobby's reason for doing that was material gain, when he first what they call turned himself out. Bobby was in Camp C and they had a guy he was in the dormitory with that used to get a lot of drugs in, and Bobby liked drugs, and I heard he turned himself out. Now he might have been getting some pressure; you never really know unless you're there. He could have been getting psychological pressure, or possibly physical. Bobby was a very good-looking person. He had real long black hair, he looked girlish, he shaved his legs, he shaved under his arms, and he had female instincts in his actions. And another thing is that in Angola, the security people don't really care. They look at it like you're supposed to be man enough to take care of yourself. People get in the penitentiary and kind of get put in certain situations where they feel like they might like a certain person, or they might just say, 'Well, I might as well be for him' or something, and turn theirself out. I believe it could be a lot better if you had more caring people up here."

From Camp C, Bobby Schriver went to Camp J, where at the time inmates were allowed an hour on the hall. "Bobby had the reputation there for being a whore," Burge recalls. "There weren't really any white guys on that tier, so these black guys controlled Bobby, and they'd come out on the hall and make him do things for them, you know. I personally take everybody individually and done had black friends and everything else, but my basic opinion is that blacks are really, really off into that, that homosexuality stuff, *heavy,* and they really get turned on by white boys. Some of them really take it like a prestige thing to have a white kid. Sometimes it's power, a lot of times."

Released from Camp J, Bobby Schriver found a protector in a prisoner named Dwayne, a friend of Mike Burge's from Baton Rouge. Dwayne shared a cell with an inmate named Randy, and shared Bobby's sexual favors with him too. When Dwayne refused to move out of the cell with Randy and move in with Bobby, Burge says Bobby *caught out* (requested a transfer) and ended up in Mag, where he again attracted the attentions of a number of black inmates. Explains Burge, "Bobby had told me out in the field not to worry about the old black guy who was talking to me about him first, and he just backed completely out of the picture. But I did find out later that they had some other black guys that were interested in Bobby, and when I came in the dorm, they were surprised. Later on, guys in the dormitory said, 'Mike, you didn't know what was going on, but them black guys resented you 'cause you come right in there and got Bobby, and they were *shooting their stick,* you know.' And Bobby didn't tell me nothing about that." It would not be the only time Bobby was not completely candid.

Even more specifically, there was an inmate named Lester Allen, a nineteen-year-old from New Orleans, well over six feet tall and weighing 175 pounds, in Angola with a life sentence on a charge of first-degree murder stemming from a bar fight. Bobby and Lester, according to Burge, had been in the dungeon together, in adjoining cells. "They would talk and everything," Mike relates, "and Lester told Bobby he was loving him and he was gonna try to come where he was at. Well, when they went to check-out court, they sent Bobby to Mag, and Lester finagled his way from Eagle and got in the dormitory with Bobby. While he was at Eagle, while me and Bobby was together, he wrote Bobby several love letters, and Bobby never did show me the letters. I remember the day Lester come in the dorm, he spoke to Bobby and Bobby wouldn't even speak back to him. I didn't know nothing about this until it was all over. One day Bobby went to work in the field, and I had duty status. I kept a lot of stuff in Bobby's locker, and I went to get something and I seen one of them letters. I seen Lester Allen's name on it, and I seen Bobby, so I read it. I asked Bobby about it, and he said, 'Man, it ain't about nothing, don't worry about it.'"

Lester Allen, according to Burge and a number of other residents of Magnolia, was part of a dorm clique consisting of black inmates, mostly from the New Orleans area, who were just a little stronger than other dormitory residents, and who, until Mike's arrival, had pretty well controlled the action in Mag 3. Says Mike, "They could be strong in Mag, but they couldn't be strong on the Walk. They were the kind of people who liked that power, and they was doing a lot of *locker jacking* (stealing from inmate's lock-boxes), and they raped a little retarded black youngster out in the field and made him wash their clothes and stuff. These guys kind of resented me because I was always by myself, and I kind of resented them because I never did have too much for no clique. I would tell them something if they messed with me. I wasn't really scared of them. In a sense, I was the only one in the dorm stood up to them."

It would be the clique's locker jacking which actually precipitated the bloodbath in Magnolia 3 Dormitory the first weekend of August 1988. Mike and Bobby shared a locker box and kept their meager valuables in it. "I'd had some cash money," Mike remembers, "and I bought some weed from the Walk. The only thing separating Magnolia from the Trusty Yard is a fence, and I knew a lot of guys on the Trusty Yard and the Big Yard, and we could throw stuff over the fence. I would throw them cash money, and they would throw me marijuana back. Most times, I would get money when I would get a visit. When I'd get a visit, I'd get it from my people. They'd have it rolled up in a rubber band, and I would swallow it and go back, and either throw it up or let it come out and get it out whenever I went to the bathroom. So we had some marijuana in our locker, some cash money, some jewelry and some blue jeans, that got stolen. The lockers were next to the beds, locked. And we found out who went in there, somebody told us. There were two of them involved in it, Lester Allen and a homosexual they call Star Child."

Star Child's name was Larry Thomas, and as a state's witness at the ensuing trial, he would admit that he and Lester had indeed burglarized Bobby's locker and had even spent Sunday evening, along with other members of their group, smoking the stolen marijuana. The rest of the black Mag 3 clique, besides Star Child and Lester Allen, were inmates Darryl Washington, Ricky Gray, Mark "Red" Vincent, Lawrence Woods, and Harold Clark, who was called Fox. In Magnolia 3 dormitory, the sixty inmates slept in four rows of beds in the back of the dorm; in the front, separated from the sleeping area by the security desk, counter and water fountain, were the bathroom on one side and the TV and game rooms on the other. Lester Allen and Darryl Washington, said to be homosexual lovers, had beds right next to each other on the same row, separated by a single bed from Robert Schriver's bed, which was just across an aisle from Mike Burge. Next to Mike's bed on this other row were the beds of Mark Vincent and Ricky Gray.

From the time of Mike's arrival in Magnolia 3, the shift in the power structure upset the clique of black inmates, who initiated a pattern of harassment which began with veiled verbal insinuations ("Gonna get some of that white pussy") and escalated to outright threats accompanied by a show of weapons. On the night of Friday, August 5, 1983, Robert Schriver said he was approached by Ricky Gray in the bathroom of Mag 3, shown a sharpened file like a long nail which Ricky had stuck in his shorts, and sex was solicited. Gray, 6'1" and 161 pounds, was in Angola on a twenty-year sentence for two counts of armed robbery in Caddo Parish, acts he claimed were committed while he was high on pot.

The following morning, Saturday, August 6, the locker jacking occurred, and Mike Burge spent the rest of the weekend negotiating with the clique for the return of his belongings stolen from Bobby's box, even offering to forget the whole thing for only half of his possessions. Strong threats were made, both in the dorm and on the Yard, with Mike told to "get his shit," "take it out in blood," "get him a knife or not go to sleep that night," according to accounts given by defense witnesses. "Have it on your mind, white boy," is what Bobby Schriver remembers Mike being told, a threat he interpreted as meaning violence was forthcoming. Sunday night, Ricky Gray and Mark Vincent switched beds, a move which placed the larger, stronger Gray, an inmate Schriver had two nights before seen in possession of a weapon, directly next to Mike Burge at bedtime. In Angola for thirty-three years on a habitual felony conviction for armed robbery after a background of numerous juvenile arrests, Mark Vincent was only 5'9" and weighed 155 pounds.

Says Mike, "The only time somebody switches beds, they usually want to talk to somebody they don't normally sleep by. But Mark Vincent and Ricky Gray slept next to each other anyway, so it don't matter who's in whose bed. I ain't never seen them switch beds before. We'd just had a whole bunch of words and they'd told me not to go to sleep, then all of a sudden they switch beds for no reason, which puts Ricky Gray next to me, and Ricky Gray was the one threatened Bobby with a knife. I could see these guys were still awake; they were facing each other, talking." The code of the penitentiary *(you don't take your problems to security)* prevented asking the dorm officer for help or transfer, even in the face of escalating threats of violence, though on Sunday Mike did telephone his father, telling him his life had been threatened, in hopes that he could get help from the warden or C. Paul Phelps (being the weekend, he couldn't reach them).

Since working inmates are aroused as early as 4:30 a.m. on workdays, lights in the dorm on Sunday night, August 7, went out at 10:30, though the television set in the TV room stayed on until midnight. Mike and Bobby had stayed in the TV room of Mag 3 until 12:00, when they went to bed, lying with their heads toward each other, whispering together across the dividing aisle, as was their nightly custom. Correctional officer James Slaven, who had only worked at Mag 3 about a week, came through the dorm to make his 12:30 a.m. half-hourly headcount, stopping along the way to write up inmate Warren Cain, called *Sweetpea* or *Wonder Woman*, for "unsanitary practices" otherwise known as masturbation, then moving into the bathroom to call his count through the window to the Walk sergeant.

The altercation began around 12:40, while Slaven was still in the bathroom area where he could not see into the dorm. According to Wonder Woman, it only took "about thirty-five seconds for all the *juggings* (stabbings) to happen." Defense lawyers would later claim that the surprise attack, well planned in advance, was made by four members of the clique . . . Ricky Gray, Mark Vincent, Lester Allen and Darryl Washington . . .

against the outnumbered Mike Burge and Bobby Schriver, with at least several weapons in the hands of clique members (weapons which Fox would dispose of after the attack by flushing them down the commode before security shakedowns of the dorm), and other clique members fully dressed under the bedclothes after lights-out, ready for action (though at least two were said to have hidden beneath their cots when the fight began). Prosecutors would claim just the opposite, that Mike and Bobby, in an act of "sensual savagery," attacked the others as they lay peacefully sleeping, Mike fatally stabbing all four with a knife taped securely to his hand the way a boxer wraps his fists, Bobby swinging a sock filled with batteries at Lester Allen.

Officer Slaven would testify at the ensuing trial that he was in the bathroom giving his head count and washing his hands for no more than sixty seconds or so before he heard sounds from the darkened dormitory as if "the beds were scooting." Exiting the shower room he encountered a bleeding Ricky Gray, who fell by the door, closely followed by Mark Vincent, who ran up and fell across the security counter. Turning on the security lights, Slaven noticed Darryl Washington throw a radio before falling onto a bed. When the officer ran to help Washington, he found Lester Allen also cut and bleeding, then heard several inmates yelling for him to get the knife. It was not until this point that Officer Slaven noticed Michael Burge standing quietly by his bed, knife in hand. Actually, he would later testify, the knife was "a file sharpened down to a knife," and it was readily relinquished by Burge as soon as security officers escorted him and Bobby from the dorm.

The weapon, Burge says, actually belonged to Robert Schriver. Mike Burge explains, "One weekend, me and Bobby were in the TV room, on weekends you could stay up all night, and Bobby goes out there by the security desk talking to this guard and then comes in the TV room and pulls out this knife, a Black Diamond file that they sharpen hoes with. It had been sharpened on a grinder to a point, sharp like a needle up the sides, about eight inches long. We'd both been smoking weed, and it freaked me out. I said 'Where'd you get that?' And he said he got it from the free man. I found out later he was lying. See, when Bobby left the Walk, she took Dwayne's super radio, and in the back of the radio was a knife. Dwayne told me later it was the same one. But Bobby must have had the free man holding it for him or something, because he didn't go nowhere but out to that desk, and when he come back he had it. Maybe he got him to sharpen it for him or something."

Bobby, according to Mike, had a sexual relationship with this particular correctional officer (*not* Officer Slaven, who had just been assigned to Mag 3), whose name Mike tried unsuccessfully to get in hopes of having him testify at the trial. "The guard's the only one in the dormitory at night, and three or four o'clock in the morning he'd go wake Bobby up and they'd go in the TV room or something. They'd do it standing up; Bobby just bent over or something like that. This same guard would let us do it, too. Sometimes we'd let a sheet hang off each side of our bed, and put a blanket under the bed and lay on the blanket, with the sheet flaps down so nobody could see in. Other people in Magnolia were doing the same, but nobody had the same pull with that guard that Bobby had. He was like everybody else; they got pickers and choosers. He might let so-and-so do it, but not let somebody else." Indeed, one state's witness at the subsequent trial, inmate Mark Duhon, whose nickname was Tadpole because he said when he first came to Angola he was so small he could get in a ditch and all that could be seen was his straw hat, would testify that the reason he'd been awake at the time of the altercation was that he was waiting for the correctional officer to either get out of sight or go to sleep so he could have sex with another dorm resident.

At any rate, the lethal file, its sharpening said to have been assured through sex with a correctional officer, entered the Magnolia compound, and the next day Bobby carried it, wrapped in cellophane, in the bottom of his tennis shoe out into the Mag yard, where he and Mike dug a hole and buried it while sitting on the ground talking. When the trouble with the black clique escalated to threats, the knife was excavated and hidden in Mike's pillow inside the dorm.

Bobby had started to get the knife once before, when he felt threatened by Dwayne's former cellmate and Bobby's former sex partner Randy, then working in the prison kitchen. As Mike explains it, "I been knowing Randy a long time, and I wasn't gonna have no problems with him behind Bobby. So I tried to get Bobby to tell Randy about us, and she wouldn't do it, so I did. Randy told me, 'You get her to come out and tell me that, and I'll accept that.' So finally I got her to go out there. And Randy accused me of coaxing her or something. Really he was wrong, because I was being a hundred times more honest with him than Bobby was, but he was really loving Bobby hard. So Randy started cussing Bobby out, said, 'When I catch you coming down that Walk, I'm gonna put a knife on you.' Bobby said, 'I'm gonna go get that knife, 'cause we gotta go into the dining hall and eat, and Randy just said he's gonna stab me.' And I said, 'You don't need that, Randy ain't gonna do nothing, and if he does, I'll just pick up a chair or something.' But I felt at that time like Bobby was trying to influence me. I was aware to an extent that Bobby had not told me everything. I don't like putting anything on him, because I feel like I am responsible for what I do, ok? I felt like sometimes he used people for their strength, but I guess I was using him, too."

Burge denies the sexual and racial motives attributed to his actions in the early morning hours of Monday, August 8, 1983. "Race didn't play a part, though it may have played a part with the blacks. I'm not saying this because I'm white, but you can take a dormitory full of white guys and you ain't gonna have all them problems. Whites are not as sensitive or as chaotic. Most of the trouble I've had was with blacks, not because they were black, but because of what they did, or what happened. That's just the way Angola is, and my reaction would have been the same in Mag if they'd been black or white. A lot of people think that when this stuff come down with this black dude, that it was behind Bobby, but I didn't look at it being behind Bobby, either. I looked at it being behind they stole all our stuff and they threatened me and told me not to go to sleep. We had had pretty strong words, and they told me I couldn't stay in that dormitory, that I was gonna have to leave. They told me not to go to sleep that night. That's a strong threat to make in the penitentiary. They're telling you that if you go to sleep, something's gonna happen to you."

Defense version of the chain of events beginning at 12:40 a.m. on Monday morning had Lester Allen starting the action by arising in the dark, kicking Robert Schriver's bed and, pointing toward the front of the dorm where the bathroom was located, telling Bobby, "Come do something for me," meaning he wanted to have sex. Bobby responded that he'd do something for him all right, jumping from his bed and hitting him with his sock filled with batteries. Mike, watching the action from his own bed, says, "Lester jumped up and went by Bobby's bed, and I took the knife out of the pillow and put on a white okra glove on my left hand. I'm left handed. That file didn't have no handle or nothing, and I had the glove to work in the field with, pick okra and tomatoes, shovel and hoe. It ain't nothing but just a cheap white cotton glove issued to inmates. Bobby jumped up and hit Lester with the batteries, and they went to fighting. When Bobby hit Lester, Ricky Gray was coming out of the bed, and he had a long spike, like the sharpened handle of a metal spoon, about six inches long. We don't get to eat with forks and knives, you know, we eat with metal spoons, and a lot of people will take the round part off the spoon, bend it back until it breaks, and that just leaves them a long piece of metal, and they take that piece of metal where they broke it off at, and they put a point on there and then make a handle for it out of a piece of wood or something. I've seen people get killed with them.

"Me and Ricky hit the aisle about the same time. We both come in the same aisle; our beds were right together. I took my right hand and put it over his right hand where he had the thing in his hand, and pushed it down. And I hit him twice in the chest with mine. Then Mark Vincent jumped over the bed and punched me, and we all three fell in Mark Vincent's bed that Ricky Gray had been sleeping in. Me and Mark Vincent rassled a little bit. I'm not even sure if he knows what I got, but I start sticking him. He didn't have no weapon, but I didn't really know that at the time. He fell back on the bed, then he got up and took off running toward the front. Both of them did. Ricky Gray fell by the front door, and Mark Vincent fell over the counter in the front where we played cards and chess and whatnot."

Dr. Emile Laga would perform autopsies on both Gray and Vincent, testifying at the trial that Ricky Gray sustained four wounds in the upper half of the body on the left side, three of which were superficial. The single external wound penetrating the chest wall between the ribs for a length of three to four inches oddly perforated the front wall of the heart twice, leaving two holes in the left cavity. Cause of death Dr. Laga attributed to the stopping of the heart due to pressure from massive internal bleeding and interference with the mechanism which makes the heart beat, and while he indicated that he presumed the victim was lying down when stabbed, the pathologist admitted he could not say so beyond a reasonable doubt. "The best you can say," Dr. Laga testified, "is that the assailant and the victim probably were in a face-to-face kind of position."

Mark Vincent's autopsy revealed two wounds, both to the chest, only one fatal. Like Ricky Gray, Vincent had one deadly penetration through the ribs into the chest wall which left two wounds inside the heart, as if the knife, once inserted, had been partially removed and then thrust back in. Compression caused by internal bleeding, collapsing the lung and making it difficult for the heart to keep beating, was said by Dr. Laga to be the cause of Vincent's death. As with Gray, the doctor initially implied that the pattern of bleeding suggested the victim might have been lying down at the time of the attack, but under cross examination admitted that he could verify only that his body *at some point*, perhaps after death, had been in a supine position, though at the time the fatal wound was inflicted he could have been sitting, lying or standing. Both Gray and Vincent were dead on arrival at the prison infirmary, though prison ambulance run reports show that the unconscious Gray was gasping for air when removed from the dormitory.

Meanwhile, back in Mag 3, Mike says, "Bobby was yelling my name, and I went over there, which wasn't but about ten feet. And they had another inmate named Darryl Washington, and he was sitting on his bed. He slept next to Lester. By this time Bobby and Lester done proceeded away from Bobby's bed, Bobby more or less backing Lester up, swinging the sock with the batteries, and they were by Darryl Washington's bed. Darryl Washington was looking at me as I was coming, and I was looking at him, 'cause him and Lester had a relationship. So Washington jumped up and he had a big long radio that had a handle on it. He hit me in the head with it, on the side, and it hurt. So all four of us was right there, standing up. So I started hitting Darryl with the knife, and I just kept swinging it and swinging it, and he went down. He went down on the floor, and I told him not to get back up. He got back up again and he still had the radio in his hand. He was swinging the radio the whole time...As many times as I was hitting Darryl with the knife, he was hitting me up beside the head with the radio. The only thing I was thinking about was I didn't want to get knocked out. I knew if I got knocked out, it was all over with...So I hit him a couple more times, and he went down and didn't get back up."

Darryl Washington, age twenty-four, a first offender serving fifteen years for armed robbery from East Baton Rouge Parish, stabbed eight times, would live, his wounds subsequently described in newspaper accounts as "minor." Lester Allen, with a fatal four-inch stab wound penetrating his liver and another on the right side of his abdomen, two cuts on the face and a forehead laceration which pathologist Dr. Debra Cavalier described as having been made by some hard blunt object instead of a knife, died shortly after arrival at Earl K. Long Hospital in Baton Rouge. The killings, according to Angola warden Ross Maggio, were the first inmate-on-inmate killings at Angola since December 1, 1981, a record for the maximum-security prison holding 4600 of Louisiana's most dangerous criminal offenders.

On the fifteenth day of August, 1983, the West Feliciana Parish Grand Jury indicted Michael Burge for the first-degree murder of Ricky Gray, Lester Allen and Mark Vincent, and the attempted murder of Darryl Washington; the case was presented to the grand jury by assistant DA Zach Butterworth. Robert Schriver was indicted for the first-degree murder of Lester Allen as well, but those charges were *nolle prossed* in late October 1984; one of Schriver's court-appointed lawyers, Jesse Means, notes that charges were dropped because of what could be considered judicial negligence, since a motion for a speedy trial had been filed for Schriver and the DA's staff (district attorney Leon Picou had had open-heart surgery in the late summer of 1984) was apparently unprepared when the trial date slipped up on them 120 days afterward. Means' participation in the case would also have an effect on Burge's prosecution, since by the time of his trial, the administration had changed, a new district attorney, Hal Ware, had taken office and named as one of his assistants the selfsame Jesse Means, giving the DA's office a conflict of interest in prosecuting a case in which a staff member had earlier worked for the defense. Consequently, from the state attorney general's office in New Orleans came a replacement prosecutor to handle the murder trial of Michael Burge, *ad hoc* DA and assistant attorney general Stephen Laiche.

Initially appointed by the court to represent Mike were two St. Francisville attorneys, Stan Branton and Charles Griffin, who at the time practiced together and convinced the judge that for both of them to be tied up in what could be a lengthy case would mean a hardship to their fledgling practice. Baton Rouge judge Mike McDonald, then an attorney with the law firm of D'Amico, Curet and Dampf, was consequently appointed to represent Burge, and was later joined in his defense by attorney David E. Stanley, also of Baton Rouge.

Convinced he had acted in self defense and recalling the time he himself was stabbed ten times by an inmate who never faced criminal charges outside the penitentiary because of that incident, Burge says he resisted McDonald's attempts to persuade him, in the face of the death penalty, to "cop out for life. And I told him, I said, 'Man, look, I'm not copping out for nothing.'" Burge also objected when McDonald pleaded him not guilty by reason of insanity and applied for appointment of a sanity commission, citing the defendant's "prior history of mental disorder having been committed to the East Louisiana State Hospital at Jackson, Louisiana, on three prior occasions for mental disorders" and "prior treatment from the age of thirteen at the state mental health facility at Mandeville, Louisiana." Says Mike Burge today, "Mr. McDonald encouraged this against my consent and my better judgment. I never wanted to go with no 'insanity plea.' I cared to go with one defense and one defense only! From the word 'go,' I wanted to go with 'self-defense.' I knew I wasn't crazy and the two doctors appointed to interview myself wouldn't do anything but agree with that finding. Unless I faked it. And I have never faked at being crazy...I felt I had a very decent 'self-defense' approach. In fact, I felt I had no other alternative. I felt by attempting a 'insanity plea' I would be showing a sign of weakness, a show of 'grasping at straws.'"

At Burge's twentieth judicial district court trial, before presiding judge Honorable William F. Kline, Jr., testimony began the eighth of April in 1985 and ended the twelfth, with McDonald at the outset withdrawing the plea of not guilty by reason of insanity and returning to the original plea of not guilty, and the charges having been downgraded to three counts of second-degree murder.

Prosecutor Laiche's opening statement advised jury members that they were going to hear "some shocking things. We are going to hear some things that are going to be revolting to you. We have to remember one thing. The state penitentiary is not on trial here today. The State of Louisiana is not on trial here today. There's only one person on trial in this courtroom today and that's Michael Burge."

However, countered defense attorney Stanley in his opening comments, "You have got to understand the conditions that these inmates were placed in at Louisiana State Penitentiary to appreciate the evidence in this case. If you don't, it will not mean anything to you...Inside the penitentiary your reputation is everything. It follows you from dormitory to dormitory, day to day, every day that you are in that penitentiary until the day that you get out or die there. It can affect your safety. It can affect your well-being. It can affect your emotional stability. If you get labeled as weak in the penitentiary, you are going to have to pay what is called 'draft' in the penitentiary. You are going to be running errands for stronger inmates. You are likely to be raped. You are going to be doing their chores. You may be washing their laundry...So to be labeled a weak person in the penitentiary, it can affect your life drastically."

After a trial he considered fraught with error, Michael Burge was convicted of three counts of second-degree murder; a polling of the jurors showed ten voting for conviction, two against, perhaps illustrating why the state opted for the lesser charge of second-degree murder, which does not require a unanimous verdict. The jury retired at 1:14 p.m. and returned a verdict, after surprisingly short deliberations, at 3:27 p.m. Darryl Washington, seemingly the most logical state witness as the only black clique member who was attacked and lived to tell about it, was cited in opening statements by Laiche as one witness who would certainly be called, but oddly never made an appearance at the trial. On May 21, 1985, Michael Burge was given three life sentences, two running consecutively with his initial 36-year sentence and the third running concurrently.

Burge's subsequent petition to the First Circuit Court of Appeal was made on grounds of nearly a dozen crucial errors, including the taking of initial statements by law enforcement officials who allowed Mike to give confessions without reading him his Miranda rights and without advising him that any of the victims had died; the presentation of inflammatory nude autopsy photographs, enlarged and in living color, showing not only fight wounds but also autopsy incisions; violations of court orders regarding sequestration of witnesses, allegedly occurring during group meetings of prosecution witnesses orchestrated by Laiche; harassment of defense witnesses, who along with the defendant were isolated and held incommunicado in the dungeon prior to the trial; improper reference, against court instructions, to the defendant's nickname in court (when the prosecutor asked Burge his nickname, the judge sustained an objection and told jurors to strike the remark from their memories, though the name *Iron Man*, not even the right nickname, had already been printed in daily newspaper accounts; wrote Mike to Judge

Michael Burge and Bobby Schriver are escorted in chains into West Feliciana Parish
Courthouse for court appearance on murder charges. Photo by Karen Didier,
furnished courtesy of the Baton Rouge *State-Times/Morning Advocate*.

Kline, "How do you strike something from your mind which has already been implanted on it, I don't really know. The jurors could only think that I must have had a hell of a nickname if it couldn't be admitted into court").

Other errors cited included failure to grant a judgment of acquittal; failure to grant a mistrial or new trial due to cumulative prejudicial effect of acts of the state and prosecution; failure to grant a mistrial after a juror viewed the defendant leaving the St. Francisville courthouse handcuffed and shackled; and admitting autopsy testimony not previously available to the defense.

The Appeals Court ruling cited Louisiana's legal definition of a justifiable homicide as being one committed in self-defense by someone who reasonably believes himself to be in imminent danger of losing his life or receiving great bodily harm, from which danger he can save himself only by killing. Killing in defense of another, the court determined, is equally justifiable when such intervention is necessary to protect the other person and when it is reasonably apparent that the person attacked could have justifiably used such means himself. The relevant inquiry on appeal, the court noted, was whether, "after viewing the evidence in the light most favorable to the prosecution, any rational trier of fact could have found beyond a reasonable doubt that the homicide was not committed in self-defense." With defense witnesses suggesting the defendant was attacked first and state witnesses testifying that Burge attacked the defendants as they slept in their beds, an account the court said was corroborated by forensic evidence and lack of defensive wounds (only one cut was noted on any of the victims' hands) which might have verified a struggle, the appeal court ruled that the trial court was free to accept or reject in whole or in part the testimony of any witness, which the jury apparently did in choosing to believe the state's version of events.

"The law cannot permit even a harassed and threatened inmate of a penal institution to take the law into his own hands, arm himself, attack his enemy with a knife, and then, because of prior threats, claim justification for a homicide which follows," the court ruled in concluding that the state had carried its burden of establishing beyond a reasonable doubt that the homicides were not committed in self-defense or in defense of Robert Schriver. Systematically rejecting each defense point, the appeal court upheld Michael Burge's conviction and sentence.

Defense attorneys would file for a rehearing, file a writ of certiorari, and would appeal to the State Supreme Court as well, to no avail. Court-appointed defense attorneys have no obligation to continue representation beyond state courts, so Mike would have to hire a privately paid attorney to appeal to the federal court system, and the only defense attorney he has consulted requested a retainer of at least $5000 just to look into filing a habeas application, money he does not have.

At no point in Mike's trial or subsequent appeals was any mention made of his violently abusive childhood, his unstable family background, the dearth of love or guidance or discipline during his formative years, though similar factors have become increasingly accepted as mitigants and/or viable defenses in criminal cases across the country. One recent study reported in the journal *Science*, conducted by John E. Bates of Indiana University, Gregory S. Pettit of Auburn University and Kenneth A. Dodge of Vanderbilt University, shows a strong correlation between childhood physical abuse and later aggressive behavior, the authors concluding that a "social information processing deficit" causes many abused children to respond to all provocative social situations in inappropriately agressive manners.

Drug abuse is another devastating spin-off from the vicious cycle of childhood abuse, according to studies done by Cathy Spatz Widom of the State University of New York at Albany, who found that early neglect and abuse can have enormous long-term consequences. Abused children are fifty-three percent more likely to be arrested as juveniles, thirty-eight percent more likely to be arrested for a violent crime, and often, Widom found, have lower IQs besides demonstrably higher risks of drug problems, depression and suicide.

If ever there were an indictment against our current system of juvenile justice, it is the life of Michael Burge, who at no point in his history ever seemed to be reached by the help he so desperately needed. Why was there no appropriate early intervention by the state, perhaps removing him while still a small child from the abusive home situation, possibly providing him with a nurturing environment offering training in areas more useful than merely how to become a better criminal? "It's best for young people to never go to reform school or prisons when they are young," Mike writes today. "It's good to reach them before that. I don't care who you are, those places have a effect on you, they leave scars."

Today Michael W. Burge remains in Angola, as does Robert Schriver. Darryl Washington has been released. Mike has corresponded occasionally with Bobby, in another part of the prison, but still has nagging doubts about the dropping of Schriver's murder charge. At Mike's trial, Bobby himself testified that he rejected a variety of deals to testify against Burge, deals offered by the prosecutor who Bobby said also threatened him with the death penalty. When the appellate court, in affirming Mike's conviction, cited some of Bobby's testimony implying that Mike's attack on Lester had come after Bobby had already subdued that inmate, Mike says he "was kinda beginning to believe that possibly he might have made a deal with Laiche. See, something happened one time, they took me and Bobby to a preliminary hearing in St. Francisville, and when they had a little recess for lunch, most of the time they feed you right at the courthouse where they got a little holding cell, but instead they brought me and Bobby to the jail and they separated us. They got like glass, and we could see each other, so these deputies go to all the trouble of taping a cardboard partition over that glass. The reason why they done that, and why they brought us to the jail to feed us, Laiche wanted to talk to Bobby."

He continues, "I didn't see that, but I thought something was funny 'cause they put that partition up there. On the way back, Bobby ain't said nothing about talking to Laiche. So I didn't find out nothing about that until Laiche was cross-examining him on the stand, and Laiche brought it up, told him 'when I talked to you in that St. Francisville jail'...And then it dawned on me, I was thinking maybe him and Laiche made some kind of deal, and he got his murder charge dropped. I don't know. You know, some people, you put them on the stand, they're so worried about covering their own tail, really you're better off if you don't put them on the stand...Since then, Bobby has told me he wasn't with nobody, but he'd been with a black guy for months. So I'm not sure if you can believe him or not."

As in the past, Bobby continues to look out for himself today, saying in a recent interview from Angola, "I've changed my life and my attitude. I've always been bisexual, but I've even put that on hold because I think it's detrimental to my freedom. I really want to get out of Angola." Referring to Mike's murder trial as a "total fabrication," he stresses that the fight had little to do with race or sex. "When we first got locked up," he confesses now, "we said it was a racial issue, we said it was a sexual issue, but it had nothing to do with none of that. Mike felt like if he used that relationship, *our* relationship, that we were lovers and that he felt like he had to help me because I was being attacked, that that would create some type of justifiable defense. So I said, 'OK, I'll say anything you want me to say.'"

What Bobby now says actually happened, however, corroborates Mike Burge's version, placing most of the blame for the altercation on the theft of items from the locker-box. "There were several people in the dormitory who I had been knowing and they told me who went in our box. Lester Allen and Star Child had went in the box," Bobby says. "So I talked to Mike about it. He went to them and nothing was settled like that, they wouldn't grasp the seriousness of the situation...This went on and went on, and I tried to talk to Mike about it, and talked to Mike. Sometimes you can avoid situations, and I could have done it, in fact I told Mike, I said, 'Look, we can do several things, we can get locked up and go to the cellblock.' That's considered jiving and cowardly, but you can do things like that if you can live with yourself, that's all that's important, because the other alternative could result in some more lives, as Mike got. But he said no."

Continues Bobby, "I think Mike always has had a concern with his image. A lot of people up here do. I think the most important thing is how you feel about yourself; I don't think what somebody else thinks is important...But Mike has always had that Iron Mike image and I think it's hurt him. It hurt him in the trial...If he hadn't killed them, I could have gone on, but he couldn't have, he couldn't accept that. It's quite possible we'd have still had some type of altercation later, but I don't believe it would have been anywhere as devastating as what happened. But in Mike's mind, that was mandatory that that happen, and at one time on Angola, that's just the way you did things. A lot of the older guys, they live by the old codes and the old principles, if somebody takes something from you, you either hurt them or kill them...But it's not necessary any more, though some people are embedded in that old philosphy, that old code, if you will. Mike wasn't used to being around a certain class of inmates that are in Mag...A lot of them are penitentiary turnouts, so they have an attitude, very few of them just accept that and are happy with that, and I have found out since that happened that two of the people that were involved were turned out up here, Lester Allen and Ricky Gray."

The death of Lester Allen, for which he was initially charged, seems the only aspect of the whole affair for which Bobby accepts any responsibility. While Mike fought with Ricky Gray and Mark Vincent, he admits, "I jumped on Lester Allen. Mike came down the aisle by where I was beating on Lester. I don't know if he was dead or not. I guess the coroner said that the knife killed him, but I've prayed and asked for forgiveness. I take part of that, that I did do that, but I don't actually know what killed him and I don't think the coroner did either."

After spending five years in extended lockdown following the August 1983 killings and his subsequent trial, Michael Burge was released to a working cellblock, Camp A-Line 21, where he worked in the field until incarcerated twenty-six straight months at notorious Camp J as punishment for a contraband charge after a knife was found in a pipechase (space containing the plumbing and heating ducts for the cellblocks) near his cell. Asserting that, though he knew the knife was there, it was not his and had been at Camp A-Line 21 long before he arrived there, Burge spent more than two years isolated, unable to work or participate in group sports or other activities, suffering what he considers intentional unnecessary abuse, constant target of verbal vilification, not to mention human waste thrown by other inmates, object of harassment as well by security officers he sees as trying to make themselves look good at his expense. As he said recently, this voracious reader and perceptive if understandably slightly paranoid observer of human nature, "I feel like some security personnel are only using me to their advantage to make themselves look good. There is a Latin saying, *Quis custodiet ipsos custodes,* which when translated into English means, *Who will keep the keepers themselves?* Which I think is a very good question."

He spent his days at Camp J painstakingly GI-ing his cell with forbidden bleach and shampoo to remove the smell of the offending waste material flung on him by passing inmates, exercising to maintain his fitness (one hundred laps in thirty minutes during his three hours weekly in the small fenced yard-pen topped with razor wire, plus forty or fifty daily sets of push-ups in his cell, half with his feet elevated on the toilet), waging incessant war against the armies of roaches, soothing frazzled nerves with music (radio headphones, he explains, blot out the constant screaming on the tier, and music becomes "the companion I don't have"), fantasizing as he turned forty about women from his past ("the years keep passing and my memories have to keep getting better"), and maintaining a voluminous correspondence with what he calls his Christian family, Nell and Malcolm Holmes.

Nationwide studies indicate the beneficial effects of religion on prisoners, and Mike's own hardwon conversion has had a positive impact, along with a natural maturation and increased self-awareness accompanying the aging process, though he remains resistant to authority. That against all odds and with negligible assistance he has grown, emotionally

Right: Michael Burge shown recently with longtime family friend Nell Holmes, whose Christian concern and interest add love and warmth to his otherwise bleak existence at Angola. Photo courtesy Mike Burge.

Below: Bobby Schriver, shown at Angola in November 1990. Photo by Anne Butler.

and psychologically and mentally, is undeniable, perceptible proof that perhaps it is not after all too late for Michael Burge. As he wrote Nell Holmes in the summer of 1990, "I always try to set goals for myself. Of course, many I set a little late in life, like after I was already in prison doing big time. Nell, I think I grew much more rapidly in my past five years, than my whole thirty-five before those five. That's a shame and a terrible waste on my part. I can't and won't make no excuse. Although I will say this, I do think I had some severe emotional problems that really dealt with me, that later on in my life I was able to conquer and learned to deal with. I educated myself these last five years. Before I never did do that. I was intelligent, but was mentally lazy and didn't push myself mentally like I do now...God, it took me a long time to understand it myself and to learn how to accept my faults and to deal properly and positively with my problems. First I had to admit I had a few problems. Which believe me, is a lot harder than it sounds....I still have faults I am not proud of. But I really think a lot more of myself now than I did in my younger days."

Expressing an interest in working with children should he ever gain release, Mike cites the satisfaction he felt voluntarily assisting with handicapped youngsters while a teenager in The Brown School. Now he feels he could become an effective voice deterring kids from taking that all-too-attractive pathway to crime. "I am really starting to believe in myself more and more now," he says, "and I firmly believe now as I never did before that if I do happen to be a free man again, that I will never come back to Angola or any other prison ever again. My whole attitude is different. I would love to go around and talk to kids in junior high and high school about my life. I think that is where it is best to reach young people at. You can steer them away better at that age from the things that are negative...I have done so many negative things in my life and hurt many people to where I would just love to do positive things and help people. I am a giver, and I learned a long time ago I enjoy very much giving. I have helped weaker inmates here many times, probably times when I shouldn't have. I kept many inmates from getting turned into sexual slaves. And I always done it without violence, just words. My words at one time meant a lot here."

Mike's father, Alfred Louis Burge, died suddenly on April 3, 1991. Before that, he regularly wrote Mike, subscribed to the Baton Rouge newspaper for him and seemed to continue to have some interest in him, but refused to accept telephone calls from him and hadn't visited his son for nearly three years. Toward the end of his life, Nell Holmes found Louis filled with heartfelt regret. He wasn't the only one with regrets. Remembers Mike, his love for his father tempered by disillusionment, "I first saw him lie when I was seven years old. He swore on a Bible to Flo in front of me that he wasn't drinking. As soon as Flo walked out of the living room, he pulled out a half-pint from his inside coat pocket and took a deep gulp. There were lots of broken promises, etc. Promises that meant a lot to me due to my devotion to him and promises which wouldn't have been hard to fulfill with a little effort, but Louis never did care to make much of an effort for others." Adds Nell with a sigh, "You know, if we don't stop in our life long enough to smell the roses while they're blooming, there's no need to go smell them when they're dried up and dead. And Louis never took the time."

Nor does Mike see other family members. The Holmes family fills the gap, visiting faithfully every two weeks, writing letters, sending necessities, providing spending money, intervening with authorities on Mike's behalf whenever possible, instilling Christian values and giving Michael Burge his only taste of love or hope in an otherwise drab and desperate existence. Mike lovingly calls Nell his "religious nut." He also calls her Mama.

Says Nell, finding Mike again and accepting the challenge of being his spiritual adviser was "just as if the Lord took a baby and laid it in my lap. We love Mike. God gave him to us. His is the saddest story of a young man that I know. It's the saddest *life* I have ever heard. When I was just a young girl, I got my first job with the state, and my desk was right next to his mother's. She liked me a great deal, even though we travelled in different lanes, and I would go over to her house and take care of little Bruce. She would call me, because she would maybe not be able to take care of him; she would drink a lot, and I would go take care of him. Or maybe Louis, the daddy, would get paid and never come home, and she'd be upset, because he drank a lot. Flo and Louis did not get along well; they fought a lot, violently, and did things that would scare a child to death. Mike's mother was murdered, and his daddy has told me that the reason Mike is like he is today is that he was abused."

Continues Nell Holmes, "And he's *still* being abused. There's no warmth or feeling for him up there at Angola. He's locked up in there like an animal. Nobody cares; nobody tries to reach out for him, and as far as they're concerned, he can rot there. I am terribly surprised that they do not have more escapes and stabbings and suicides at Angola, because what do the inmates have to look forward to? Now I know Mike did wrong, and he has gone to his Lord to ask forgiveness in my presence. But he's been treated so badly, and now he feels like there's just no hope for him. All he wants to do is get out of isolation so he can work."

Increasingly concerned by Mike's growing feeling of isolation, hopelessness and despair, Nell Holmes has talked to correctional officers and top-level administration at the Louisiana State Penitentiary at Angola about Mike's case. She has talked to former wardens and retired state corrections officials. She has talked to coroners and federal judges and professional psychologists, including one who said he recently quit Angola fearing for his own safety after crossing officials by daring to suggest that Mike Burge might safely be released into the general prison population. Recently she even approached Governor Buddy Roemer's secretary of the Department of Public Safety and Corrections, former gentleman-farmer Bruce Lynn, and was horrified by his casual uncaring response to her visit on Mike's behalf. Says Nell with a sigh of despair, "He told me he didn't care if they *all* committed suicide, because the less there were up there, the easier it made his job." With an attitude like that at the top levels of state corrections, what hope is there, indeed?

2009 Update:

Michael Burge remains in Angola.

III

"May His Soul Burn in Hell": Death in the Electric Chair

Wednesdays would prove to be the momentous days of Faith Colleen Hathaway's life. It was on a Wednesday, May 21st in 1980, that this pretty eighteen year old with the naturally curly brunette hair and dancing dark eyes would graduate from Mandeville High School in the town where she had spent much of her childhood. Born in December 1961 in Orlando, Florida, she moved when she was six to this quaint coastal resort area of Louisiana, called "across the lake" by harried New Orleanians who have only to traverse the twenty-four-mile-long causeway over Lake Pontchartrain, the world's longest continuous over-water bridge, to find themselves in another world, far removed from the urban bustle and accompanying violence of life in The City That Care Forgot (*care* may have forgotten it, but crime most certainly did not).

Faith would leave Mandeville only temporarily in the late seventies, when her stepfather Vernon Harvey took the family to spend a couple of years in Haiti and Ecuador where he was building ports, and it would be these trips which aroused her interest in foreign languages. Living and attending school with the locals, in Haiti she picked up some French and the Creole dialect spoken by the unlettered of that poverty-stricken country, as well as Dutch learned from family friends who'd come there from Holland, and in Ecuador she learned to speak passable Spanish as well. Faith's facility for learning new tongues and her interest in foreign cultures led her to enlist in the U.S. Army, the branch of service she felt offered the best foreign language programs.

Setting her sights on learning Russian and perhaps serving her country as a translator, Faith was to report for active duty on another Wednesday, May 28th, one week from her high school graduation. She never made it. It would turn out that, fatefully, that particular Wednesday had been the last of her short life. Her battered body would not be found until the following week, on yet another Wednesday, June 4th.

Retracing her steps revealed that Faith had spent Tuesday, May 27, with her mother in the huge shopping mall in nearby Hammond, breakfasting at McDonald's before purchasing support bras which her recruiting sergeant had mentioned would not be supplied by the army. Returning to the Mandeville apartment complex managed by her mother, where Faith and a girlfriend shared a unit separate from that of her mother, stepfather and younger half-sister, Faith spent an enjoyable afternoon in the pool, swimming until she had to report for work at a local restaurant. It was not actually her night to work, but she was covering for a fellow employee who had final exams the next day, a girl who had in turn worked for Faith while she went on her senior class trip.

68

Getting off work around 10 p.m., Faith visited a school friend, then went to the Lakefront Disco, where another of her classmates worked as disc jockey. Celebrating her last night as a civilian and bidding friends goodbye with what must have been mixed regret and excited anticipation, Faith spent most of the night partying in this popular club on the lake in Mandeville. And then, in the words of her mother Elizabeth Harvey, "It was just like in the middle of that crowded room, she vanished from the face of the earth."

The following morning, Wednesday, May 28, Faith's surprised mother found that her daughter's bed had not been slept in, nor did her roommate know her whereabouts. "Faith usually came over to our apartment every morning, and she was there every afternoon," Elizabeth Harvey recounts. "I was trying not to check on her real closely, since she was trying her wings by living in her own apartment, but I knew her recruiting sergeant would be coming by at any time. I knew she'd be going far away where she'd have to be responsible for herself, yet I was still trying to keep an eye on what kind of decisions she was making. It's kind of hard to let go, but you know you've got to. You back away but try to stay close enough to see that your children are keeping in mind what you tried to teach them, especially the safety part."

Harvey called the friend Faith had visited before going to the disco, hoping that perhaps her daughter had spent the night there. She had not. The recruiting sergeant dropped by to leave Faith's army enlistment papers, mentioning that 6 p.m. was her deadline for reporting in New Orleans before making the trip to Missouri. He didn't seem to be concerned. Elizabeth Harvey, on the other hand, *was*. "I guess I kind of walked the floor," she remembers, "not knowing exactly which way to turn, trying to contact everybody I knew. It's hard to say to yourself that you don't know where your child is. That's just something that you hear about on radio or television, or read about in the papers; it doesn't actually happen to you. I always knew where Faith was. If she went anyplace, she'd call, and I was never any farther than the other side of the telephone from knowing where she was."

Looking back today, Elizabeth Harvey with the benefit of hindsight wonders whether some odd sense of foreboding might have propelled her daughter into trying to squeeze the experiences of a lifetime into her last year. "It seemed like," she says now, "when we looked back after the shock of everything was over, that there were a lot of things Faith tried to do in the last six months that were extremely different from her usual activities, as if she had to rush to see if she could do these things, like she might not otherwise get a chance to do them. At the time I didn't realize what was happening, but there were so many things that changed so quickly, it was as if she rushed to try her wings because she knew she never would have a chance later to see if she could."

Harvey dreaded notifying her husband Vern, working in New Orleans. "I hated to think about him driving across the causeway after I told him, because he and Faith were so close," she says. "Faith would go and talk to him about something before she'd come to me, their communication was just that easy. I felt kind of jealous about it at first, I

Faith Hathaway as a high-school senior.
Photo courtesy of Elizabeth and Vernon Harvey.

think, but I was glad to know she was talking to somebody, and I knew what kind of information she would get from him, straightforward answers without any beating around the bush. So I was glad she was at least coming to one of us so we knew what was on her mind. She generally did tell us what was on her mind; we never had to wonder."

Vern began contacting people who might have seen Faith at the Lakefront, an old theater which had been turned into a bar, while his wife sat at home in the desperate belief that if her daughter could get to a telephone, she would call home. At 6 o'clock in the evening, the time Faith was due to report for active duty, her recruiting sergeant arrived at the Harvey home again and promised to extend the deadline, giving her another week to report. "I thought it was so she wouldn't be AWOL," Elizabeth Harvey now says. "I didn't realize that if he moved the date back, the army wouldn't be involved in the search for her. At 6 o'clock we reported to the Mandeville Police Department that she was missing, and at 10 o'clock we reported it to the St. Tammany Sheriff's Department. Vern rode the streets between the two departments. And it was still hard for us to say to ourselves that we didn't know where Faith was."

On Thursday a multi-state alert was put out by law enforcement agencies, and by Sunday personal articles belonging to Faith had been discovered in a remote 47-acre tract called Fricke's Cave south of Franklinton, a rugged hilly area of deep eroded gravel pits with red clay domes just off the Bogue Chitto River. A secluded area popular for camping and recreational use as well as for parking by privacy-seeking young lovers, Fricke's Cave is in neighboring Washington Parish in the toe of boot-shaped Louisiana, 35 or 40 miles north of Mandeville.

"A family from Franklinton was picnicking and picking blackberries there," Vern recalls, "and their seven-year-old daughter came back with some lipstick. When her mother inquired as to where she got it, the child said there was a whole bunch of cosmetics down there in a plastic case, and some other things. So they went and found some of Faith's clothes and a piece of carpeting that had come out of a truck, and her driver's license was in her purse. It seemed awfully funny to them, so when they got back to Franklinton, they took these things to the sheriff's department. When the deputies found her driver's license in her billfold, they called the sheriff's department in Covington and wanted to know if there was a Faith Hathaway missing. And of course they said yes."

While a search party was organized to scour the Fricke's Cave wilderness, the Harveys remained unaware of the discovery. Vern was searching the banks of some canals in another area on advice of a psychic when Elizabeth heard that someone in the apartment swimming pool had mentioned that Faith's clothes had been found. "I got on the phone and called the sheriff's department," she recalls, "and the man who is now chief of police in Mandeville came out and told me that her clothes, neatly folded, and her purse had been found. And I said, 'Why haven't you let me know this, I told you all along that my daughter was missing and that I needed help, to please help me find her, and you didn't believe me, did you?' And he admitted that he hadn't. And I said, 'You believe me now that her purse and clothes are found, you believe me that she's in trouble and that I need help.' And he said he did. 'At least now you believe me, why on earth wouldn't you let me know?' I asked him. He said they wanted something more to tell us. And I said, 'Don't you think it would have been a relief to me to know that at least now you finally believe me that my daughter is in trouble?' I said, 'You all have said that she's eighteen years old and probably got cold feet about going in the service, that she's just off doing her thing.' And that's exactly what they thought. Vern's sister overheard one say she was off somewhere shacked up."

Says Vern, vehemently, "You'll find some police officers who are very compassionate, but by God, there are some who are very cruel, whether they mean it or not. They don't have any compassion toward the victims. There's a bunch of victims in any crime. In a murder crime, there's a victim who's been killed, and all the family of the one who's been murdered are victims, too. But the police don't seem to want to accept anybody but the corpse as a victim." Adds his wife, "They don't have to answer to the corpse, and if they don't consider us victims, then they don't have to answer to us either. To begin with, we had to fight to find out any information at all. We had no one to help us, and it was like we had a contagious disease in Mandeville, like if anyone got near us, it might happen to them, too."

The Harveys and other family members joined law enforcement officials at Fricke's Cave the following day, Monday, June 2, and searched until dark. "Going down to Fricke's Cave, it was so steep you had to go in a trot," Elizabeth Harvey recalls. "It wasn't far until we started finding other things that had fallen out of Faith's purse. We found a bag that she had gotten some freeze-dried bananas and pineapples in, some matches, a few other things. They said we had to get out of there when it was about to get dark, and they asked us not to come up on Tuesday as they were going to bring dogs in."

It would not be until Wednesday, June 4, that a body would be found some two hundred yards through thick underbrush from where the clothing and personal items had been discovered on Monday. Mike Varnado, an investigator for the Washington Parish district attorney's office, found the unclad victim, and on Thursday parish coroner Jerry Thomas identified the remains as those of Faith, telling newspaper reporters that the results of an autopsy in New Orleans, plus evidence found on and near the body, led to the identification. Though the exact cause of death was difficult to determine due to the length of time the body had lain in the woods, Dr. Thomas indicated that she had been brutally raped and then murdered by having her throat slashed.

Body frozen in death in the spread-eagle position in which she had been held, bent legs forced apart, arms stretched above her head with several fingers severed trying to defend herself, Faith Hathaway had been stabbed repeatedly in the neck with a large knife; there were at least seventeen stab wounds. She had a large deep cut so savagely inflicted across her throat that her favorite necklace, the one with the medallion inscribed "Class of 80" and "Dawn of a New Decade," was imbedded in her flesh. Paul McGeary, LSU

School of Medicine pathologist who performed the autopsy, indicated that death was not immediate but instead took an excruciating stretch of time filled with suffering, before being caused by extensive bleeding and difficulty in breathing as the opened windpipe filled with blood.

Faith's family was not allowed to view her remains, something which continues to fill Elizabeth Harvey with regret. "I now know that I wanted to see Faith. I now know that I had the right, that I *could* have seen her, to know that that was her that I was burying. But they absolutely told me that I could not." Filled with misgivings and doubt, hoping against hope that some tragic mistake had been made, Harvey could not accept the initial identification. "If she had been cremated, her teeth couldn't have been identifed and we wouldn't have known that that was her, so it's a good thing she hadn't been cremated. There's no way we would have known if that was her."

"*I* knew it was her," interjects Vern sadly. But his wife continues, "After the coroner told me what all had happened to the body, I asked if he had done a dental check, and he said no. I said, 'You expect me to bury this body and yet you tell me that you cannot look and tell if that's her or not, that the only way you can tell if that's Faith is by a dental check and you didn't do one, that you couldn't get fingerprints or anything else, that she has no face left or eyes, that the body is all decomposed, and animals. . . .And you want me to bury this body?' And I repeatedly asked. I said, 'They aren't looking for her, they've stopped looking for her, what if this is not Faith?' I said, 'I don't wish this body on another living soul on this earth, but I've got to know whether this is Faith or not before I can bury this body and before I can stop searching for her.' And I called and called, and could not get them to do anything. They took her ring and watch off of her body, and we had to end up getting a judge's order to be able to see them, and I never did get to see the contents of her purse or anything."

Harvey finally accepted the identification of Faith's body only when her younger brother, a Virginia dentist, arrived and confirmed through dental records that it had indeed been Faith who had been murdered. "My brother, he had to search through two bags of lime that they had in with her body, trying to search for her teeth to be able to identify her," she recounts painfully. "He was real close to Faith, because he was still at home when Faith, the first grandchild, was born, and I lived close to home. When he had been drafted into the service, he refused to bear arms, and the trouble that they gave him about that was quite harsh. Now, he owns a gun, which he never did before, and he said he could take it and blow the heads off the ones who killed Faith. I didn't realize what I was asking him to do, but it was the only way then that I knew of to get Faith identified. I know now that I could have gone to the district attorney's office and demanded that someone identify her."

Before the military funeral in Mandeville, Faith Hathaway's tragic murder case had become associated with another which bore striking similarities. On Saturday, May 31, a mere three days after Faith's kidnapping in the wee hours of the morning on May 28, another abduction would take place in the same area. Mark Allan Brewster, aged twenty, of nearby Madisonville, was parked in his car on a secluded oak-shaded lover's lane along the Tchefuncte River on the north shore of Lake Pontchartrain with his sixteen-year-old girlfriend, a student at Covington High School, when they were accosted by two armed men. Locking Brewster in the trunk, the two drove eastward into southern Alabama, raping the young girl repeatedly. On an Interstate 10 exit road near the community of Wilcox, in Baldwin County, Alabama, the car was stopped and a struggling Brewster was taken into a wooded area, tied to a tree, shot twice in the back of the head with a .22-caliber pistol and slashed across the throat.

Leaving Mark Brewster for dead, the abductors then returned to Louisiana, continuing to abuse the girl until she was finally released at the urging of a third man in whose trailer they had been hiding near Folsom, La., about halfway between Franklinton and Mandeville. After notifying the St. Tammany Parish sheriff's department on Monday, June 2, Brewster's girlfriend was miraculously able to lead authorities to him, even though she had been locked in the trunk while he was shot, and by Tuesday he was in guarded condition after undergoing surgery in the University of South Alabama Medical Center hospital in Mobile to remove bone fragments from his head.

At the same time Brewster was being operated on in a desperate attempt to save his life and minimize permanent damage from two gunshot wounds to the head, several suspects in his abduction were being arrested in Hope, Arkansas, just northeast of Texarkana, where they were recognized from teletype bulletins by an alert state police trooper near a bus station, allegedly on their way to Denver. Taken into FBI custody were Robert Lee Willie, twenty-one, of Covington, Joseph Jesse Vaccaro, twenty-eight, of Pearl River, and Thomas Leslie Holden, twenty-six, of Folsom. At the time of the Brewster abduction, Willie had been armed with a sawed-off shotgun and Vaccaro with a .22 pistol, but they offered no resistance at the time of their arrest.

Willie and Vaccaro were charged in the kidnap-rape of Brewster and his girlfriend, while Holden, who was said to have talked the others into sparing the girl's life after they brought her to his trailer, was charged as an accessory after the fact. Apparently the trio had been provided by Willie's mother and stepfather with transportation out of the state, and had hitchhiked through Mississippi after catching a ride along Interstate 55 near McComb; the parents, Elizabeth Oalman, thirty-eight, and her husband Herbert Oalman, Jr., would eventually be charged as accessories as well.

Not until the body of Faith Hathaway was found on Wednesday, June 4, the day after the Brewster kidnap suspects were arrested in Arkansas, was there speculation that the two crimes might well be related, particularly after Brewster's girlfriend identified the spot where Faith was killed as one place she was taken and repeatedly raped by her abductors after they returned with her to Louisiana. Sheriff's deputies and investigators from the DA's office in both St. Tammany and Washington parishes flew up to Arkansas in a state police helicopter to interview Willie and Vaccaro, who were being held on federal charges under $500,000 bail each. Willie, who hadn't been very cooperative with FBI interrogators, opened up immediately to St. Tammany deputy Donald "Duck" Sharp, who'd known him since childhood and shared his enthusiasm for trucks.

"If you ever wanted Willie to talk to you, you could talk about trucks, and then he'd talk about killing people," Lt. Sharp says today. "When we got to Arkansas, the FBI agents came and told us they'd be glad for us to talk to Willie, but he wasn't going to tell us anything. Well, me and Willie talked for thirty minutes, just about things happening around here, and he told me, he said, 'Well, I messed up this time.' And I said, 'Yeah, you did.' And we talked about different things, and I told him the reason I was there was about Faith Hathaway. I had a picture of her, and I said, 'Tell me what you know about her.' He said, 'Killed her.' And I said, 'Well, I know that, I know you killed her, but tell me how.' And then he went into detail about how they killed her, that he didn't actually kill her but Vaccaro cut her throat with a knife. We talked for about an hour, and then I got Vaccaro back in there and let him listen to Willie's statement. I said, 'Now, tell me if he's lying or telling the truth.' And he said, 'He's telling the truth with the exception that I wasn't the one that cut her throat, he was.'"

Sharp today continues to believe that Willie, though, was the one who actually killed Faith Hathaway. "From my dealings with Robert Lee Willie, and I know his background well, from the time he was a little devil about ten years old packing a pocket knife which he kept plenty sharp, Willie would hurt you with a knife and a gun, but he was quicker with a knife and he didn't mind cutting somebody. Faith Hathaway was cut, her throat was cut and her fingers were cut, you could tell even though the body was so decomposed. When I showed Willie the pictures of her body, he said, 'Yeah, see her fingers cut, she grabbed the knife when Joe was trying to cut her.' He kept saying *Joe,* and Joe kept saying him. I asked him, 'What did you do, Willie, when Joe was cutting her throat,' and he said, 'Well, I finally reached up there and grabbed her hands,' and his exact words, and this is what made the jury just shudder later, were, 'I told her to behave.' I said, 'You mean you told her to *behave* while you were cutting her throat?' And he said, 'Yeah.' There is no doubt from what I know of Willie that Willie cut her throat."

Sharp continues, "The statements in the newspapers that Faith Hathaway begged them to kill her quickly came from Willie and Vaccaro. They said she told them to let her die in peace, and they just sat around and watched her for a few minutes and then got up and walked on off. Willie told me that Joe jugged her once or twice in the throat, but the evidence was that it was a cutting wound and possibly some jugging too, just in the throat. Each one pointed at the other about rape. Vaccaro said he tried but couldn't; Willie said Vaccaro did, that they both did, but Willie said that she *wanted* to have sex with him. Willie also said he'd never seen her before, that they had picked her up and she had told them she was out celebrating before going into the service."

Sharp says today that a third woman, besides Faith Hathaway and Mark Brewster's young girlfriend, almost became a victim as well. "It all took place in a very short period of time, just a matter of a few weeks," he recounts. "Willie told me that what set this off was that he and Vaccaro had been in jail together, and when they got out, on the same day, they stayed drunk and smoked marijuana and took every kind of drug they could get ahold of. He said they didn't hardly sleep. I asked him why, and he said they were just making up for lost time. They made an attempt at a woman in Mandeville on the same night as the Brewster kidnapping, and she screamed and hollered and they drove away. There's no doubt it was them, because she described them to a T."

Robert Lee Willie was no stranger to the police when he was arrested. Born in 1958, at twenty-one he was a tall slim blond boy with more than thirty tatoos snaking around his torso . . . zigzags, swastikas, brick walls, spider webs, female heads and a bracelet chain of skulls which would figure prominently in later interrogations. He completed only the ninth grade in school, and was constantly in trouble even before dropping out. Vern Harvey says Willie had seriously cut a young classmate with a pocket knife in the first grade, when he was only seven. His official juvenile record begins by age fourteen with arrests for shoplifting and truancy; before his fifteenth birthday he'd been sent to reform school for horse theft and being an ungovernable delinquent.

Graduating to more serious crimes, Robert Lee Willie was arrested for auto theft, trespassing, disturbing the peace, criminal damage to property, aggravated assault, several counts of theft and simple burglary, as well as contributing to the delinquency of a juvenile, all before he turned eighteen. Before his arrest in the Brewster case, he'd piled up additional charges throughout his late teens for such offenses as carrying a concealed weapon, resisting arrest, unauthorized use, criminal damage to public property, battery, public intimidation and aggravated escape, once reportedly leaping from the courthouse roof and breaking his leg in a failed bid for freedom.

Says St. Tammany sheriff's department chief deputy Wallace Laird today, "Willie started out with petty theft/burglary type situations and then it just started to increase with his involvement with other problem people and going on to narcotics. Robert was one of these kids that anything he did was just animalistic, not something that a good sane reasonable person would think about doing. But he wasn't a reasonable person, not after he got into drugs. And when they picked up this little girl on the street down here, they had been drinking and taking drugs for a period of time, and I think that all of the reasoning was gone from their minds. Robert was proud of being an outlaw, and he was proud of his daddy's legend, so to speak, although they were two completely different individuals."

Robert was born when his mother, Elizabeth Jenkins Willie, was only seventeen and his father, John Kelton Willie, a good ten years older, was in the Louisiana State Penitentiary at Angola, where his nickname "Snitchin' Willie" attested to his propensity for helping the administration gain information in return for protection. The Willie family has a long history in this neck of the woods, always with a few rough edges but only recently on the wrong side of the law. In fact, John Willie's grandfather, John Avery Willie, was a deputy for some thirty-five years with the St. Tammany Parish sheriff's department, and John's father, Kelton Willie, spent nearly two decades in the same job while raising eleven children, eight of them girls who doted on the baby boy

Right: Robert Lee Willie in March 1983. Photo courtesy of *The Angolite.*

Left: Robert Lee Willie's father, Angola veteran John Willie, shown in 1954. Photo courtesy of *The Angolite.*

John, especially after the only other two brothers drowned and the mother followed them to the grave. Recalls Chief Deputy Laird, "John's grandpa was one of the first deputies in this parish. He was shot by a black man one time, got his arm shot off. Of course, way back then, the black man went missing, and no one ever found out where he was. It was a pretty rough family, and I think some of them took care of that situation. There's a lot of good people in the family, but some of them had some problems."

John Willie, according to Laird, had his own long history of problems with the law, but of an entirely different sort than his son's. Arrested mostly on battery charges and once for cattle rustling, John Willie was sent to Angola several times for murder or attempted murder. He was involved in a number of barroom fights and even shot his own brother-in-law at one point, but Laird is quick to point out the difference in type of offenses committed by father and son.

"John was a kind of legend in the community," Laird says today, "and although nobody was proud of what he was doing, everybody held him in a little bit of awe. I don't know if Robert drew from that that people were proud of him or what, but that did seem to have some effect on him. I think Robert began to see his daddy as some sort of hero just from hearing people talk, but they were quite different in the way they were. John was the type individual who would strike out in fear if he thought somebody might hurt him, but he didn't go out and *seek* people to hurt; he was just overly protective of himself to the point where he would shoot you or cut you or whatever he thought was necessary to get out of a frightening situation. Whereas Robert, as it turned out, was a type individual who *would* go out and seek somebody to inflict harm on. He never expressed any remorse, none whatsoever, and I don't think there's any doubt that had Robert gotten out of Angola, he would have killed somebody else. I don't doubt that whatsoever. He needed to be removed from society."

Part of the contrast in crimes committed by John and Robert Willie can be explained by substances they used and abused, and part of *that* difference can be explained by changing times, for St. Tammany Parish is now crisscrossed by several major interstate highways, not to mention the causeway from New Orleans. These fast-paced links with the Crescent City and the Mississippi Gold Coast have had the effect of bringing to this rural area the drugs and violent crimes once more closely associated with overpopulated urban communities and the wide-open gulf coast resorts where urbanites traditionally indulged in high-stakes gambling and other illegal recreations.

"I would say drinking caused many of my crime problems, it shore have," says John Willie today. "A lot of it is high temper and drinking." Robert Lee, on the other hand, did more than drink, and as the modern-day drug user is considered by law enforcement officials to be more volatile, more unpredictable and more violent than the alcoholic, so his crimes escalate to unspeakable brutality and unnecessary cruelty. Says John Willie of his son, "He got hooked up with the wrong group, using drugs and drinking too, and I guess that led him to the crime he did. They'd drink, smoke that dope, marijuana, get high on pills, and they'd just go. He started doing drugs in his teens, when I was still in the pen, and you name it, what they didn't do. He'd get a job, work about a week or so, get enough money to buy dope with, and that's it. He got bad when he got to be a teenager, and he just rocked right on. His mother, she just died of cancer at forty-seven years old, she was as sweet as she could be to him, she and my sisters, but he just wouldn't listen."

Expressing regret at the course of his son's life, especially during his own absences at the state penitentiary at Angola, John Willie nonetheless draws a strong distinction between his own career and Robert's. "One way," he says, "I couldn't help it, 'cause I was away from him and didn't raise him, which I hated. But I was sorry that it happened, sorry it turned out like that. It's a sad thing to think about a son doing something like that. I've killed people in my time, but not like that. Naw, I wouldn't do nothing like that. I mean, I wouldn't do *no way* nothing like that!"

By the second week of June 1980, Robert Lee Willie and Joseph Jesse Vaccaro had been indicted by a federal grand jury on charges of conspiracy and kidnapping, and also faced state murder, attempted murder, car theft, rape and other charges in connection with the Brewster and Hathaway cases. Willie was transported by a U.S. marshall from Arkansas to New Orleans on June 11, and Vaccaro, married and the father of at least one child, would follow shortly.

In October, their unique murder trials would begin in Franklinton in the Hathaway case, two trials conducted simultaneously before different juries and in separate courtrooms of the same courthouse. On Monday, October 20, 1980, two juries, each consisting of eight men and four women, were seated, chosen from a venire of two hundred. Robert Lee Willie would be tried in the basement courtroom before District Judge Hillary Crain, with District Attorney Marion Farmer prosecuting and lawyer Samuel Austin McElroy of the St. Tammany indigent defender office representing the defendant, while Vaccaro's trial was held on the second floor of the same courthouse before Judge A. Clayton James, prosecuted by an assistant district attorney and lawyer Reggie Simmons representing the defendant. Defense motions for changes of venue, restricted news coverage and other matters were denied. Yet another trial was scheduled for later in the month in Covington to try the two defendants on kidnap, rape and attempted murder charges stemming from the Brewster case; a change of venue motion would remove this kidnap trial to Baton Rouge.

The trials in Franklinton were dramatic. Elizabeth Harvey, present for every moment of every court procedure for four long years, recounts how Mike Varnado of the DA's office lay on the floor before the jurors, unforgettably duplicating the exact pained position in which he had found Faith Hathaway's body. Jurors were not shown the gruesome photographs of Faith's body, but the prosecutor did manage to introduce one picture of her, taken during graduation ceremonies, showing her wearing during happier times the necklace which was found imbedded in the flesh of her mangled throat.

Robert Lee Willie was found guilty and sentenced to death. Later invalidated by an appeals court because of a comment made by one of the DA's staff, the sentencing phase had to be repeated at a later date, when Willie was again sentenced to death by a second Washington Parish jury. Vaccaro, also found guilty, received a life sentence when one juror held out against the imposition of the death penalty, capital punishment requiring unanimity. Among the courtroom spectators were Elizabeth and Vernon Harvey, both disappointed at the actions of Vaccaro's jury. Said Elizabeth to the news media at the conclusion of Willie's trial, "We felt a sense of relief that he would not be able to murder anyone again."

Vernon, on the other hand, was incensed that Vaccaro did not share Willie's sentence, and thought he knew why. "Vaccaro got off," he says today, "because of one woman on his jury who was picked originally for Willie's jury. When they were choosing jurors downstairs for Willie's case, they had turned this woman down when she said there was no way she could vote for the death penalty or even consider the death penalty. So they discharged her off of that jury, and they put her name right back in the pot. She went upstairs to the jury room and they put her on that jury. I went up there and looked during a break in Willie's trial, and there she sat on the jury. Right away I told the assistant DA who was trying the case. I said, 'What's *she* doing on the jury?' And he said she had been picked. And I said, 'Well, downstairs, she said she couldn't consider the death penalty,' and he said, 'Well, she said she *could* here.' He said there wasn't anything they could do about it because she'd already been sworn in. I know better now; I could have got her thrown off because she perjured herself."

Vernon continues, "She got sick when it was time for the sentencing, and when they brought the jury in, she was all redfaced. She held out altogether all the way through the sentencing phase, and it takes twelve jurors in agreement for the death penalty. So it was eleven to one when they polled the jury, and it wasn't hard to tell she was the one. I researched the records and they showed she had perjured herself. I don't know why she wanted to be on that jury. She has two little girls, and I would never wish anything on those little girls, but I would sure like to see her have to suffer some of the pain that we suffered over this."

John Willie is oddly in agreement with the Harveys, at least about the inequity of Vaccaro's sentence when compared to the ultimate price paid by his own son. "What hurt me was they didn't execute the other man, Vaccaro," he says. "Far as the crime, like I told Robert, if I do a crime, I'll pay for it, I wanta pay the debt to society. If two men done a crime, I believe both of them should pay the same way. I don't believe one man should die and the other live. I believe a murderer should die just like the victim, that's the kind of man I am this morning."

Calling himself a hard old con ("I ain't no *inmate;* an inmate might turn out to be a little *girl* or something"), talkative John, grayhaired at fifty-nine and suffering from colon cancer, expounds on his unique sense of rightness and order in the criminal justice world. "Now if a man gets in an argument with another man and he shoots and kills him, now that's one kind of crime, but if a man is jealous over his wife and kills another man over that, that's another crime altogether, and I think he should pay for it, 'cause a man ain't got no business being jealous over his wife, 'cause there's too many women in the world today for a man to kill other men over women. He found *her*, why can't he find another one? Me, I've been married three times."

John says Robert told him, during a visit on Death Row, that he wouldn't mind paying for his crimes either, but that he hadn't been the one who killed Faith Hathaway. Recalls John, repeating the highly unlikely scenario sketched for him by his son, "He said, 'Daddy, I didn't kill her, I just held her for Vaccaro to kill, 'cause the girl fell in love with me that night and didn't want nothing to do with Vaccaro, and Vaccaro got mad.' In my mind, I can't say for sure, but I believe Vaccaro done the killing. I admit that that boy of mine helped him, but I believe that Vaccaro done the stabbing. I think both of them are responsible for her body, and I think both of them should have got the death penalty." Nearly as preposterous as Willie's claim that the terrified rape victim "fell in love" with her abuser is his insinuation that Faith voluntarily shared drugs, including LSD, with her abductors; knowing she was to report for induction into the service the following morning, it is highly unlikely that she would have wanted to risk having illegal substances in her system.

Lt. Donald Sharp repeats, with emphasis, "There is no doubt, from what I know of Willie, that Willie cut Faith Hathaway's throat." Elizabeth Harvey adds, "When Faith was found, her hands were still gripped from Vaccaro holding her down and some of her fingers were cut off from her fighting, but Willie admitted that he was between her legs when her throat was cut. Vaccaro couldn't have been holding her hands and reached over and cut her throat; the person had to be facing the other way to cut her throat." Interjects Vern, "It was one just as guilty as the other. I don't know which one cut her throat, and I don't care." But his wife insists, "Yes, well, I *do*, because Willie admitted that at the time her throat was cut, he was between her legs, and the coroner said that the person who cut her throat couldn't have been above her head. And her hands in death were still in that gripped position, held above her head."

And yet, adds Elizabeth, it matters not which suspect cut her daughter's throat; both were equally guilty in causing her death, and both should have paid the same ultimate penalty for that. "Both of them admitted that they raped her," she recalls with anguish, "and the first thing that the coroner told me when he came to my house was that she was so brutally raped and torn up that they would never have saved her even if they hadn't split her throat. Her insides were torn up that badly. Willie said Vaccaro had split Faith's throat, and Vaccaro had said Willie split Faith's throat. But to me it made no difference, because the coroner said she had been so brutally raped they never would have saved her, and both of them admitted that they raped her."

The trial process proved so painful that the Harveys almost regretted the decision to go through with it, and media publicity brought them hate mail like the letter from one Kansas inmate threatening, "Even if Willie did kill your fucking daughter, what good did it do to burn him. That makes every one of you blood-thirsty bastards worse than him. . . . Some day when I get out of the joint I'm going to show you fuckers how it feels to face death. . . . Maybe then you fucking do-gooders will see the other side."

Armed guards atop the courthouse from the beginning of pretrial hearings bespoke community concern; Elizabeth Harvey thought it indicated concern that Willie might again attempt escape. Vernon, on the other hand, thought the safety precautions more likely represented concern that he himself might give vent to his frustrated rage and attempt to kill the defendants. "Both Willie and Vaccaro were scared to death of me," recalls Vern with no small degree of satisfaction. In court each day he had to surrender the gun he carried as a part-time Mandeville police assistant. "But," he says, "I am not a killer. One time they took Willie to the bathroom and when he came back by me in the courtroom, he said to me, 'Man, it'll never happen, it'll never happen,' meaning that he was pleading to federal charges so that he wouldn't face the state death penalty and wouldn't go to the chair. 'You son of a bitch, I'll see you burn,' I told him. And I *did.*"

"They wouldn't let us know when the defendants were coming to the courthouse or anything else," Elizabeth says. "When they were being brought back from Arkansas in the very beginning, we got a telephone call, asking if we wanted them taken care of or delivered to our door. I told them I wanted to see what the judicial system could do. That's the way I felt. Of course then I was very innocent about the system." Puts in Vern, "The system just plain stinks."

His wife continues, "Well, I have a lot of respect for the system in a lot of ways, but it needs a lot of improvement. There's a lot of work to be done. The rights of victims have improved, but I don't know if I would have waited for the criminal justice system now, as much as I know about it. Only a few cases even get to court, and those that do, getting a sentence is even harder. So I don't know whether I would go down that same road again."

Elizabeth Harvey has thrown herself into working with a national organization called Parents of Murdered Children (100 E. Eighth St., Cincinnati, Ohio 45202), begun in 1978 in Cincinnati by the grieving parents of nineteen-year-old Lisa Hullinger, beaten to death with a sledgehammer in Germany by a fellow exchange student. The Louisiana chapter (Parents of Murdered Children, 465 Fairfield Ave., Gretna, LA 70053) was started in 1982 in New Orleans by Carol Deutsch, whose twelve-year-old daughter was killed by a teenaged neighbor. Providing a long-needed vehicle for the sharing of ideas, dissemination of legal information and proffering of support to meet the needs of crime survivors in individual communities, PMOC operates at least partially under a grant from the U.S. Department of Justice's Office of Victims of Crime, hosting training sessions, displaying a memorial wall, publishing newsletters and maintaining a national office to assist local chapters.

From helping, the Hullingers found, comes healing, and they based their group support programs on a quote from William Shakespeare:

> *"Give sorrow words; the grief that does not speak*
> *Whispers the o'er-fraught heart and bids it break."*

Victims often feel they are brutalized twice, Harvey explains, quoting from Daniel Popeo, the general counsel for the Crime Victims Program of the Washington Legal Foundation. They feel, and often rightfully so, that they have been brutalized once by the crime and then again, less understandably, by a criminal justice system which is only beginning to accord to the survivors rights equal to those mandated by law for the criminals. Experienced PMOC members help new victims penetrate the cold wall of incomprehension surrounding the court process, explaining every step of the way, from investigation and arrest through initial arraignment and preliminary hearings to grand jury consideration, arraignment, pretrial hearings, trial, sentencing and the seemingly interminable appeals process. Only in some of the more progressive states have *victim's bill of rights* laws been enacted, assuring survivors of being kept informed of court proceedings and notified in advance of possible parole hearings, allowing victim input as to the impact of the crime, and facilitating access to restitution or compensation funds.

POMC groups also help survivors endure the inevitable and indescribably painful grieving process, too often misunderstood by well-meaning but impatient relatives and friends who prove less than helpful in encouraging a too-quick return to normalcy. Remembrance cards go out to survivors on death anniversaries, and newsletters give upcoming parole hearing dates on offenders so that fellow members can write opposing early release. Mostly, POMC members *understand*. Only one who has gone through it can know the devastation of losing a child, especially to an unprovoked violent crime, and confronting the suffering that that child endured before death can be unbearable for an anguished parent.

Says Elizabeth Harvey, "If someone had asked me before if I would have survived a daughter being murdered, I would have said no. They'd have been burying me pretty close right after her, if not *with* her. It was an ordeal just to breathe, the pain was so heavy on my chest, and how easy it would have been not to try my next breath. But you think of your husband, your other daughter. And then you have to take each moment. Each minute seems like an hour, each hour seems like a day. The first three years, you just make up the beds and do the dishes and wash and stuff, because that's what you've been doing. When you look back, there's so many things you can't remember doing that you wonder how they got done. People don't realize how many of us are just walking around not really aware what we're doing, just doing it automatically, with so much built up inside. It didn't help that we were treated as if we had some contagious disease, and speaking Faith's name was absolutely something that they didn't do."

Faith's younger half-sister, Lisabeth, only fourteen when Robert Lee Willie was executed, penned a heartfelt poem to express the grief and regrets typical of family suffering in every violent crime. She called it "Looking Back":

> *How we take things for granted. Now here lies my sister, the breath taken from her body, so unfair does it seem. Yet how many times did I tell you how much I love you.*

Holding you, wishing that I could have told you. Oh God, how it hurts,
the pain almost unbearable. Oh Faith, how I wish you could hear me.

Peace on your face, knowing no more suffering will come your way. Still
if only I could have told you I love you, and why I did not I could not say.

So many times we take our family members for granted, and tend to forget,
here today, gone tomorrow. Hear these words, if it's the last words you hear,
tell your loved one you love them today before you can't tomorrow.

Elizabeth Harvey's dedication to the cause of victims' rights has earned her a seat on the state Crime Victims Advisory Board, and she says, "I hope that with everything that the criminal justice system has taught us, we can help a little bit. It does help to have someone who *knows* beside you. When we went down that road, we didn't know that we had any options whatsoever, but there are a lot of options for victims of violent crime now, ten years later. For one thing, there's up to $10,000 in the victim restitution fund which can provide help with burial expenses or medical treatment. You know, there are many people who do not even have the money to bury their own child. It's pretty rough when you go down this road feeling like you have no rights at all, but when you know you have choices to make, it doesn't seem so rough. Maybe you don't want to open that door, but just knowing you have a choice about whether you want to open it or not, then it feels a lot better."

It was partially because of her sensitivity for the suffering of others that Elizabeth Harvey felt she had to join her husband in seeking permission to watch the carrying out of Robert Lee Willie's death sentence in Angola's Death House, a sentence which was stayed some five times during appeals. She says, "I felt like if Willie escaped from prison after the state had sentenced him to the electric chair, and he killed your child, when you said to me, 'You knew what kind of person he was, why didn't you push it,' I felt like I had to do what I could under the law so that I could look you in the face and say, 'I *tried.*' I felt like I had to live with myself, and that I had to be able to tell you, 'Yes, I did everything that I humanly could do to see that he served the sentence that he got.' And I would be glad to know that he was dead, glad that he could not kill again." And she also wanted to see that death with her very own eyes, which was not an easy goal to attain.

"At one court appeal," she recounts, "the lawyer was mentioning that Willie could not be brought back to Louisiana for execution because of his federal sentences which had to be served first. And one of those supreme court judges asked, 'What says he cannot be brought back to the state for execution?' The lawyer said nobody had ever been brought out of federal prison until they had served their sentence there first, and the judge kind of leaned up and he said, *'This just might be the case.'* We went through Congressman Bob Livingston and the president of the United States. Bob Livingston was having a town meeting and Vern asked him how we could bring Willie back out of federal prison, and later he told Vern to get together records of all Willie's crimes and he'd see that the information got to the president."

Vern picks up the story, recounting an exhaustive search for every possible shred of evidence of criminal activity engaged in by Robert Lee Willie throughout his short lifetime, then relates with glee his receipt of the presidential phone call. "What would you do, you're trying to mix yourself a drink, you've just come in from work, it's hot summertime, you just drove sixty miles after working heavy construction outside all day long, and the telephone rings and someone says, 'Hold for the president.' I says, 'President of what?' I just about started to hang up, thinking it was some practical joker, when Ronald Reagan came on, and I recognized the man's voice. I can't remember just the words he said, but he told me if he ever wanted information on somebody, he'd never ask *me* for it because I'd send him too much. He said he'd been reading this thing over and that Willie would be coming back to Louisiana for execution in the very near future, soon as the U.S. Supreme Court turned down his last appeal. And two days later the court turned him down." It was not long before Robert Lee Willie was returned to Louisiana from the maximum-security federal penitentiary at Marion, Illinois.

Granted permission to be among state witnesses at Willie's execution, along with Mike Varnado of the DA's office and one of the prosecuting attorneys, the Harveys were cautioned to show no emotion and make no comments while in the Death House. "We were told that we were state representatives," Elizabeth recalls, "and we wanted to be careful not to make any gestures or do anything that might prevent somebody else from being allowed to witness an execution at a later date." That didn't stop Vern, he says with some satisfaction, from silently responding to Willie's last statement. "Willie said, 'Mr. and Mrs. Harvey, I hope you get some satisfaction from my death, but the killing is wrong, whether it's the state, individuals or society, the killing is wrong.' And I gave him a big smile. *Yeah*, I got some satisfaction out of where he was going."

Elizabeth comments that Willie's last statement reflected not so much his own beliefs as the sentiments of his spiritual adviser, Catholic Sister Helen Prejean, longtime dedicated opponent of capital punishment. "Willie's last words was words from her mouth," Elizabeth says. "Sister Prejean came and visited us before the last pardon board hearing, and everything she had talked to us about, she used against us at that hearing, turning everything around as though every twenty-four hours seven days a week our whole existence was dedicated to seeing that Robert Lee Willie would be executed. But you know, of course, life has to go on, you have to earn a living, bills have to be paid, a house has to be cleaned, clothes have to be done, meals have to be cooked. She thought that the only thing we tried to do was see that Willie was executed, not that justice was done. But the pardon board said, when someone tried to say it was up to them whether he was executed or not, and this made me feel better than anything else in this whole wide world, they said, 'We are not executing Robert Lee Willie; Robert Lee Willie put himself in that electric chair the day that he murdered Faith Hathaway.'"

Dying to Tell

Saying she had counselled Willie on Death Row and that he had ultimately concluded that after death he would be received by God in heaven (Vern all the while adamantly insisting that he would instead burn in hell), Sister Helen Prejean would tell the press gathered for the execution, "I think these are very dark days in our history and people are operating out of a lot of fear, hoping that if we execute people it's going to make murder and crime and violence go away." But the electrocution of Robert Lee Willie, Elizabeth Harvey insisted, would surely make at least *some* murder and crime and violence go away. Said she, "Robert Lee Willie will never be able to murder again, he won't be able to add any more victims to his list, and it's a long list."

It was indeed a long list, having grown considerably longer than even law enforcement officials might have suspected during the appeals process on the Hathaway and Brewster cases, when two other killings would be revealed by Willie in a casual, almost offhanded fashion, murders for which he would receive additional life sentences. Detailed to accompany Willie to court in Washington Parish for re-sentencing in the summer of 1982, deputy Donald Sharp of the St. Tammany parish sheriff's office was astounded to be told by the offender that he wanted to tell the officer "something good about a body." Willie, who Sharp described as somewhat simple but extremely street-smart, then proceeded to describe in vivid detail the four-year-old killing of one Dennis Buford Hemby of Missouri during a drug deal.

Willie insisted that his cousin Perry Taylor had done the actual killing in late May of 1978, after the pair purchased a couple of one-ounce bags of Columbian marijuana for $35 a bag from Hemby, but added that he had helped in the slaying and would plead guilty if the charge were reduced to second-degree murder. On June 29, 1982, the skeletal remains of Hemby, still wearing tan cowboy boots, were located under a towering pine tree near the river in which he had been drowned, exactly where Willie said he would be. Taylor, sent to Angola over this case, insisted that Willie had been the one to do the actual killing.

By August of 1982 Robert Lee Willie, already in custody more than two years, was also charged with the murder and armed robbery of St. Tammany sheriff's deputy Sgt. Louis Wagner in June of 1978, a crime to which he also pled guilty and which he said had been committed in company with three other young men, one of whom he said had done the actual shooting of the twenty-six-year-old deputy, who was married and the father of two small children, the last one born posthumously. The parish grand jury indicted Willie, Richard Lott, Perry Phillips, Jr., and Bobby K. Raney in that murder. In his statement to the sheriff's office, Willie related that he and his co-defendants followed Sgt. Wagner's truck through town and pulled alongside him on LA Highway 21 as Willie waved a shotgun. Ricky Lott, according to Willie, then shouted, 'Every dog has his day and today is your day,' as he shot the deputy.

But charges against Lott, Phillips and Raney were *nolle prossed* in early 1983. Donald Sharp says, "In my mind I know who killed Sgt. Wagner. Willie didn't actually pull the trigger, but he was there. The three people we had in jail were the guilty parties." John Willie too says his son denied being the one who actually killed Wagner. "About three days before he was executed, I was up to see him at Angola on Death Row, and he told me he didn't do it. But he said, 'I won't tell you who *did* it, because I know you would go back and tell somebody.' So he never would tell me who done it, who killed the deputy sheriff, but he said he didn't do it. He said, 'I was with the people that killed him, but I didn't shoot the man.'"

But Robert Lee Willie, Lt. Donald Sharp insists, was involved in other murders as well, murders which to this day remain unsolved, and the details of these crimes have gone to the grave with the perpetrator. It all goes back to that incriminating tatooed bracelet of skulls, modern-day equivalent of a gunfighter's notched gun grip proclaiming his infamy throughout the Old West.

"Willie owed me two more," Sharp says. "He killed Dennis Hemby and Faith Hathaway, kidnapped and shot Mark Brewster, raped his girlfriend but didn't kill her because he said she was too pretty. Once up in the jail I asked him about that bracelet. I said, 'What are the skulls for?' And he said, 'Think about it, man, you got to think about things.' That's the way he was, he'd give you a little something and let you do some legwork, he'd run you to death, and once you found out something and came back and showed him what you had, he'd say you were right. That's the way he was. He had a skull for each person he killed, and there was a breaking link in the bracelet. There was a skull for Hemby, one for Faith Hathaway, one for Louis Wagner, and two which are unsolved. Willie said he didn't figure he'd killed Brewster, though he figured he might die later in the hospital."

Sharp continues his incredible story. "Willie told me he'd killed two other people, but he wouldn't never tell me where they were at. He said we were gonna work on one at a time, and when we got through with the Wagner case, we'd go on to another one. He said he ran over one of them. Willie was bad about stealing dope, he'd buy a bag from somebody and see they were holding a bunch, and come back later and steal it, looking at it that they couldn't go tell the police. He stole this guy's marijuana, ten bags he told me, threw the guy out of the car, the guy threw a brick through the windshield and Willie turned around in the road and ran over him. Buried him in the woods, he said. Another guy he threw in a gravel pit when he was driving a gravel truck. Said it was for a good reason, that the guy was a hitchhiker and had a hundred dollars, and he wanted it."

If ever there were anyone who deserved the death penalty, it was probably Robert Lee Willie, who had the dubious distinction of earning a grand total of six state life sentences and several thirty-year federal sentences in addition to one death sentence, having killed at least three known times, viciously violated two young teenaged girls, kidnapped and assaulted and partially paralyzed a promising young man just entering his prime. Boldly refusing to beg for mercy at his final pardon board appearance before being executed, Willie almost boasted in a subsequent interview, "I'm an outlaw. I've been an outlaw most of my life. . . . If I had it to do all over again, I'd be an outlaw. . . . I lived a pretty good life. I've done almost everything there is to do—drugs, sex, rock 'n roll, travel, football, school—about everything. I've had a number of women, drugs. I've experienced about everything there is to experience. I've been in the drinking scene, the drug scene. I've had a pretty good life. So I'm ready. I'm ready."

At age twenty-six, Robert Lee Willie had done it all, he said. The state could just go ahead and kill him, for all he cared. And so it did, after four years of stays of execution, on December 28, 1984. Buried in blue jeans and a t-shirt so his tatooed arms could show to best advantage, a scarf over his shaven head, rebellious-to-the-last Robert Lee Willie, who blithely blew kisses to his surviving rape-kidnap victim (now a successful teacher) as she courageously testified in court, had no apologies, nor any apparent regrets. Should the state have had any? Certainly not in the view of the victims of Robert Lee Willie's heinous crimes. Said Faith Hathaway's grieving stepfather, after witnessing with his wife Willie's execution, "I think that little jolt of electricity that they gave him over there that killed him . . . was just the beginning of the heat that his soul is going to have to put up with for eternity."

The death penalty, of course, is nothing new, having been imposed since biblical times by means of such cruel methods as stoning or crucifixion for crimes ranging from murder and adultery to the disobedience of a child to its parents. Though present-day perception of biblical justice leans toward the grim eye-for-an-eye measures extracted even today in some mideast cultures, turbaned enforcers plucking out offending tongues and whacking off sticky-fingered hands, in actuality the law in earliest history leaned more toward restitution than retribution, especially after the vicious vengeance of the Old Testament was softened by the loving forgiveness of the New.

In colonial America, criminal justice was decidedly harsh and usually swift, combining as it did English and Mosaic justice, with crowd-pleasing public executions by hanging or firing squad. Capital crimes varied from colony to colony and included such diverse offenses as slaying by poisoning, rape, kidnapping, murder and cussing one's parents. The first execution in this country was the 1608 shooting of a colonist dubiously convicted of treason for spying for the Spanish crown. In New York in 1665, the death penalty was mandated for anyone denying the true God, and Virginia ordered capital punishment for stealing grapes or killing horses or chickens.

Some effective early defenses against the application of the death penalty included pleading hunger (to excuse the stealing of foodstuffs or other possessions) and what was called "the benefit of clergy," a sentence reduction originally available to the clergy alone and later only to those who could read, which consisted of the offender reading *Psalms 51:1* from the Bible, *"Have mercy upon me, O God, according to thy lovingkindness: according unto the multitude of thy tender mercies blot out my transgressions."* Even today in Khartoum, Sudan, the current interpretation of the 1350-year-old *Islamic Sharia,* an ethical, criminal and civil code, allows murderers to escape the death penalty by paying to the victim's family what is called *diyyah* or blood money in the amount of one hundred camels or a negotiated equivalent which has recently been legally standardized at close to $17,000.

In the Quaker-influenced colonies of Pennsylvania and New Jersey, only two crimes were considered capital offenses, treason and murder, while in other colonies judges and governors often granted pardons, especially if the public cried out for mercy. Sham sentences were sometimes handed down, the judge ordering the imposition of a so-called death sentence which might be carried out almost to the very final moment, even to the point of having a firing squad shoot above the quaking criminal's blindfolded head, before he was exhorted to change his ways and clemency was granted.

In the several decades before the Civil War, anti-gallows societies formed and some states abolished the death penalty altogether, while others at least admitted the need for more uniform and humane application of capital punishment. The zeal for reform was soon swallowed up by the anti-slavery movements sweeping the northern sections of the country, however, and it would be a century before there would again arise widespread and effective national opposition to the death penalty.

In the late 1880's, New York State instituted a sweeping study of capital punishment, including investigation of the thirty-four diverse methods of judicial killing which had been employed since history began. The study commission, all too aware of gruesome tales of separated heads bouncing off the gallows and crowds of excited onlookers patronizing concession stands, broken ropes and long loud agonizing deaths twisting in the breeze, soon eliminated hanging, calling it a potentially horrible public death scene fraught with possibilities for error caused by offenders' theatrical resistance, executioner incompetence and the misconduct of tumultuous crowds of bloodthirsty bystanders cheering the histrionics or heroics of the condemned.

Indeed, one double hanging in 1880 in Murfreesboro, Tennessee, had attracted more than 15,000 onlookers from twenty surrounding counties. The nineteenth-century write-up of this February 20th hanging of John Hall and Burrell Smith, quoted in a series of articles *The Tennessean* based on the fascinating findings of researcher Watt Espy of the University of Alabama, enthused, "Murfreesboro was a scene of great merriment that day, the bartenders doing a great business and a large barbecue being held for the witnesses." A huge amphitheater was erected for the excited spectators, whose numbers were so great that the stands collapsed, causing a near-stampede, but from all accounts, "everyone had a terrific time and was thoroughly entertained." The condemned had requested that their bodies be delivered with dispatch from the gallows to a group of local doctors in hopes of being revived by means of galvanic batteries or some such method; alas, the resurrection attempts proved fruitless and the bodies were then dissected to further the knowledge of medical science.

Before long, the New York commissioners, determined to be done with such public spectacles as that "enjoyed" by the multitudes at Murfreesboro, had narrowed the field of choices down to four . . . newfangled electricity, prussic acid or other poison, beheading by sword or guillotine, strangulation by the garrote . . . and eventually recommended that the state mandate death for its condemned from "a current of electricity of sufficient intensity to destroy life instantly."

The New York state legislature, after dramatic debate, passed the bill calling for electrocution effective January 1, 1889, and by August 6, 1890, the first electrocution in America would take place at Auburn State Prison, the unlamented death of drunkard and huckster William Kemmler for the gory hatchet slaying in Buffalo of his unfaithful mistress Matilda Ziegler. "Papa hit Mama with the hatchet," testified the pair's four-year-old daughter, and indeed Matilda had suffered twenty-six gashes on the face and head, as well as five wounds on the right hand, arm and shoulder. Said Kemmler boldly, "I wanted to kill her, and the sooner I hang for it the better."

During defense appeals to the Supreme Court arguing that the substitution of electricity for the gibbet was unconstitutional and cruel, the lack of general knowledge concerning this new power called electricity was vividly demonstrated by witnesses like one Mr. Alfred West, struck by lightning in 1880 and revived, he insisted, only when the power was *drawn out* by placing his feet in warm water while a rescuer "pulled on Mr. West's toes with one hand and milked a cow with the other," according to court records (some folklorists insist that this is not as ludicrous as it sounds, and that a certain amount of static electricity is indeed discharged by soaking one appendage in warm water while opening up the joints of the fingers). Other methods of resuscitation from electric shock described at court during Kemmler's appeals included the injection of brandy and the application of traction on the victim's tongue, whereby it was held firmly and drawn forcibly forward for a quarter of an hour, inducing a supposed diaphragmatic reflex response.

Nevertheless, William Kemmler was electrocuted by the State of New York in a heavy oak armchair previously tested only on luckless animal subjects, using the new alternating current system of George Westinghouse, at the devious urging of his rival Thomas Edison, who himself used only the continuous or direct current system in his new incandescent lamp and electrical systems. Testifying before state officials, Edison blithely insisted that his own system of low-tension direct current was "harmless as a spring breeze" and totally unsatisfactory for executions, while Westinghouse's competing alternating current "would kill men like flies." Hoping the ensuing bad publicity might put his competitor out of business, Edison even went so far as to bring an engineer to the state capital at Albany to put on a grisly demonstration in which a dog was killed by means of alternating current, and subsequent demonstrations at Sing Sing using a Westinghouse dynamo brought boasts that electrocution would usher in a new and humane era in the history of mankind. The making of history was not lost on Chicago sideshow promoters, who vainly telegraphed the warden at Auburn with extravagant offers to purchase the body of the first murderer to die in the electric chair.

The actual execution of Kemmler was alternately described in newspaper accounts of the times as "a disgrace to civilization," "fiendish torture" under "the most revolting circumstances," and, at the other end of the spectrum, "the grandest success of the age." Firmly bound to the electric chair by eleven straps across his body, arms and legs, with a wired headpiece attached by leather bands over his forehead and chin, his clothing cut away at the base of the spine for the attachment of a second electrode, Kemmler was dispatched at daybreak as Warden Charles F. Durston, saying, "Goodbye, William," signalled for the switch to be thrown. Wires connected the chair with a dynamo in an adjoining room. Some 1700 volts coursed through Kemmler.

"He's dead," declared one of the witnessing physicians, no doubt with relief, as excited comments on the ease and success of the proceedings distracted attention from the slumped body in the chair. The desired goal, reported the New York *Herald,* had been the development of the machinery of death capable of instantly rending soul from body, and that hope appeared to have been realized. Doctors began removing the electrodes, readying eagerly for examination of the corpse, which would eventually be divided into several parts to allow those interested the opportunity for investigation.

"My God! He's alive!" shouted a horrified voice. Kemmler appeared to breathe heavily, his breast heaving against the bonds. "Strong men fainted and fell like logs upon the floor," reported the *Herald.* More current was applied, and not until eight minutes after the start of the ordeal was Kemmler finally declared dead, burst capillaries vividly coloring his face, hair singed, a blue flame playing about the base of his spine, his brain baked, blood turned to charcoal, and the awful odor of burnt flesh assailing the nostrils of those witnesses hardy enough to retain consciousness.

"A brutal affair" better done with an ax, commented George Westinghouse, though the brutal affair would unexpectedly prove much to his benefit. The fact that it had taken two long doses of alternating current to finally dispatch poor Kemmler discredited Edison to the extent that his costlier direct-current system lost favor, public support swinging to rival Westinghouse's AC when it came to wiring homes and commercial spaces for the newly harnessed power of electricity. Said Westinghouse, "The alternating current will kill people, of course. So will gunpowder and dynamite, and whiskey, and lots of other things; but we have a system whereby the deadly electricity of the alternating current can do no harm unless a man is fool enough to swallow a whole dynamo."

Kemmler's would be far from the last botched death by electricity. Nevertheless, legal electrocution soon became one of the more popular forms of capital punishment, adopted by some twenty states (including Louisiana in 1940) and utilizing electric chairs similar in many ways to that first one in which William Kemmler took his leave of this life, though electrodes would later be attached to the head and the calf of one leg rather than the spine. The advent of the new technology of death brought an ensuing need for modernized vocabulary, with Edison suggesting that death by electricity should be called *ampermort, dynamort, electromort, electricide,* before public usage finally settled on *electrocution.* Perhaps, it was proposed only half facetiously, the word chosen should be the name of his old rival Westinghouse, adequately expressive as either noun or verb, the criminal being said to have been *westinghoused* or *condemned to the westinghouse* in much the same way the guillotined criminal in France provided perpetual tribute to that method's inventor Dr. Joseph Guillotin.

During the century following the first electrocution, more than twenty thousand condemned would be legally put to death in the United States, the youngest a mere child of twelve years of age, the circumstances varying from state to state according to local laws and customs as well as the wishes of the deceased. Besides usually being granted the enjoyment of one last meal of their choosing, a few, like wife-killer Frank Brenish in 1890, were allowed to drink themselves into a stupor before facing the gallows, giving him leave to protest in words foreshadowing many a later defense, "They oughtn't to hang a man when he ain't to his right mind!"

Many of the condemned have been allowed the soothing strains of melodies of their choice as well, being dispatched to meet their maker to the tune of favorite hymns like *In The Sweet Bye and Bye*. During the forties and fifties in Tennessee, a talented inmate singing group called *The Prisonaires* performed special requests for those about to be executed in the electric chair housed in the state penitentiary.

Watt Espy's Capital Punishment Research Project for the University of Alabama has turned up memorable examples of the tasteless headlines with which the contemporary press sensationally saluted news of many nineteenth-century executions. Fourteen-year-old Willie Bell of Georgia, for instance, was said in 1892 to have " . . . Gwine to Glory," and other headlines trumpeted, "Jerked to Jesus," "Stretched Hemp," "Danced in the Air," "Swung into Eternity" and "Burned to a Crisp," revealing, no doubt, the public perception of punishment well deserved by condemned considered little more than wild creatures.

It would be a hundred years after the botched Kemmler execution in New York before another court case would again strongly question the humanity of electrocution, specifically, as a constitutional means of judicial execution. Federal appeals made by the Loyola Death Penalty Resource Center for Louisiana condemned killers Frederick Kirkpatrick and Robert Wayne Sawyer explicitly (and unsuccessfully) challenged the state's electric chair in 1990, citing design flaws and previous executions which resulted in unnecessary suffering and mutilation to the bodies of inmates Robert Wayne Williams (verified by post-mortem photographs published in *The Angolite)*, Dalton Prejean and Wayne Felde, whose sister, a veteran nurse, described deep head burns clear through to the skull, the left ear almost burned off and chunks of skin missing.

Williams' pastor, who witnessed his 1983 execution as the first man to die in the state electric chair after the reinstatement of capital punishment, testified before U.S. District Judge Henry A. Mentz, Jr., to seeing smoke and fire rising from Williams' head as fiery red sparks flew from his leg; the Reverend J. D. Brown, pastor of Faith Chapel Church of God in Baton Rouge, also testified that a horribly offensive odor of burnt flesh clung to Williams' body even at the funeral home, and that, strangely, Williams' penis "was busted." Mention was also made of the May 1990 Florida electric chair execution of Jessie Tafero, from whose head flames, smoke and sparks dramatically shot as his throat gurgled for an interminable four minutes, causing a temporary postponement of subsequent executions by the governor.

When electrical engineering expert Dr. Theodore Bernstein of Wisconsin examined Louisiana's electric chair at Angola as part of the appeals process, he found the design of the electrodes, which pass electric current through the body, to be seriously flawed. Fastened to leather straps and saltwater-soaked sponges attached to the head and leg, the electrodes could cause current to jump from them to the skin, thereby allowing more burning than necessary, Dr. Bernstein testified. There was also a problem with voltage; the electrocution was supposed to be carried out by the application of a 2400-volt jolt of electricity for ten seconds, followed by 480 volts for twenty seconds, then a repetition of the entire cycle, but the control panel on the electric chair at Angola only put out 1800 volts, Bernstein found, perhaps because of a bad connection or overloaded transformer.

Nevertheless, Judge Mentz ruled that, while *damage* may be inflicted upon the body of the accused during the execution process, unnecessary *pain* is not. What bodily damage is done by Louisiana's electric chair, Mentz stated from the bench, is in his opinion caused *after* the initial application of current to the brain has resulted in disruption of its function, rendering the condemned unconscious and hence unable to experience pain and suffering. "The fact that Louisiana's design of its electric chair is subject to improvement does not mean that Louisiana's implementation of the death penalty is unconstitutional," the judge said in his ruling, nonetheless adding, "To meet constitutional muster, an execution, as much as humanly possible, should minimize the risk of unnecessary pain, violence and mutilation."

While a dozen states at the close of 1990, a full century after the country's first criminal electrocution, continue to sentence their condemned to death in the electric chair, others utilize a variety of alternate methods, six states even providing for prisoner choice. Some thirty-six states continue to have legalized capital punishment, though some have not carried out an execution for several decades; fourteen states and the District of Columbia have done away with the death penalty altogether. Three states still use the gas chamber for executions, and New Hampshire continues to carry on its books the penalty of death by hanging.

Regardless of the outcome of court cases challenging the legality of its electric chair, the state legislature voted to carry out capital punishment in Louisiana, as in eighteen other states and in federal cases, by lethal injection beginning in mid-September 1991. Angola officials removed for display in the Louisiana State Museum in New Orleans the infamous chair in which some 77 condemned were put to death after hanging was abolished in 1941, and let a contract to an outside firm for the manufacture of the gurney upon which the condemned would receive the fatal injection after inmates in Angola's metal shop refused orders to build it themselves. Described as substantially painless when administered properly, death by lethal injection, first practiced in Texas in 1982, begins with the administering of a rapidly acting anaesthetic like Sodium Pentothal or Thiopental, which induces sleep within ten or fifteen seconds, followed by an injection of Curare or Pancuronium Bromide which paralyzes the muscles and a third injection of Potassium Chloride, which immediately stops the heart.

Painless or not, however, death by lethal injection raises its own unique questions, many of a moral and ethical nature, particularly for the medical community. Strapped to a hospital gurney and wheeled into the execution chamber where a trained technician inserts a needle into a vein and begins an intravenous drip which will carry the massive overdoses of anaesthetics into the bloodstream, the condemned looks for all the world like any ordinary patient about to undergo lifesaving surgery. It is just that similarity which chills the enthusiasm of the medical profession, to the extent that the American Medical Association has drawn an ethical line forbidding the participation in executions of physicians, who have after all sworn to uphold the basic principle of the Hippocratic Oath, "First, do no harm."

"A physician, as a member of a profession dedicated to preserving life when there is hope of doing so, should not be a participant in a legally authorized execution," the AMA declared, though the doctor may make a final determination of death.   Added Texas physician Nancy W. Dickey, AMA trustee who chaired the organization's Council on Judicial and Ethical Affairs, in a *Washington Post* article on lethal injection and medical ethics, "Medical technology should be used to relieve suffering and return people to better health. Obviously this (lethal injection) is subverting it for something totally different."

To the AMA guidelines, the American Psychiatric Association has added an even more strongly worded directive, necessitated by court cases like that involving thirty-six-year-old Michael Owen Perry, condemned by the State of Louisiana for the chilling murder of his parents, two cousins and a two-year-old nephew he insisted had to be a devil because he was too smart for his age. Perry suffers from a schizoaffective disorder, a mental illness so severe that he must continually be forcibly medicated with the anti-psychotic drug Haldol in order to be legally considered competent enough to be executed, in the face of Supreme Court rulings that executing the insane violates the Eighth Amendment's ban against cruel and unusual punishment. Said the APA of cases like Louisiana's *Catch-22* attempt to mandate the medical maintenance of Perry's mental competence just so he can be killed, "The physician's serving the state as executioner, either directly or indirectly, is a perversion of medical ethics and of his or her role as healer and comforter."

With the professional physician restrained from participation in death by lethal injection, the potential for error rises, especially since many of the condemned have histories of longtime drug abuse with accompanying deterioration of abused veins. In some executions the catheters have been known to pop from weakened veins, leaking lethal fluid onto the execution chamber floor, and in one case, the condemned killer, a drug addict, had to himself help technicians find a useable vein so they could kill him.

So what, bristle legislators like Louisiana state representative Peppi Bruneau, who asks, "Why should we be concerned about doing it in a humane manner? Shouldn't we be doing it to set an example instead of saying you just fall asleep and go away for killing people?" Yet surely the *intent,* in a sophisticated modern-day society like ours, is for the state to carry out the legal sentence of death painlessly and swiftly, not to *torture* to death. The psychological torture, according to Sister Helen Prejean, is bad enough, given that the condemned, unlike most of us, knows the exact day and hour of his death and has plenty of time to dread its approach, regardless of the method by which it will be imposed upon him.

Even when all goes well with executions by lethal injection, however, opponents of the death penalty insist the highly touted "humanity" of the method merely masks the fundamental fact that all state-ordered killing is barbaric and ultimately inhumane. Asks longtime death penalty opponent Joseph B. Ingle, director of the Southern Coalition on Jails and Prisons, a United Church of Christ minister who has twice been nominated for the Nobel Peace Prize, "The original murder was terrible. Should we compound the tragedy by killing again in the name of justice? Is murder—the premeditated taking of a human life—any less coldblooded when carried out by employees of the state following the instructions of government officials?" To dedicated Joe Ingle, the death penalty is a racist charade, a "systematic killing process that is unworthy of a democratic people and that shames us in the eyes of the civilized world and in the sight of God."

He is joined in this view by many, including nationally respected author William Styron, who introduces Ingle's moving book *Last Rights* by insisting that the death penalty, imposed mainly in "America's chief killing ground" of the South upon a "wretched minority" unlucky in "the lottery of capital punishment," is a deadly blight upon our democracy. The truth, Styron says, is "that the death penalty almost never deters a criminal, that it is visited overwhelmingly on the indigent and those disadvantaged by race and class (and too often, unbearably, on minors and the mentally retarded), that it is applied with callous inequity to the point of randomness, and that a significant number of those who are later proved innocent go to their doom." Continues Styron, "If it is wrong to destroy a human life, vengeance compounds the wrong. The wrong of the crime of killing is in no way redressed by the state's own vengeful murder." Or, as one of the fateful thirteen Death Row inmates Ingle worked so desperately to save throughout *Last Rights* said to him, "It's not the *dying*, it's the *killing* . . . bothers me."

Even Styron, however, admits to being out of step with current feeling in this country. "The overwhelming majority of Americans," he laments, "favors the death penalty. They appear to favor it with a vehement passion." And undeniably, he is right. This present passion for executions is reflected not only in the passage of legislation and the assumption of political platforms tough on crime; it is also reflected by our judicial systems, all the way up to the highest court in the land.

During the seventies, when public support for the death penalty had been low for a decade, the U.S. Supreme Court's re-examination of the constitutionality of the death penalty granted a hiatus which resulted in freedom from death for capital cases awaiting execution at the time and mandated specific guidelines governing future cases in which the death penalty could be considered appropriate. The respite, however, would be brief, and from a low point in 1966 when the Gallup Poll found only forty-two percent of

Americans favoring the death penalty, support for that ultimate penalty had risen to seventy-nine percent by 1988.

The pendulum of public opinion, at a time when an all-time-high prisoner population inhabits Death Rows across the country and overcrowded prisons bulge at the seams, seems indeed to have swung with a vengeance back to a thirst for blood. Says writer E. J. Dionne, Jr. in an article appearing in *Corrections Today*, "Capital punishment, which was once outlawed in most of the United States, is becoming part of the normal fabric of American life again and scholars who study the question say there is one main reason why: The people want retribution."

Vengeance is no longer merely ascribed to the Lord; the victimized American public is ready to fight back, and wants to see justice done here, now, and in living color. At least one California television station has petitioned the court for permission to videotape and then televise executions; in June 1991 a federal judge upheld the state's ban on cameras at executions, though allowing for other press coverage. That particular state just happens to have an eighty-two-percent approval rating for the death penalty, according to a March 1990 Field Institute poll, nearly double the approval rating of the mid-fifties. For an especially heinous crime, the approval rating jumps to eighty-four percent.

Why? "Deterrence was the argument in the early 1980s," says Leigh Dingerson, director of the National Coalition to Abolish the Death Penalty in a recent article in *Vanity Fair*. "Now that argument has been refuted by any number of studies, and what remains in this country is this sense that 'they deserve it.' Retribution is the argument of the nineties." Adds one defense lawyer, "It's the 'politics of death' in California."

Continues this attorney, Robert R. Bryan, "The fact is that those who wind up on death row . . . aren't necessarily those who commit the worst crimes. The common denominator is that they're all poor. Add to that the uneven quality of public defenders, doctors, police, sometimes the political agenda in the county where the crime was committed, how much money the prosecution has to spend on a case, the judge, the makeup of the state supreme court in a given year—of course it's arbitrary, and little wonder that an innocent man could end up on death row."

The public doesn't seem to care. *Corrections Today*, calling the shift in attitude toward capital punishment one of the more striking changes in public opinion over the last quarter-century, cites a *New York Times*/CBS News poll conducted in the spring of 1990 which found that of seventy-two percent of Americans favoring the death penalty, only fifty-nine percent actually considered it to be a deterrent. Besides not verifiably serving as a deterrent to future crime, the death penalty has been shown time and again to be ultimately unfair in its application, with variables like the race and social class of both victim and offender, the resources and skills of defense attorneys, location and just plain luck playing major roles in determining exactly which cases would end in capital punishment and which would receive lesser sentences.

Just this randomness of capital punishment in Louisiana was vividly illustrated by results of a three-month *Times-Picayune* study which involved computer analysis of hundreds of murders as well as interviews with attorneys, criminologists and law professors. The study found that not much had changed since 1972, when the U.S. Supreme Court denounced the death penalty as unconstitutional, calling it cruel and unusual punishment because there was little meaningful basis for distinguishing those few cases in which it was imposed from the many cases in which it was not. Though the new capital punishment laws approved in 1976 were designed to ensure uniformity, reduce the number of crimes punishable by death and provide new opportunity for appeal, the *Times-Picayune* study concluded that the death penalty since re-instatement in 1977 continues to be the same old lottery, with the race of the victim more than any other factor influencing whether a sentence of death will be returned. Tulane University sociologist M. Dwayne Smith, who assisted in the New Orleans newspaper's study, puts it bluntly: "All other things being equal, the victim's race proved the most influential factor in who did and didn't get the death penalty," a pattern consistent with that found by other researchers in other states.

"In every type of first-degree murder," Smith continues, "no matter where it happened or under what circumstances, the murder of a white victim is more likely to result in the death penalty than the murder of a black victim. This particularly holds true in southern states, which, of course, are where the majority of the nation's executions occur. It's ironic when you realize that crime statistics show that a higher percentage of blacks are murdered than whites. If anyone needs protection, it's blacks."

Times-Picayune criminal justice writer Jason DeParle, analyzing study results, found that while racism might account for part of the discrepancy in sentencing (capital punishment juries in Louisiana are generally predominantly white as is the state's population, and prosecutors often exclude potential black jurors as less likely to vote for death), much of what appeared to be racial discrimination was actually discrimination along economic and social class lines. The murders of white middle-class victims, usually unprovoked, receive more outraged press coverage and more vigorous prosecution, especially in suburban and rural areas, and consequently more often result in death sentences.

This is even more likely when the economic status of the offender requires him to rely on court-appointed defense attorneys, overworked and underpaid, lacking the resources to mount a proper defense, hire expert witnesses or thoroughly investigate background influences or mitigating circumstances. According to figures provided by the Loyola Death Penalty Resource Center, two-thirds of all death sentences are reversed by the courts in this country, and once a death sentence is affirmed on direct appeal, the condemned first-degree murderer is entitled to review in state and federal courts. But free legal representation extends only to the initial trial and direct appeal phases. While a private lawyer might require a $25,000 fee for a murder defense, court-appointed defense attorneys receive a laughably inadequate $1,000 maximum, for which they are expected, in the words of LDPRC director Nicholas Trenticosta, to become social worker, psychiatrist, investigator and attorney all wrapped up into one in order to present the entire compelling picture of those he calls "society's throw-aways," offenders with psychological and mental illnesses and problematic or abusive backgrounds who, had there been proper state intervention at some point in their lives, might not be on Death Row, people Trenticosta sees as "a product of a lot of the ills of our society and a lot of the ills of the way the government treats people who need help."

"If anything changes the public will, it will be the perception not only that capital punishment is not a deterrent, but also that it has not been administered fairly. And that, ultimately, it may be *impossible* to administer fairly," says writer Mark MacNamara in *Vanity Fair,* emphasizing that of 291 condemned men on California's Death Row, some thirty-five percent are black, although blacks account for a mere 7.5 percent of the state's population.

Yet it is unlikely that anything will change the public will, especially since support for the death penalty has been demonstrated to closely parallel the crime rate. Since re-instatement of the death penalty nationwide in the mid-seventies, proponents of capital punishment might expect an accompanying drop in crime. Instead, the national crime rate in the eighties and nineties soared to terrifying new heights, blowing all to hell the tenuous theory of death penalty as deterrent, especially in light of the fact that an increasing number of crimes are committed by offenders high on alcohol or drugs and hence operating with diminished capacities to make the cause-and-effect connection between crime and consequence.

The national murder rate per 100,000 people rose from 5.6 in 1966 to a record high of 10.2 in 1980, nearly doubling. Violent crimes of all kinds are on the upswing, rising from 430,180 in the United States in 1966 to nearly three times as high in 1988, some 1,566,200 crimes. Even among the shockingly young, arguments which once were settled with harsh words or flying fists are now settled, and settled permanently and irreversibly, with guns, and life is cheap.

New York City leads the country in murders, exceeding six each and every day, and the city's deputy police chief attributes it all to the ready availability of drugs and handguns. "In 1960, 19% of all our homicides were committed by handguns," New York City deputy police chief Michael Markman has said. "In 1990, . . . 69% of all the homicides were committed by the use of handguns. In 1960, you had the Saturday Night Special, a $25 gun. It fired a .22-caliber, if it fired at all. It bounced off your jacket half the time. It would fire one round and that was the end of it. Now, we have nine millimeters. They carry maybe sixteen rounds, eighteen rounds, they work all the time, they're more powerful; you don't have to be a good shot when you fire sixteen rounds."

The FBI annual crime report shows that across the country violent crimes . . . murder, rape, robbery and aggravated assault . . . jumped 10% in 1990, each crime with a victim whose personal experience contributes to the lust for vengeance and the growing general disenchantment with the criminal justice system. *Corrections Today* writer E. J.

Dionne, Jr., concludes that this profound shift in the way Americans view crime, punishment and retribution has much to do with the increasing acceptability of executions, making support for the death penalty popular with politicians determined to show a vengeful voting public they too are tough on crime.

This trend appears to be nationwide, the past decade of conservative national politics and accompanying conservative court decisions extending the wave of executions across the country, though the south continues to claim the dubious honor of killing the highest number of offenders, accounting for all but a dozen or so of the hundred-plus executions since the U.S. Supreme Court cleared the way for resumption of the death penalty in 1976.

Says Dionne, "The growing popularity of retribution as justification for the death penalty marks a major transformation in the debate over capital punishment, a change that has worked against the death penalty's foes. Years ago, when popular support for the death penalty was declining, opponents asserted not only that it was morally repugnant, they also raised complex statistical arguments to challenge the idea that the death penalty deterred capital crimes. But in recent years the appeal of deterrence has been supplanted by a frank desire for what large majorities see as just vengeance."

Vengeance, once the Lord's, now belongs to the prosecutors, the juries, the judges, the courts, even the victims or their grieving survivors. Said Faith Hathaway's mother after watching the execution at Angola of her daughter's rapist and killer, Robert Lee Willie, "I wish this day would come for all the victims out there. Robert Lee Willie will never be able to murder again."

And yet, in each and every capital case, the application of this ultimate penalty must be free from doubt and error, for a state cannot in the name of its people shoot the juice to the wrong offender and then hope to rectify the mistake with an "Oops, sorry!" Can we say without a shadow of doubt that the offender has been justly convicted, that he is without question the guilty party, that he is guilty of the particular crime with which he is charged? Can we be sure the judicial process has been without error from beginning to end, that the accused has had benefit of effective legal counsel and been accorded even-handed justice, that no under-the-table deals have been made and no informant given the opportunity to avenge some prior grievance? Can we affirm with strong conviction that a second wrong, which many consider any man-mandated killing, piled atop the first makes a right?

There are many who would join Faith Hathaway's parents in offering affirmative answers to these questions. But in a pair of letters written from the federal penitentiary at Leavenworth, Kansas, to the Bogalusa *Daily News*, Joseph Vaccaro in the summer of 1990, a full decade after the murder of Faith Hathaway, claimed that the state of Louisiana had electrocuted the wrong man, that Robert Lee Willie had merely watched from the truck as he killed the girl.

"I have been in the Penitentiary for 10 year's now," wrote Vaccaro at age thirty-eight with poor penmanship and poorer grammar and spelling, "and I have giveing this matter alot of thought, and I think I have heled this in long enought. Are sould I say, as long as I could. I always thought I was mentally perpared for anything and everything. *But* I was wrong. After living with the death of Miss Hathaway on my mine, I fined it hard to remain sane. And now since the death of Mr. Willie I fined it even harder. My only hope is to keep my sanity in here by teling the *true* in the Hathaway case."

The "true" facts presented by Vaccaro in his letters are that he and Willie, riding around in a borrowed pickup truck, gave Faith Hathaway a ride around 4:30 a.m. the day she was murdered, then took her to Fricke's Cave an hour later, where he says what happened "may be a little bazaar." He relates that the two men had "been on drugs, LSD for about a week," and that as he looked at Faith in the act of sex, "she didn't look like a gril [sic] anymore, I was on LSD. Hallucinating is what LSD is all about. I looked down at her and she had a head, in the form of a goat, and legs of a deer with wings on her back. All I could think to do was to kill her. I stab her two are three times, and then she looked like Faith again, and then back to what I seen again, and I stabed her until she was dead. Willie was still in the truck, and he could see us."

Because of the legal protection against double jeopardy, Vaccaro cannot be tried again for the crime for which he was sentenced to an automatic life term when his jury could not reach a unanimous verdict for death. His own former defense attorney, Thomas Ford, discredits the claim and suggests it might well be an attempt to win a free trip home or to cast doubt on the capital punishment system itself, pointing out that LSD was never mentioned by either defendant during the trial process and that the thick underbrush of the death scene made it impossible to drive close enough to watch anything from a vehicle. Ford's comments are echoed by former district attorney Marion "K.O." Farmer, who says Willie was generally considered the leader who called the shots and would hardly have been likely to assume such a passive role as waiting patiently in the truck. Adds Covington lawyer Bill Alford, who prosecuted Vaccaro and handled Willie's second sentencing phase, "Please spare me the flowers. . . . Both were animals and my regret was that a jury spared Vaccaro's life."

Nevertheless, Vaccaro wrote, "It's a tragedy that someone died for something he didn't do." And so it would be. But it is no less a tragedy that someone, Faith Hathaway whose name is legion, also died for doing nothing.

2009 Update:

Throughout their lives the Harveys remained vociferous in their support of the death penalty. The case lives on in print and in the movies, where it formed the basis for part of the composite main character in Sister Helen Prejean's anti-death penalty book/movie *Dead Man Walking*, as well as one investigator's book (*Victims of Dead Man Walking*) and one surviving victim's compelling memoir (*Forgiving the Dead Man Walking*).

IV

"You Can Kill the Messenger":
Death of a Vietnam Vet

In the steamy jungles of Vietnam, bad bush they called it, the point man was that unlucky member of a patrol elected to go out alone ahead of the group in the falling darkness to assess the dangers lurking there . . . booby traps, snipers, land mines, NVA soldiers, Viet Cong . . . a grab-bag of potential surprises, all bad. When, as often happened, an ambush was sprung and the point man was cut off from his buddies, his screams would echo throughout the still jungle night. His sleepless comrades knew he was either being painfully tortured by the enemy or excruciatingly burned by napalm strikes they'd called in, napalm or the white phosphorous the troops called "Willie Peter," which burned into the skin until it had to be literally dug out. Either way, there was nothing they could do to help him, and listening to his screams meant they shared in his agony. Torturing the point, this was called.

Wayne Robert Felde, even after the war, continued to serve as something of a point man himself, leading the way for the legions of psychologically war-wounded, and the agony he endured as a spokesman for the cause of Vietnam veterans suffering similar after-effects was no less torturous for being played out in prison cells and packed courtrooms rather than on hot sticky jungle trials.

Felde's was the first Louisiana capital case to use as a defense Post-Traumatic Stress Disorder resulting from the horrors of combat in Vietnam; some of the subsequent cases would be successfully defended, but not Felde's. Because the syndrome was so little known at the time of Felde's August 1980 trial, having just been recognized officially by the American Psychiatric Association in its third diagnostic manual, released that same year, newspaper accounts of courtroom proceedings were full of such misconceptions as PTSD being the result of drinking rainwater contaminated with the highly toxic defoliant Agent Orange.

Besides the unfamiliarity of the psychological stress defense, three other aggravating circumstances were weighed against the mitigating factor of obvious mental problems to almost guarantee that Wayne Felde's Louisiana murder trial would result in the death penalty. The first was that the victim had been a police officer acting in the line of duty. The second was that the defendant had taken a life before, in Maryland, under circumstances which remained questionable. And the third and most crucial was that both the defendant and his attorney asked for death in the event the jury could not find Felde innocent by reason of insanity.

For Felde, that plea was made in all sincerity, for, as he told distraught jurors, they

Left: Teenager Wayne Felde as a high school student in the mid-sixties. Photo courtesy of Kay Smith.

Right: In October 1968, Wayne Felde was a cocky but grim gunner facing death on a daily basis in Vietnam. Photo courtesy of Kay Smith.

would almost surely have innocent blood on their hands if they did not execute him in the absence of the treatment he so badly needed. For the attorney, the plea may well have been a gamble, a card played early in the game in hopes of subsequent higher-court reversal, and it would not be the only gamble which didn't pay off for him (that he died after being struck by lightning while boating is verifiable; that the bolt resulted from an unwise challenge flung heavenward may be mere coincidence, however oft repeated as gospel).

Expert testimony in the trial challenged the jurors to grasp complicated new psychiatric theory, but the most compelling evidence of all had to be the pictures. If they understood nothing else, the jurors, who were often in tears, must have been touched by the progression of madness in the sequential photographs of Wayne Robert Felde, shown as a carefree smiling high school student aiming for college and a career as a veterinarian, then as a grim-faced young combat veteran in Vietnam ferreting out the enemy in dark dangerous tunnels and trying frantically to replace the intestines spilling out of mortally wounded comrades, and finally as a desperate and wild-eyed prison inmate, bearded and scowling and bound for the electric chair after several suicide attempts and a fifty-eight-day fast which left him near death without bringing the hoped-for understanding and support from organized veterans' groups.

The point man had indeed been tortured, and his screams of agony reached across the land as he himself calmly and courageously walked into the death chamber at Louisiana State Penitentiary at Angola in the wee hours of the morning on Tuesday, March 15, 1988, ironically the Ides of March. Dressed in t-shirt, blue pants and beige slippers, Wayne Felde carefully studied each witness, then read a powerful statement: "You can kill the messenger, but you can't kill the message. Sooner or later, you have to acknowledge what it means, not for what you want it to mean." To his dear friend Kay Smith he would write at the end, "I know I'm going to a better place, so fear not and know a message to the country was needed. I was a mere messenger." The message to which he referred was what combat in Vietnam had done to him and to thousands upon thousands of other veterans.

This message may have fallen on deaf ears in the Oval Office, where President Ronald Reagan (Felde called him Rambo Ray-Gun) declined to answer Felde's letter pleading for treatment, as well as local, state and federal appeals courts, pardon boards and the Louisiana governor's office where newly seated Governor Buddy Roemer, sworn in at high noon March 14 and from the same area as the slain policeman, refused last-minute requests to stay the execution. Still, Wayne Felde's message was not silenced by the blasts of electricity which ended his life at 12:14 a.m. Perhaps best exemplified by the proliferation of outreach treatment centers for troubled veterans and the rousing welcome given forces returning from the Persian Gulf as compared to the Vietnam vet's reception, the results of Felde's case have been far-reaching, results for which he calmly and willingly gave his life.

But then Wayne Felde at age thirty-eight viewed his visit to the death chamber as a passage to peace, for he considered death nothing new, its sting no more frightening or painful than what he'd endured for years. It had been a lost twenty years since he'd shipped out to Vietnam. He may not have been shipped back in a body bag, but he might as well have, for Wayne Felde left his mind and heart and soul in the jungles of Southeast Asia just as surely as any of the 58,175 casualties chronologically memorialized on the impressive black monument in the nation's capital. Said writer Doug Magee, articulate opponent of the death penalty, "There should be a special section of the Vietnam Veterans Memorial for people like Wayne Felde, for those who died in Vietnam and lived to tell about it."

He didn't have to go to war, this sole surviving son of a veteran, but he finagled his way into the service anyway, collaring an unknown colonel in the halls of the Pentagon to fix things for him, volunteering for Vietnam. His father, Christ Felde, was a World War II medic in the South Pacific who would later develop drinking problems and have nightmares about his wartime experiences. He lived through the war to die at age forty-eight by his own hand in Sheboygan Falls, Wisconsin, where he had worked as a mail carrier. Wayne's mother Ruby had filed for divorce the previous summer, moving with her son to Benson, Louisiana, where her father lived, and then to Langley Park, Maryland, where they lived with her brother, a Washington, D.C., police officer.

In high school in Maryland (and Texas, where he stayed briefly), Wayne Felde was a typical teen, carefree, happy-go-lucky, and for several years deeply in love with Kay Smith, two years younger. When Wayne was fourteen, he was walking through the suburban Maryland housing development where both he and Kay lived and exuberantly threw a dart high into the air. As fate would have it, the dart landed square in the thumb of twelve-year-old Kay. The two were introduced by the mutal friend with whom Wayne was walking, and from that time on were inseparable for several years, developing such an intense relationship that Wayne begged Kay to promise to marry him whenever she turned eighteen. Says Kay, "It is absolutely inconceivable that the Wayne Felde I knew at fourteen and fifteen and sixteen and the Wayne Felde I would come to know again at the end on Death Row would ever have, without the impact of his experiences in Vietnam, become a killer."

With the bittersweet poignancy of all first loves, Kay remembers Wayne well, for their relationship would take another fateful turn later, its strength after all the years irresistibly drawing them back together again just before his execution, when she happened by chance to pick up an old newspaper in Maryland and read, for the first time, of his troubles with the law in Louisiana and his scheduled execution. Married and with children, she would nonetheless feel compelled to spend the last two weekends of his life visiting Felde at Angola and would talk to him by phone just before his execution, his first love becoming his last, returning to him once more the power to feel joy and to experience love, for which he expressed tremendous gratitude.

At fourteen and fifteen, Kay says, Wayne was a completely normal teenage boy (if there *is* such a thing), playful, mannerly, a little bit shy, laughing and loving and living up to the high standards hardworking Ruby Felde set for her children. Ruby's daughters would follow her into the nursing profession, and her close relationship with her son may explain Wayne's attraction to the field of veterinary medicine as well. At any rate, upon graduation from DuVal High School in June 1967, Wayne wanted to go to college but couldn't afford it, so he enlisted on August 15, 1967, with hopes of eventually completing his education through the G.I. Bill.

After training, Felde arrived in Vietnam on March 25, 1968. It was his nineteenth birthday, and he was assigned to Company D, Second Battalion, 35th Infantry, Fourth Infantry Division, arriving at Fire Base Polly Ann near the Cambodian border right in the middle of a big fire fight. A mortarman and M-60 machine gunner who soon earned the nickname Mouse because his small stature and quiet demeanor made him ideal for the terrible high-turnover job of tunnel rat, descending into dark dangerous tunnels searching for enemy soldiers and arms caches, Felde would later describe his first experiences in Vietnam to writer and fellow veteran Philip Caputo, whose intensive interviews with Felde after his murder conviction formed the basis for an excellent *Playboy* article in 1982.

Felde said of his fiery initiation, "We were flown out to Polly Ann, me and a few other replacements. Company D was running patrols off another fire base out in the bush, and they'd run into an NVA ambush that day. The big guns on the fire base were firing like crazy, there were air strikes, and we heard the napalm was hitting both because the fighting was close up. The chopper couldn't fly us out to the company. The LZ was too hot. We waited around until it was getting close to dark. Another chopper came into Polly Ann. We had to drag four bodies off to get on. They were our own guys and they were all bloody and burned from our own napalm. The bodies smelled because they were burned, and the smell made me sick. I threw up. The guys with me threw up, too. There was blood all over the floor."

The experience had to be horrifying for the green recruits, who finally joined their company and endured their first major fire fight. Said Felde to Caputo, "I was scared shitless. It lasted on and off all night. The woods were on fire from the napalm. The woods burned for days. You could smell the burned bodies. I was scared. The point man was out in the woods. The NVA had let him through before they sprang the ambush. He was cut off from the rest of the company. He was screaming because he was burned by the napalm. Some guys said he was being tortured by the NVA. We couldn't get to him because of the NVA and because the woods were on fire, so some other guys in the company opened up on him and shot him to put him out of his misery. Come daylight, the fighting was over. We had to pick up pieces of our guys to send home. Arms and legs and three quarters of a whole person. Me and some guys got to the point man, and when we went to pick him up, his arms came off because he was burned so bad. The smell was bad and we got sick again. We sent him and the other pieces back. I thought about their moms and about my mom, and someone offered me a little reefer. I'd never smoked it before, but I smoked it then and from then on."

Happy birthday to Wayne Felde, nineteen years old and scared to death in the service of his country. For the duration of his tour of duty along the dangerous Cambodian border, in the northern part of Pleiku Province and the lower and middle part of Kontum Province, scenes of some of the heaviest fighting in the war, he performed his job well and stored in his memory plenty of similar experiences. There was the soldier who jumped right out of a helicopter onto a mine, another who leapt off a truck to take a leak and landed on a mine. There was the friend who took a direct hit from a rocket and the medevac brought him in . . . at least what was left of him, a chunk of arm and part of a leg in an army boot.

Then there was the time Felde and his squad were crossing a rice paddy on security patrol when schrapnel hit a nearby soldier midsection, spilling his guts out, Felde trying frantically to replace them. "I grabbed his insides and tried to shove them back," he remembered. "It looked like afterbirth, and it just slid through my hands, and the guy died. It didn't take long. Then we took some small-arms fire from a village. I don't remember if it was much, but we charged the village and started shooting. It was near dusk, and all I could see were muzzle flashes and grenades going off, just noises and flashes, like the Fourth of July. Everyone started shooting. There was total panic. You know how it is when something like that gets started. You can't stop it. There was nobody in charge and everyone was shouting and shooting, shouting, 'Shoot this, shoot that,' and I went into a hut that was filled with people and sprayed it.

"We wasted everyone and everything in that village. We wasted the women and the kids and the old men and the dogs. I swear to God, the dogs looked like VC to me, the dogs had slanted eyes. Then we burned the village to the ground. It was the most awful thing, and I still dream about it. Listen, man, I dream this shit almost every night. I see the flashes and hear the gunfire and the explosions, like the Fourth of July, and when I wake up, I don't know where the fuck I am. I don't talk to anyone for hours, days sometimes. I try to block it out of my mind, but I can't."

The horror of these moments would never leave Wayne Felde, not even when he was thousands of miles from the Central Highlands of Vietnam, which he called in a letter the jungle of the dead. Forever after he hated rice and loved the rainfall, taking a measure of contentment in walking for hours in the pacifying showers. It had been the frequent downpours, sometimes occurring ten or fifteen times a day during the rainy season, which stopped the battles, at least temporarily. Terrifying nightmares interrupted his restless sleep, while equally vivid flashbacks colored his waking hours, replaying wartimes over and over again, with exploding shells and the ghastly screams of the dying, with endless rivers of blood running and intestines spilling out into the rice paddies. The faces around him would turn, inexplicably, into the Oriental features of marauding Viet Cong, and there was no one to talk to, for Wayne Felde returned from Vietnam to a country torn apart by war protests, unappreciative and suspicious of its returning warriors.

Hitchhiking to his next assignment at Fort Dix, New Jersey, after returning from Southeast Asia, the uniformed Felde thought a driver had stopped to offer him a ride;

instead he was sprayed in the face with a fire extinguisher and called a killer. It would happen over and over. Said Felde, "Everybody was running around burning American flags, burning draft cards, colleges were protesting, throwing bottles, calling us baby killers . . . I heard that all the time. I couldn't wear my uniform on the street without being called a baby killer, a woman killer, but I'd shrink away, because I knew it was true. It was true, but you had to do it. It was a survival thing and you had to live with it."

It just may have been too big to live with, though, and Wayne Felde's life was never again really his own, never again completely in his control. Though honorably discharged, even decorated for his service, Felde had trouble in the military after returning from Vietnam, wrecking a new car and piling up three AWOLs. He had even more trouble in civilian life. He tried college, but not for long, and three times quit Lincoln Technical Training Institute in Washington, D.C., where he'd hoped to train as an auto mechanic.

In 1971 he tried marriage, but not for long, beginning a string of separations as early as six months after the marriage and finally divorcing Rita Skolnik in 1974, describing life in their apartment as turbulent, to say the least: "I mean, mustard jars went off the walls, mayonnaise jars went off the ceiling. I broke two television sets. I tore up a dresser. I ripped cabinets off the wall. And it cost me more money to repair that apartment than I think they paid to get it built." He tried working as a grocery clerk, brick mason, backhoe operator, mechanic and carpenter, but never kept any one job for any length of time.

He was arrested several times for drunk driving, his tolerance for alcohol diminished by what would later be suspected as liver damage from exposure to dioxin, the highly toxic Agent Orange, liberally sprayed as a defoliant in Vietnam before mid-1970. He was irritable, moody, explosive, depressed, withdrawn, unpredictable, paranoid, argumentative, self-destructive. When he looked up Kay Smith upon his return from the war, she found him strangely detached. "His body was physically present, but his mind was somewhere else," she says, looking back.

His oldest sister Maria's husband, David Krebsbach, with whom Wayne at different times both lived and worked, would comment on the difference between his behavior before and after Vietnam. "Before he went to Vietnam, he was . . . jovial, happy-go-lucky-type kid when he was young . . . and when he come back, he was . . . quite moody . . . more irritable and didn't seem to enjoy life like he did before . . . His sleeping habits, when he come back from Vietnam, were . . . quite erratic. If he'd be asleep . . . during the day or something and you'd try to wake him up on the couch, you had to be careful how you woke him up because . . . you never knew what he would do."

Maria herself would later testify to seeing her brother throw his service medals in the trash can, and when she asked him what he was doing, he replied that "they weren't any good anyway, that it was a disgrace that he had to go over there and fight, that nobody appreciated it, that everyone thought he was terrible for being over there, it wouldn't bring his buddies back, they were blown to bits, and he started crying and I quit talking about it then because he got so upset with me."   His sister said, "Before Wayne went (to Vietnam), he was . . . such a good kid and he was fun-loving, fun to be around, happy-go-lucky, the kids (her children) were crazy about him, and when he came home he was so moody you got to where you didn't know if you should even speak to him because he was so moody and depressed. You never knew what to expect, what's going to happen from him."

He was, she said, "just like a clock, he could be fine one minute and when the clock would reach a certain click, he'd go off. You just never knew when it was going to happen and he'd do a lot of strange things then that no one understood." He also knocked her halfway across the room once when she touched his arm to wake him for supper, then cried in sorrow and horror at the realization of what he had done. "The next time I woke him up," Maria Krebsbach testified, "I used a broom handle. I wasn't going to get right up close because . . . I thought he was probably having a nightmare. I didn't want to get knocked across the room so I took a broom handle and poked him with it from a distance."

Wayne's mother Ruby would testify that "before he went to Vietnam, he did not have this feeling that everybody was after him, but after he came back, he was just jumpy, nervous. He could not sit still. He could not find himself any place that he could stay any length of time." Maria added, "Mother and I both knew something was wrong. I felt like I had sent one brother over there and a different one had come back, like he almost was a stranger." To no avail Wayne's mother, a registered nurse, begged him to get psychiatric help, begged his military superiors to get help for him. Two people would be dead before Wayne Felde knew there was a name for his condition or that it was shared by thousands of returning veterans.

By no means did Wayne Felde stand alone, for, as Bonnie Green, director of the trauma stress service at Georgetown University Medical Center in Washington, D.C., says, "Without a doubt, combat changes people." "There are psychiatric casualties in every war," says Seattle psychologist Gerald Rosen, "and a lot of the combat veterans experience the feeling of being unplugged from life." By 1980, the figures for Felde's fellow sufferers would be of such magnitude that the problem which came to be known as PTSD could no longer be denied . . . more than 70,000 Vietnam combat veterans incarcerated, a divorce rate among these same vets twice that of comparable peers, a suicide rate a third higher, a tremendous amount of substance abuse, and some twenty percent unemployed, unable to hold jobs.

Unlike the shell shock or battle fatigue of earlier wars, symptoms now were showing up not during or immediately following combat, but sometimes years later, timed-release results from trauma suffered in combat returning to haunt the veteran who thought he'd made a successful adjustment and gotten on with his life at home. Said Caputo, "Every now and then, we read about some French farmer, plowing the fields of Verdun, getting blown up by an unexploded mine or shell that has been buried for decades. Something like that is happening in the minds of Vietnam veterans: experiences and emotions long repressed are detonating unexpectedly, frequently with catastrophic results."

He quoted results from an extensive three-year study of the war's after-effects by Dr. John P. Wilson, Cleveland State psychologist who would be called to testify as an expert witness in Felde's murder trial in Louisiana. Wilson in 1982 put the number of Vietnam combat vets afflicted by PTSD at 500,000, while other researchers went as high as 700,000, all noting that it was the veteran who had seen heavy combat, not the one who'd been behind the lines in relative safety providing support services, who suffered the most stress and manifested the most severe problems. By 1988 when the second edition of Dr. C. B. Scrignar's comprehensive book, *Post-Traumatic Stress Disorder—Diagnostic, Treatment, and Legal Issues*, was released, it was noted that as many as a million Vietnam combat veterans were claiming a delayed PTSD, perhaps as many as half of the 2.8 million American men and women who served there. Even a congressional study in 1988 found some 479,000 Vietnam vets afflicted with serious cases of PTSD, another 350,000 with more moderate symptoms.

The staggering numbers caused the American Psychiatric Association in 1980 to finally concretely define the malady for the first time in the third edition of its *Diagnostic and Statistical Manual of Mental Disorders*, the definitive catalog of mental illnesses, revised in 1987 as DSM-III-R. "The essential feature of this disorder is the development of characteristic symptoms following a psychologically distressing event that is outside the range of usual human experience (*i.e.*, outside the range of such common experiences as simple bereavement, chronic illness, business losses, and marital conflict). The stressor producing this syndrome would be markedly distressing to almost anyone, and is usually experienced with intense fear, terror, and helplessness. The characteristic symptoms involve re-experiencing the traumatic event, avoiding stimuli associated with the event or numbing of general responsiveness, and increased arousal."

DSM-III-R notes that the disturbance must be of at least one month's duration. The most serious traumata involve a grave threat to the life or physical integrity of oneself, one's family or friends, or the sudden destruction of home or community, or the sight of another person recently injured or killed in an accident or physical violence. The trauma may be experienced alone, as in the case of rape or assault, or in a group, as in military combat. Such stressors may include natural disasters like floods or earthquakes, accidental disasters like automobile accidents or plane crashes, or deliberately caused disasters like bombings or death camps. Some stressors produce the disorder more often than others, but those of human design seem to produce more severe and longer lasting results.

Experiencing the traumatic event may occur many ways, most commonly in recurrent and intrusive recollections or distressing dreams. Sometimes there are accompanying dissociative states, lasting from seconds to days, during which the event is relived so completely that the traumatized person behaves as though experiencing the event at that very moment; he *is* back in combat, or in a plane crash, or whatever.

Events similar to the original trauma, and stimuli associated with it, can cause intense psychological distress, evoking avoidance reactions like a general numbing of responsiveness. The sufferer becomes detached from other people, loses the ability to enjoy activities or feel emotions, and may experience symptoms of increased arousal like difficulty sleeping, hypervigilance and an exaggerated startle response. Recurrent nightmares replaying the trauma disturb sleep.

Says DSM-III-R, "Many report changes in aggression. In mild cases, this may take the form of irritability with fears of losing control. In more severe forms, particularly in cases in which the survivor has actually committed acts of violence (as in war veterans), the fear is conscious and pervasive, and the reduced capacity for modulation may express itself in unpredictable explosions of aggressive behavior or an inability to express angry feelings. Symptoms characteristic of Post-Traumatic Stress Disorder, or physiologic reactivity, are often intensified or precipitated when the person is exposed to situations or activities that resemble or symbolize the original trauma."

The manual explains that symptoms of depression and anxiety are common, impulsive behavior can occur, and in the case of a life-threatening trauma which was shared with others, it is not uncommon for survivors to have persistent painful guilt feelings that they survived when others did not. "Impairment may be either mild or severe and affect nearly every aspect of life. Phobic avoidance of situations or activities resembling or symbolizing the original trauma may interfere with interpersonal relationships such as marriage or family life. Emotional lability, depression, and guilt may result in self-defeating behavior or suicidal actions."

In other words, there is an initial traumatic event which is outside the range of usual human experience and which would be markedly distressing to anyone. This traumatic event is persistently re-experienced, either through repetitive recollections, distressing dreams, a sudden acting or feeling as if the traumatic event were recurring (including a sense of reliving the experience, illusions, hallucinations, and dissociative or flashback episodes). Intense psychological distress at exposure to events symbolic of the trauma results in the persistent avoidance of such stimuli and a general numbing of responsiveness, an accompanying disinterest in significant activities and feelings of detachment from others, as well as increased arousal indicated by sleeping difficulties, irritability and difficulty concentrating, hypervigilance and an exaggerated startle response.

Dr. Scrignar, professor of psychiatry at Tulane University School of Medicine in New Orleans as well as adjunct professor of law and psychiatry in its law school and school of social work, has studied hundreds of PTSD sufferers and been called as an expert forensic psychiatric witness in many court cases; he conducts seminars on PTSD throughout the country for attorneys and forensic clinicians. Noting that PTSD is one of the few psychiatric disorders listed in the DSM-III that are defined in part by environment, Scrignar explains that any outside stimulus, if perceived as dangerous, can be traumatic enough to precipitate PTSD, which is a multifaceted anxiety disorder involving not only post-traumatic stress but disruptions in other areas of personal functioning as well.

Says Dr. Scrignar, "Some have criticized the concept of PTSD, especially the publicity which emphasizes its ubiquity, but it is hard to deny the environment's potential for causing physical and psychological harm. To place the issue in perspective, most people who are exposed to situations which pose a serious threat to life or limb do not develop PTSD, but in the past this stress disorder has been overlooked and underdiagnosed." The determining factor of development, apparently, is the impact of the trauma on the individual's autonomic nervous system.

One of the most important factors in maintaining PTSD, Scrignar explains, is the persistence of encephalic processes, described as being the thoughts and visualizations of scenes related to the trauma which result in retraumatization of the patient when confronted with environmental stimuli associated with the initial traumatic event. It is the encephalic events, says Scrignar, which distinguish PTSD from other anxiety disorders. These cognitions, the functions of the brain having to do with thoughts, visual images, flashbacks, assumptions, beliefs, perception of external events and dreams, he calls the *sine qua non* for PTSD.

"Following a trauma," he explains, "encephalic events play a major role in the development, furtherance of symptoms, and the sustainment of PTSD. Anxiety rises and is maintained when intrusive thoughts and frightening visual images related to the traumatic incident periodically erupt into consciousness. These upsetting memories, like the sounds and images on a tape cassette in a video recorder, are extremely vivid and realistic. When these 'videotapes of the mind' are activated by stimuli reminiscent of the trauma, the resulting scenario, portraying the themes of serious injury and death, generates and sustains pathologic anxiety, thereby retraumatizing the victim." Pathologic anxiety can initiate or accentuate accompanying physical symptoms, which serve to remind the patient of the initial trauma and stimulate further encephalic activity which retraumatizes him in a spiral effect compounding and prolonging the problem.

While many traumas . . . the battering of women, the abuse of children, the taking of hostages, rape, torture, criminal coercion, earthquakes and fires, car wrecks and plane crashes, exposure to toxic substances and the threat of radioactivity among many others . . . can set off PTSD, the most prevalent in this day and age seems to be combat. Says Scrignar, "Wars, the most intense and destructive of human enterprises, traumatize and damage minds and bodies of antagonists. The battlefield, a microcosm of trauma, is a ghastly place which assails all five senses. The sounds of battle—the discharge of weapons, the fierce shrieks of soldiers, the wailing of the wounded—all merge into a terrifying cacophony. The sights and smells of war assault the eyes and insult the nose and are no less frightening. The maniacal look on the faces of the enemy, together with the sight of broken and bloodied bodies of combatants and the pervasive stench of death, overpower the minds of soldiers and civilians alike. Battles inflame thoughts of imminent death or impending injury, so the trauma of war becomes firmly embedded into consciousness."

War, though, is certainly nothing new, nor is its effect upon young soldiers, as indicated by the first studies of symptoms by Dr. Jacob Mendes DaCosta during the Civil War. From "DaCosta's Syndrome" in the nineteenth century and "Soldier's Heart and the Effort Syndrome" or "Neurocirculatory Asthenia" in WWI to "Traumatic War Neurosis" or "Combat Neurosis" in World War II and Korea, the effects of war on man have been noted. But there is something different about the conflict in Vietnam, something deadly which has increased the incidence of delayed stress reactions a thousand fold.

For one thing, the age of American combatants in Vietnam was markedly younger than those in previous conflicts; the average age of the World War II soldier was 26, the average age of the Vietnam soldier only 19. Young, idealistic, often away from home for the first time, these teenaged warriors marched off to fight for their country, then found themselves and their efforts appreciated neither in Vietnam nor at home. The enemy was not easily identified, and the tiny child shyly appoaching American GIs often turned out to be boobytrapped, the friendly dog wagging his tail wired with plastic explosives. There were no clear battlelines, and territory once captured often had to be retaken again and again, frustration mounting with the futile repetitiveness which denied any clear sense of accomplishment.

All-out victory seemed not to be part of the battle plan, and many soldiers felt like they were fighting with one hand tied behind their back. The actions of some groups of soldiers, actions in the heat of battle after undeniably terrible experiences, were not ones of which they could be proud . . . fraggings, or the indiscrimant slaughter of innocent civilians in villages which may or may not have harbored the enemy, an enemy which became increasingly difficult to differentiate from the supposedly friendly farmers and villagers.

For the most part, the soldiers, ambivalent about their actions already, returned from Vietnam quickly and alone once their tours of duty were up. Soldiers in previous wars trained and shipped out and came back as part of a closeknit company, returning on slow troop ships with time to decompress amid the comaraderie of colleagues who'd been through similar experiences, and when they got home, they received jubilant welcomes expressing the heartfelt thanks of a grateful nation. The Vietnam vet instead found himself flying back by airplane on his own and moving swiftly from jungle war to family home in a matter of mere hours.

Finding little acceptance or understanding at home and often downright condemnation, these disappointed young warriors stopped discussing wartime experiences few civilians could comprehend; they repressed these memories, which often puzzled them as well, relegating them to shadowy spaces behind the closed doors of the mind, only to find that it was difficult to keep them there. And as these combat memories and the recollections of atrocities burst through the doors of the mind and increasingly affected their daily lives back home, the Vietnam vets withdrew from loved ones and divorced, they medicated themselves with alcohol or drugs, they lost jobs and friends, they committed crimes and they committed suicide in unprecedented numbers.

Wayne Felde was one of their number, though it would be years before he began to fathom the depth of the problem or understand just what was happening to his life, helped through reading everything on the subject he could find, corresponding with other vets, and contact with interested activists across the country. Before the understanding and the diagnosis, however, came the symptoms and the manifestations.

It was in the fall of 1972 that Felde, then twenty-three, supposedly shot a friend in the head with an M-1 rifle and held off arresting officers for more than forty minutes, shooting wildly and screaming about Vietnam. Felde worked in Prince George's County, Maryland, with William "Butch" Blackwell, a twenty-seven-year-old ex-convict on parole from a ten-year sentence for assault who had also been charged with rape, and the two had gone out drinking on Tuesday, November 28, 1972, after work at Wrathall and Ovalie construction company. They then stopped by Felde's apartment in Greenbelt, still drinking beer and smoking marijuana, reportedly to discuss which weapons to take on a deer hunt they were planning. An argument erupted, soon escalating into a serious fight and a struggle for Felde's M-1 carbine which both knew was in a closet; the gun was not a wartime souvenir, but had been given to him by an uncle in Texas when he was a high school junior. Felde told Caputo he remembered "an exploding sound inside his skull when Blackwell hit him, and that inner detonation setting off a succession of others, *boom-boom-boom,* like grenades, just like grenades, and he was *there* again, in that village."

Concluded Caputo, "He was 're-experiencing,' a term the psychiatric manuals define as 'sudden acting as though a traumatic event was actually occurring because of association with an environmental or ideational stimulus.' When you drop the turgid jargon, that means that the tension of the argument and Blackwell's violence and the talk about guns made Felde snap. He heard the grenades and the gunfire, the Fourth of July, and then he and Blackwell struggled for the carbine. Felde got hold of it and sprayed the apartment, the way he had sprayed the hut in the village, shot the place up."

Blackwell lay dead on the floor of the closet and Felde, shouting "Vietnam, Vietnam," and "Come on in and I'll show you what Vietnam is like," held police at bay until his mother arrived on the scene and talked him into surrendering. She would later describe him as looking like a wild man and making the sounds of a wild animal. As Ruby Felde testified at her son's Maryland trial, "His voice was mumbling. He sounded like a wild man. He did not know what he was saying and I turned around to the policeman and I said, 'He's wild. He does not know what he is doing.'" Wayne's sister Maria testified that he "looked wild-eyed and like he was way off. He . . . had a distant stare on his face." But as Felde emerged from the apartment, according to Caputo, "He returned from the village and was back in Greenbelt. Handcuffed, he put his head on his mother's shoulder and cried, 'Ma, wipe my tears. Ma, wipe my tears.'" She took the Kleenex from her pocket and tenderly did so.

Post-Traumatic Stress Syndrome had not yet entered the collective vocabulary, and Felde's defense counsel, from a law firm which would later be revealed as having once represented Butch Blackwell, pled only intoxication, ignoring symptoms now recognized as classic. Felde's mother testified that his initial panicked phone call had begged her to come quick because, "I think there's a man in there that was shot in the head. I think I've killed some man," no longer even consciously recognizing his friend and co-worker, while the psychiatrist who examined Wayne soon after the incident, Dr. Guillermo Olivos, testified that the defendant seemed so divorced from the reality of the situation that he had to ask the doctor, "Did I do it or how did I do it? Did I do it in self-defense or what?" The doctor prescribed Valium.

Shown an article from the Washington *Evening Star and Daily News* about the incident by his sister later, Wayne Felde would ask, "Did I say all that? The newspaper must've printed that wrong." And even later, during his Louisiana trial, Felde would testify that he had shouted about Vietnam in Maryland because, "I've been in Vietnam ever since then and I still am to this day, and I think I'll be in it the rest of my life."

Sentenced for manslaughter for the slaying of Blackwell and assault for firing through the apartment door over the heads of police officers Seger, Crizer, Travers and Valltos, Felde's initial second-degree murder conviction had been reversed and he was promised a light sentence in return for a guilty plea to the lesser charge; he got twelve years, ten for one count of manslaughter and four two-year sentences for assault, one to run consecutively and the others to run concurrently with the ten years.

After serving three years with a good record, Felde was denied parole in 1976. He left anyway, walking away from the minimum-security prison in Hagerstown, where he was on a work detail at a disposal plant, travelling mostly at night, crisscrossing the Potomac and making his way through the mountains for three days until he came to a highway, then hitchhiking to Grand Cane, Louisiana, where his mother had moved to care for her dying father and work as night nursing supervisor at DeSoto General Hospital in Mansfield. Felde later testified that his mother was the only person who actually knew that he had escaped from the Maryland penal institution; everyone else in the family thought he was out on bond awaiting re-trial, he insisted.

Even so, his eighty-four-year-old grandfather had apparently talked enough about Wayne's problems to make it impossible for him to find work in the community. Consequently, for several years Wayne drifted around and used the alias Harold W. "Harry" Hershey. Lacking a Social Security card or identification when he first arrived in Louisiana, he had taken his actual birth certificate, taped the made-up name of Harold Hershey over his real name, and gone down to the library in Shreveport, where he made photostatic copies, then copies of copies, over and over again until the outline of the tape faded enough to send the birth certificate to Baltimore and request a Social Security card for Harold Hershey.

He drifted from Louisiana to California to Nevada to Colorado and points in between, working for as long as he could stand to stay in one place, some twelve to fifteen jobs a year, none held for over a few months and some for only a single day. The one constant in his life was his mother Ruby, to whom he was devoted, the only one he trusted implicitly enough to have called out for during the seige when Blackwell died.

This 1983 mug shot shows the terrible transformation Wayne Felde had undergone in less than two decades. Photo courtesy of *The Angolite*.

But in the early fall of 1978, Wayne was contacted in Colorado by his sisters. The news was bad. Ruby Felde had been diagnosed with cancer and did not have long to live. Wayne rushed to her side, sitting with her around the clock in the hospital as her last few weeks passed in pain. To please her, he resumed the use of his real name, dropping the Hershey alias; she wanted, she told him, to be able to tell everybody he was her son. Said the dying Ruby Felde, "He's my son and I'm proud of him. If it took my life to straighten him out, it was worth it."

At 9:30 on Friday night, October 13, 1978, Ruby Felde, primary anchor of Wayne's increasingly detached life, died. On Sunday, October 15, 1978, she was buried. On Monday, October 16, 1978, an argument erupted over whether friends of Wayne's who'd just arrived from Colorado could stay temporarily in his dead mother's trailer until they could find an apartment; the sheriff's department in Mansfield was contacted and asked to send a deputy, but the patrol car was at the other end of the parish and Wayne left, so the request for police assistance was cancelled.

On Tuesday, October 17, 1978, Wayne Felde had a minor automobile accident in South Mansfield on Highway 171, cooperated with the chief of police in filling out the wreck report, and was scheduled to appear in court in November. On Friday, October 20, 1978, Wayne Robert Felde asked his family to save him the burial plot next to his mother's. He then left his carpentry job at the Whitaker Construction Company's site at Continental Car Wash, on Mansfield Road across from Burger Chef in Shreveport, having been informed that the police were looking for him and noticing a police car parked near the site.

From the car wash construction site, he went to Lorant's Sporting Goods to purchase from clerk Amos Mustin a .357 Magnum pistol and some bullets, the total purchase price being $174.29; the purpose of purchasing the gun, he would later testify, was not to harm anyone "except possibly myself." He then settled down to wait for his two friends from Colorado, who had promised to pick him up and get him out of town. The friends, dark-complected mustachioed Larry Hall and his girlfriend Cheryl McKenzie, had been living in a pickup camper parked in the K-Mart lot across from Continental Car Wash, where Hall worked with Felde. They were supposed to go to Mansfield to pack some of Wayne's clothes and other supplies for a hurried trip to Houston, where Cheryl had relatives.

The Colorado friends were then to meet Felde in an hour in front of the Cinema VI movie theater behind the Pizza Inn and the Dragon Lounge at 7500 Mansfield Road. They never came back. Wayne would divide his time for the remainder of the day between the restaurant, where he ate pizza, drank a pitcher of beer and rested his head on the table as if asleep, and the Dragon Lounge next door, where he drank some more, waiting for six interminable hours with growing frustration and hopelessness, getting "pretty loaded."

When a despairing Wayne Felde, dressed in jeans and a red football jersey with the number forty-five on it, took the gun from the waistband of his pants in the men's room of the Dragon Lounge, contemplating suicide, another customer reported him and the police were called by bartender Beverly Jean Carter. It was the beginning of the end, but it came heartbreakingly close to never happening. The two Shreveport policemen who arrived around 9:24 p.m. in separate cars, Officer Donald R. Norwood and Officer Thomas Glen Tompkins, were not the officers to whom the directive to proceed to the Dragon Lounge was first issued, but since they were nearby, they volunteered to answer the call. They would not normally have been alone in their cars, either, except that Shreveport police chief Kenneth Lanigan would later explain that an officer shortage at the time resulted in even rookies patrolling alone.

Upon arrival, the officers first frisked the wrong man, Alfred J. Brown, who also happened to have on a red shirt and blue pants. When the waitress pointed out Felde, who by then had asked that a cab be called for him and was leaving the bar, the policemen then searched him, encountering no resistance. They found a box of bullets but not the gun. The Yellow Cab driver, Meyer Schwartz, a thirty-six-year veteran cabbie, left. One of the policemen went after him to try to persuade him to drive Felde home; Schwartz refused, saying Felde "looked like he was about sixty-five percent drunk to me, and I don't like to haul drunks."

In the subsequent trial of Wayne Felde for the murder of one of the arresting officers, Schwartz would provide the few light moments, managing to impart to the jury his entire life story in between explanations of how he refused to drive what he perceived as a drunken passenger that fateful night . . . boasting that he had two twenty-five-inch color Curtis-Mathes consoles at home with cablevision, HBO and twenty channels, so he rarely went to movies now (the attorney was attempting to elicit from him an admission that his eyes might have needed a few moments to adjust, coming outside from the dark bar interior, just as movie patrons usually did); and how he no longer saw many movies anyway, though at one time before his marriage he had seen as many as eight shows a day in New Orleans while on vacation from the barbeque place where he worked in Shreveport, spending entire days watching movies and eating dozens of oysters ("But when you got nine kids, you can't afford oysters anymore," he volunteered to the court, unasked, to which one of the attorneys replied, "Maybe that's why you got nine kids").

But wasn't the lounge interior dark, persisted the attorney, to which Schwartz answered that he'd been in there himself back when he used be a drinker, confiding that after six beers he'd be "drunk as I can be" and had at times been discovered by his irate wife on the front porch in his underclothes. Did he recognize his wife in his state of inebriation, the attorney queried? "I found out after she hit me for getting that drunk," Schwartz replied, adding that now at nearly sixty-four he drank no more, having promised his dying mother eight months before that he would quit, and admonishing the lawyer not to try to get him twisted up, "because I'm Jewish and you'll never do that."

When talkative Meyer Schwartz drove off into the darkness in his Yellow Cab, Wayne Felde refused to allow the officers to call him another cab, tried to leave and was arrested for simple drunk, the lightest charge possible, one which would not have entailed fingerprinting or photographing and might well have meant merely an uncomfortable night in the drunk tank before release. He was handcuffed with his hands behind his back, and placed in the back seat of the patrol car of rookie officer Thomas Glen Tompkins, age thirty-one, on the force just eight months. It had been Officer Tompkins who had followed the departing cabbie as he left the Dragon Lounge, trying to talk him into driving Wayne Felde. Schwartz would later testify, "He told me that I could have him, if I wanted him. And I'd told him absolutely no. I said, 'Ya'll got him first, ya'll keep him.'"

Why, Felde would be asked later, did he not surrender his pistol at the time of arrest? "If you don't want to hurt anybody, why don't you give them the pistol?" asked prosecutor B. Woodrow Nesbitt, Jr. "Because I wanted to hurt myself, Mr. Nesbitt," answered Felde. Consequently, with Felde in the backseat, still armed, Officer Tompkin's patrol car pulled out onto Mansfield Road at about 9:40 p.m., bound for the city jail.

After driving only a few hundred yards and still within sight of the Dragon Lounge, a struggle of some sort ensued, four gunshots were fired, the patrol car hit a guard rail, and Officer Tompkins staggered out and fell dead, face down in the ditch across the road. The prosecution called it cold-blooded murder. The defense contention was that Felde had taken out his gun, again contemplating suicide, his hands still cuffed behind his back, Tompkins had slammed on the brakes while leaning over the car seat trying to wrest the pistol away from his prisoner and was killed by a richochet bullet which hit a seat spring first before severing a vital blood vessel in the officer's right flank, in the lower part of his body. "Glen Tompkins, in effect," said defense attorney Graves Thomas in court, "lost his life trying to save his prisoner."

Concluded Caputo after interviewing Felde about what happened in the car, "He was a fugitive. His life had been a nightmare since Vietnam. He was on his way back to jail. He wanted to die. Working his manacled hands around to his side, Felde gripped the butt of the revolver and drew it from his waistband. Tompkins apparently saw the gun through the rearview mirror, because, as far as can be determined, he turned around and grabbed hold of Felde's wrist. The revolver went off twice, both bullets plowing through the roof of the car, and as soon as Felde heard the terrific blast, he was back in the village. Grenades going off. Machine guns. Muzzle flashes. Men shouting: 'Shoot this, shoot that.' The Fourth of July. The Magnum went off three more times, one through the floor board, two through the front seat, which, according to ballistics tests, richocheted off a spring and struck Tompkins in the side. He bled to death within minutes."

In his trial testimony, Wayne Felde described what he remembered happening in the car like this: "We started going down the road. And a whole lot of thoughts ran through my mind. My mother ran through my mind. Prison ran through my mind. Vietnam ran through my mind. And I wasn't going back to prison." His hands were cuffed behind him, the gun was stuck in the front of his pants. Reaching around, he said, "I got the gun out and I bent down and I was going to shoot myself, and I remember being pulled forward and I got throwed back, and then I remember explosions . . . (witness crying) . . . muzzle flashes, gunfire . . . "

Still handcuffed and in the throes of what the defense would describe as a classic delayed stress reaction, Felde managed to get out of the car, though the backseat doors of Shreveport police cars had no inside handles (nor did they then have screens between officer and prisoner), and ran through the Wray Ford car dealership lot into a residential neighborhood, becoming almost immediately the object of an extensive manhunt as some fifty to seventy-five law enforcement officers from Shreveport and the surrounding areas rushed to find the killer of a fellow patrolman.

Were Felde's hands still cuffed behind him at this point, or had he somehow managed the contortions required to slip them to the front? Had he managed to grab the box of bullets from the front seat of the patrol car? Could it have been physically possible for him to exit the car, scale a fence and reload the Magnum on the run, hands still in cuffs? During the subsequent trial, upon a challenge from the defense counsel, the prosecutor attempted to demonstrate how the pistol might be reloaded with hands cuffed, at least until the anxious foreman of the jury expressed reservations about the safety of the re-enactment.

Officers who soon found Felde testified that he was crouched beside some garbage cans in a driveway at 7120 West Canal St. The officers said Felde was in a firing position, his .357 Magnum reloaded and ready to fire, held in front of him with hands still cuffed together. Officer J. B. McGraw of the Shreveport police department was said to have been the only police officer to shoot at the suspect, firing his shotgun two times from about eighteen or twenty feet away, after issuing several warnings to Felde to freeze and drop his gun.

After taking two full rounds of .00 buckshot to the body, by 10:10 p.m. Wayne Felde, hit in at least twenty-seven places, was no longer crouched, no longer in a firing position if he had ever been. He lay in a fetal position beside the garbage cans, and the gun lay beside him, bloody, on the ground. Allegations made during the trial suggested the pistol might have been reloaded and cocked after Felde's death, that more than one officer might have shot him from more than one direction, that his inert and bloody body might have been kicked and battered before he was transported to LSU Medical Center in Shreveport.

Felde himself had no recollection of anything between the time of Officer Tompkins' shooting and the time of his own. After describing his thoughts in the patrol car immediately preceding the shooting, he said his next conscious awareness was "laying on the ground and I was all bloody, and I couldn't keep my eyes open and I knew I was dying, and that's all I remember except waking up in the Emergency Room . . . It seemed like a matter of seconds . . . I felt kind of relieved inside, yes . . . it was finally over."

During his frantic treatment after he arrived by ambulance at the emergency room at 10:15 p.m. and during his subsequent three-month hospitalization, he underwent surgery a number of times, lost a kidney and part of his liver, had a colostomy, suffered a ruptured spleen and ruptured pancreas as well as a perforation of the stomach and small bowel, lost part of his intestines, had sciatic nerve damage causing continuous permanent pain, and had a shattered right ankle which proved permanently crippling and which caused his right leg to atrophy. His Louisiana State University Hospital medical record consisted of 644 pages.

Besides his physical problems, there were problems with law enforcement, with overzealous policemen and deputies and guards understandably grieving for a fellow officer, showing that grief in thoroughly unprofessional ways. During Felde's emergency room treatment there were shouts from police officers to let him die. During his hospitalization, he was shackled hand and foot to his hospital bed, with guards periodically jerking the shackles on his shattered ankle and roughly jostling his mattress in what they said were searches for contraband. The lights in his room were never turned off, even when medical staff requested it, and snapshots of his mother's gravesite were torn up in front of his eyes by police. While a patient, Felde was not permitted visits from surviving family members for an incredible two full months.

Later incarcerated at Caddo Parish Jail, he was refused access to pain medication in a timely fashion and kept from obtaining a needed leg brace for months; most inhumanely, his colostomy bag was purposely punctured by deputies, resulting in excrement leakage all over the prisoner and his bedding. Felde was often prevented from keeping follow-up medical appointments; on those occasions when he was grudgingly transported to the medical center, he was placed unattended in a loose wheelchair in the rear of a careening police van, the wheelchair wildly rolling and crashing into walls and several times overturning with the helpless patient shackled to it. When Felde wrote a local judge complaining of his treatment at the hands of one officer, the letter was turned over to the object of his complaints, and it took federal injunctive relief to finally allow the removal of the nearly golfball-sized tumor which had appeared on Felde's breast.

It was no wonder, then, that the Louisiana Supreme Court intervened in Felde's case and, for the first time in history, ordered a change of venue in a criminal case from Caddo Parish after three district court denials of defense venue motions. Wayne Felde's first-degree murder trial was transferred to Rapides Parish after he was found capable of standing trial by a Caddo Parish sanity commission, made up of the parish coroner who had performed the autopsy on the dead officer and a couple of present and former deputy coroners, seemingly in violation of the Louisiana Code of Criminal Procedure Article 644, which expressly prohibits more than one member of such a commission being the coroner or any one of his deputies.

One sanity commission member, Dr. Norman Mauroner, clinical associate professor of psychiatry at the School of Medicine in Shreveport and employed by the state of Louisiana as a psychiatric program administrator, when asked to describe his knowledge of the mental defect of Post-Traumatic Stress Disorder and its listing in DSM III, replied, "None whatsoever. I'm not familiar with DSM III because we have not been directed to use it. I work for the state, and within the state system we don't use it."

If one good thing had come out of Felde's experiences in Caddo Parish, it was the enrollment of N. Graves Thomas as defense counsel, replacing court-appointed attorneys about whose lack of interest and experience Felde worried. In later stages of the case, Felde, who enrolled with Thomas as co-counsel, would be assisted in presenting his defense by such well-known lawyers as Millard Farmer of Atlanta, Bill Quigley of New Orleans, J. Michael Small of Alexandria, and Wellborn Jack Jr. of Shreveport, who would be the defense counsel engineering the state's first successful use of PTSD in a capital case (*State of Louisiana* v. *Charles Heads*) in 1981, ushering in a new era for the insanity defense.

A new understanding of PTSD would within a few years make it possible for attorneys to explain to juries that while PTSD sufferers are generally in contact with reality and symptomless, some of them, especially those subjected to extreme stress, can develop dissociative reactions with episodes of depersonalization or derealization, and occasionally criminal behavior may result. Since a person's cognitive state may be impaired during a dissociative reaction, when the PTSD sufferer may feel unrestrained by reality and unable to control his behavior (for example a Vietnam vet committing criminal acts while reliving traumatic war experiences during a flashback and uncontrollably engaging in violent behavior typical of a combat soldier), it has been shown possible to prove to juries that the defendant did not appreciate the criminality of his behavior, could not control his actions and regulate them according to the requirements of law, and therefore should not be held criminally responsible. But this would all come later, when it was too late to help Wayne Felde.

During the summer preceding the trial in Alexandria, Thomas, who said he entered the case "to see a man who has served honorably over there and who has had his life destroyed for doing it receive some justice," had several nationally respected psychologists evaluate the defendant. Their decision? Wayne Felde had a classic case of chronic Post-Traumatic Stress Syndrome. Said Dr. John P. Wilson, psychology professor at Cleveland State University and director of the Forgotten Warrior Project on Vietnam Veterans as well as of the National Outreach Center for the Disabled American Veterans, in July 1980, "I conclude that because of mental disease and defect, Wayne Robert Felde was unable to conform his behavior to the law and lacked the requisite capacity to distinguish right and wrong." Said Donald K. Gucker, clinical psychologist, on July 10, 1980, "Based on my examination I believe that Wayne Robert Felde was unable to distinguish right from wrong with respect to the conduct in question at the time of the offense in question." Said Dr. Charles R. Figley on July 31, 1980, "Based on my examination, I would conclude, with respect to the conduct in question, that Mr. Felde was unable to distinguish between right and wrong at the time of the offense."

The stage was set for a landmark court case, a case the defense attorney would call "perhaps one of the most difficult cases that has ever been tried in this state," the first attempt to use the newly recognized mental condition called Post-Traumatic Stress Disorder as a criminal defense in Louisiana. Suffering from the disorder, not in touch with reality at the time of the offense, unable to distinguish right from wrong, his body in a patrol car but his mind in the midst of a frantic fire fight in Vietnam, Wayne Felde was, his attorney pleaded, not guilty by reason of insanity.

Ninth judicial district judge Guy E. Humphries, fearing a trial which newspaper reports speculated could last weeks and cost up to $50,000, sequestered the jury and set a rigorous schedule for court proceedings, holding sessions on weekends as well as weekdays and often not adjourning for the evening until after 10 p.m., once not until well after midnight.

The judge was requested by defense counsel to include among his jury instructions the following: That the defendant, who has the burden of providing his insanity at the time of the commission of offense by a preponderance of the evidence, must establish that it is more likely than not that he was insane at the time the crime was committed; that insanity at the time of the crime exempts the offender from criminal responsibility; that if circumstances indicate that because of a mental disease or defect the defendant was incapable of distinguishing between right and wrong with reference to the conduct in question, the defendant must be found not guilty by reason of insanity; that intoxication at the time of the commission of the crime is usually no defense, but if the intoxication was involuntary and such condition was the direct cause of the commission of the crime, defendant can be exempt from criminal responsibility, as he can if his intoxicated condition precludes the presence of the requisite specific criminal intent; that for a finding of first-degree murder, the offender must have exhibited specific intent to kill or inflict great bodily harm.

Some of the most telling testimony in the Felde murder trial, which began Monday, August 11, 1980, came from Dr. John P. Wilson, brought in from Ohio as an expert witness on PTSD and a sensitive doctor who had examined several thousand Vietnam veterans. Dr. Wilson had served as consultant to both the Disabled American Veterans and the Veterans Administration national outreach programs for Vietnam veterans, setting up outreach centers to help vets suffering from PTSD and other problems. As director of the Forgotten Warrior Research Project, he had conducted extensive investigations into the impact of the Vietnam War on the psychological adjustment of veterans and the necessity for developing treatment facilities for vets suffering residual problems from the war. Widely recognized as one of the foremost national experts on PTSD, Dr. Wilson served as consultant to the President's Commission on Mental Health Special Task Force on Vietnam Veterans, often testified before Congress and its various veterans subcommittees on PTSD among Vietnam vets, and served as consultant for numerous medical schools and psychiatry departments about PTSD.

Dr. Wilson examined Wayne Felde on August 30, 1979, at the Caddo Parish jail for four and a half hours along with Dr. Charles Figley, Purdue University psychologist who had studied more than 3500 Vietnam vets and was the founder of the Consortium on Veteran Studies and author of *Strangers at Home: The Vietnam Veteran Since the War and Stress Disorders Among Vietnam Veterans*. Dr. Wilson's opinion following interviews and the administration of a number of psychological tests was firm. "My opinion is that, unequivocally, Wayne Felde has Post-Traumatic Stress Disorder, a chronic form." Dr. Figley concurred; so did Dr. Joe Ben Hayes, Pineville, Louisiana, psychiatrist.

Describing the disorder for the edification of the jurors, Dr. Wilson continued, "Post-Traumatic Stress Disorder is a recognized behavioral disorder, a mental defect, by the American Psychiatric Association . . . recognized as a kind of mental disorder that has a number of components to it . . . 'Post-traumatic' means just that. It's a post-trauma stress response . . . And it can happen to Vietnam veterans who have been in life-and-death catastrophically stressful situations as a combatant is in a war, but it also can happen to a lot of other people, for example the survivors of the atomic bomb at Hiroshima . . . Likewise, the survivors of the holocaust in Nazi Germany exhibited many of these symptoms of post-traumatic stress. Survivors of terrorists' hostage holding, survivors of naturalistic disaster such as a hurricane or a dam break or things like this often exhibit the same kind of symptom, okay, and that's why it's called Post-Traumatic Stress Response; and the symptoms include: depression, flashbacks to the trauma, an inability to control one's impulses, often a kind of violent explosive behavior, there's frequently suicidal thoughts, recurring nightmares of the event.

"There is often memory impairment, an inability to feel close to people, this is a very common symptom, this one in particular. There is a great deal of what is termed 'emotional numbing' or psyche numbing where the person loses their capacity to be sensitive to normal events . . . These kinds of symptoms are what really define Post-Traumatic Stress . . . Dr. Figley and I having examined Mr. Felde came to the conclusion that he, as a Vietnam veteran and one who was in extensive combat during the war, does show these symptoms and others of the Post-Traumatic Stress Disorder."

Why, Dr. Wilson was asked in court, do some Vietnam veterans experience post-trauma stress problems and others do not? "I wish we had the answer to that," answered the psychologist. "The best we can come up with, in terms of our data, and this also was borne out by the research during World War II, is that the younger individual seemed to be more severely affected by the nature of the combat experience than was an older man who had more experience in life and brought to the combat situation more skills of adaptation . . . When we talk about Vietnam . . . the average soldier was nineteen in combat and I think this is, again, very much connected with the fact that, that age is one of identity formation and, therefore, the stresses of war had a very profound impact on this normal developmental process of forming a coherent identity in the individual."

Wilson cited exhaustive studies by Darrel Care, director of the office of Veterans Affairs in Washington, D.C., showing that on a national basis, twenty-five percent of those incarcerated in both federal and state prisons were Vietnam veterans, some 70,000 inmates, with an additional 200,000 out on bail, parole or probation. He added that the suicide rate of Vietnam combat vets was nearly forty percent higher than non-vets of similar age. "Another statistic I would add here," he said, "that I find, frankly, just frightening and very sad, is that the VA data indicates that the alcoholism rate among Vietnam veterans is sixty percent higher than it was for veterans of World War II or Korea. So we're seeing both, a lot of suicide and a lot of use of alcohol, in destructive ways."

Wilson quoted studies conducted by the Center for Policy Research, with funding from the VA and National Institute of Mental Health, which showed nearly forty percent of Vietnam veterans have persistent, chronic problems, including depression, suicidal thoughts, alcohol abuse and other symptoms of PTSD; among combat veterans, those actually involved in fighting, the figures jump to sixty percent with chronic, persistent emotional problems. Multiply that by the 1.1 million Vietnam veterans who were actually combat soldiers, said Wilson in 1980, "and you end up with at least 500,000 and possibly as high as 750,000 Vietnam veterans suffering at this time from Post-Traumatic Stress Disorder."

Felde's rootlessness after the war, drifting from state to state and from job to job, Wilson found to be a common symptom of PTSD. "I think that the root of it is this," he explained to the jury, "that when we try to examine the effects the stress had on a developmental process, that is, the formation of one's own identity . . . normally, this occurs in our lives when we're late adolescents, that we have to figure out who we are and what we want to be when we grow up, and we begin to make commitments to choices and decisions that we make about ourselves, this is a part of what forming a sense of our own identity is about. Well, for those young men who went to Vietnam at eighteen and nineteen, often the stresses of war sort of exacerbated this process of trying to get a root on who you are and what you can commit yourself to. And what I've seen a great deal of, in fact everyone who works in the Outreach Program has seen this with individuals in PTSD, that they report they have a hard time committing themselves to a job, to another person, to the choices they make, and they feel anxious about it, and eventually they avoid the kind of conflict that comes with those decisions by moving on."

Why then, Dr. Wilson was asked in court, did Felde not simply move on, once he found that the Louisiana police were looking for him as an escapee from Maryland corrections; why did this troubled man purchase a gun? From interviews he and Dr. Figley did to construct a history of Wayne Felde, Dr. Wilson related, "He had a very close relationship to his mother. But after he came back from Vietnam and began to exhibit these symptoms of PTSD, he didn't feel good about himself. In fact, Wayne told us that he felt that he was worthless in some ways and that everything he touched, and this is a quote, I don't say this to offend any of you, but what he said is, 'You know, everything I touch turns to shit. I'm just no good. Nothing turns out well for me.' So I think what we have is a person who feels badly about himself, he has a very negative self-image, he's depressed, he feels helpless, he has a lot of residual war stresses and his life doesn't go well . . . The most significant support person for Wayne was his mother . . . He wanted to please his mother, respected his mother and loved his mother enormously because she cared for him, worked hard as a nurse to support the family and rear the children, so this was the central, significant, emotional person in his life."

Continued Wilson, "He's an isolated kind of person; and now he is scared. The police are coming. They're tracking him down from being an escapee from the prison in Maryland. At that point in time, it's my judgment, my opinion, that he began to react again as a combatant; tremendously scared. I think he felt helpless. Helpless, I want to point out, in, I think, the same way that one would feel helpless if you were walking through the jungle in Vietnam and didn't know where the next booby trap was, you know. When is it going to get you? You know, when is the person coming? Are you going to die? Are you going to survive the experience? And, at that point in time, feeling this impending kind of threat and helplessness, I think that's why he wanted the gun. Many Vietnam veterans still sleep with their weapons, carry their weapons. It's a security piece. If you had nothing else in the jungle, you had your weapon and, if you were going to get blown away or fight, that was the last bit of security that you had."

But the gun, for Felde, represented several different types of security. Wilson explained, "Wayne is buying this weapon for two reasons. One is, it represents the kind of security against an impending threat like he felt in Vietnam, you know. He is like, again, sort of a trapped and caged animal. He is running. He is scared. Tremendously scared at this point in time. The second reason is, I think he wants to kill himself, that he had no reason to live at this point in time, that he had been to prison, he'd been divorced, his mother died, the war had messed up much of his life. He had all these difficulties. He felt totally helpless.

"So I think the prospect was this. That if the police had found his identity, you know, Wayne Felde and not Harry Hershey, his alias, he would face going back to prison in Maryland. Rather than be incarcerated again, you know. And, again, incarceration means more helplessness, you know, in this kind of situation. I think he was making a decision to kill himself . . . And I think . . . when he began to purchase the gun and when his friends did not come back to pick him up, I think that triggered once again this dissociated state, like we saw in the Maryland case in 1972. He's in an altered state of consciousness. He's confused. He's scared. He's disoriented . . . I think he wanted to kill himself . . . I think if there was a struggle, it intensifies the fact that he is going to react with combat-like tactics, survivor tactics."

While many Vietnam vets can have flashbacks and still maintain perfectly normal functions, others enter a completely dissociative state, removing themselves from their present situations altogether. How could the difference in reactions be explained, Wilson was asked by defense attorney Graves Thomas? "The more controlled the environment, the more predictable the environment, the better," he answered. "That is, the more stable relationships, the more consistent things are in the individual's life, the more there is a kind of routine, the better. What seems to precipitate flashbacks or even, in the more extreme cases, these dissociative reactions, where there is sort of a radical change in a person's functions so that they begin to behave like a combatant again, is, if there's stress in the person's life, he may have, he may be divorced, he may just lose a job . . . "

The death of one's beloved mother and subsequent removal of all semblance of stability would certainly fall into the category of stresses capable of precipitating problems, triggering flashbacks or even dissociative reactions during which the victim is precipitated abruptly back to being a combatant again in a war zone, Wilson explained. So would a combat situation, especially a fight involving a struggle for a gun in which shots were fired, which certainly covered the incident in Maryland and may well have covered the incident in the Shreveport police car as well. "If the person had PTSD and were placed into a situation where they had to fight," Wilson concluded, "they are going to use what they know how to use to defend themselves in that situation, and what we see for Vietnam veterans is that they begin to act with survival tactics again." The PTSD sufferer would also be in such complete dissociation that he would be removed from reality to the point of having only spotty recall of his actions in the dissociated state, Wilson explained.

With the fragmented memory of events typical of Post-Traumatic Stress Disorder, Felde related to the examining doctors what he remembered of the incident in the Shreveport patrol car when Officer Tompkins was fatally wounded. "I was in the back of the car and I thought I'd blow my brains out," Felde told them. "I tried to turn the barrel towards my face. I remember the jerk, going forward . . . Then I saw flashes, flashes, like incoming round hits, like firecrackers, hearing machine guns, I heard machine guns, I heard rifle fire, I heard more explosions and I couldn't move. I was happy because I knew I was going to die."

A similar interpretation of Felde's actions in the Maryland incident with Blackwell may be made, Dr. Wilson said. "That's a classic dissociative reaction in which the struggle, the whole struggle precipitates him responding again as if he were in a combat zone. In other words, he's using survival combat tactics in that situation. But he's also in an altered state of consciousness. That is, he is dissociated. He is not fully cognizant of all the events around him. He is acting like a caged animal, okay. He's in a survival mode, which is interesting, because it . . . corresponds to the description of him as a wild animal. So that kind of description is consistent with what we would see and what I have seen, by the way, on a number of other occasions, as a dissociative reaction precipitated by stress." During such a dissociated state, Wilson concluded, the defendant "couldn't discriminate right from wrong and he couldn't conform his conduct to the law. I think he was totally disoriented."

It would be Felde's mother who returned him to reality after Blackwell's death. Explained Dr. Wilson, "In dissociative states, with that kind of stress and trauma, one of the things that will bring the person out of the state is to have contact again with a stable, trusted individual who can ground the person, you know, who can bring them back in touch with where they are."

Ruby Felde's gentle presence snapped her son back from the incident in Maryland; her death and removal of her stabilizing love and steady comfort may have set the scene for the second fatal encounter in Louisiana. During his Louisiana trial, Wayne would weep at the mere mention of his mother's name. He also stuffed cotton in his ears to block out the sounds of Vietnam during the showing of army training films to help the jury understand just how he had been taught to function in combat, covered his head and cried during psychiatric testimony, and refused a courtroom request to face the jury, saying, "I don't want to look at them. I'm sorry, but it's just been too much said. . . . "

And when the prosecutor, assistant Caddo district attorney B. Woodrow Nesbitt, Jr., brandished Felde's gun and questioned his suicidal tendencies, the defendant offered to blow his brains out right in the courtroom if Nesbitt would hand him the weapon. "If you'll load that gun right now, Mr. Nesbitt, I'll blow my brains out right here. I will. Go ahead and load it," he said, and he meant it. His attorney knew it, too. "I was afraid he was going to hand him the gun," Graves Thomas said to the jury. "I had no doubt in my mind, from my association with that man over the last year, that he would have done it because he is not rational."

Felde's self-destructive and suicidal tendencies were common symptoms of chronic PTSD, Dr. Wilson explained, though he added, "I don't want to give the impression that all Vietnam veterans suffering Post-Traumatic Stress Disorder are necessarily self-destructive. That is not the case, and that would be an injustice to the decent Vietnam veterans that we have. But we have a chronic, you know, a very severe form of this disorder. There often is an underlying suicidal ideation, that the person wishes to die. Many, many, many Vietnam veterans have told me that they feel that they actually did die or a part of them died in Vietnam, and they're kind of just a body, a shell walking around today. And, in some situations, where they feel helpless, feel that they have nothing to live for, the person may act in a way, a self-destructive way, often a suicidal way to try to end their life since they feel that they have nothing left; that they really died ten years or fifteen years ago in Vietnam."

Longterm group psychotherapy with other Vietnam veterans and longterm intensive individual psychotherapy in a controlled setting could successfully treat Wayne Felde, Dr. Wilson testified. What, the doctor was asked, would be the results should Felde be denied treatment and released? "I think," he replied, "if Wayne were put on the street immediately, he'd kill himself and if he didn't kill himself, I think there's a high probability that he would, he could aggravate a situation to get himself killed or in the process kill another person."

Just that probability was used by the prosecutor in his summation before the Louisiana jury, an unflattering appraisal of the ethics and mentality of both medical professionals and judges alike. "If you find him not guilty by reason of insanity, he is not going up to Michigan, or wherever his experts came from," Nesbitt told the jury, "and sit around with a bunch of Vietnam veterans and talk about things. The judge will tell you, he is going to a state hospital until the doctors recommend he be released, and then a judge will decide when that will be, six months or a year, five years, whenever a judge decides in the future, upon recommendation of doctors at a state hospital, he must be released, and the judge's decision is reviewable by the Supreme Court as to the merits of that decision. And if he lines up two or three, I mean, goes around, patting them on the back, I'm doing fine, acts real nice, just like he did in the pen, do it two, three, four years, take his medication, act great, recommend his release. And, you know, you can't keep him in jail because he is not going to be in jail. He's going to be in a hospital. He's escaped from the penitentiary. He wants to go to a hospital. He doesn't want to go to the pen for life or possibly face the death sentence. He wants to go to a hospital where he can get out. And, just like he testified, when they didn't give him parole, he got out. And what will he do when they don't turn him loose the first time he wants out?"

Nesbitt disparaged the Post-Traumatic Stress Disorder defense. After hearing the experts called to testify by defense attorney Graves Thomas, he told the jury, "But, you know, anything that is not explainable, the defense would have you believe, oh, that's consistent with a Post-Traumatic Stress Disorder. If it's not explainable, that's consistent." He disparagingly told the jurors that the experts had come looking for PTSD, and so it was no surprise that they had found it. "When you are told what you are supposed to be looking for, you may be more apt to find it, especially, when you are dealing in things as subtle as alleged disorders. We are not talking about psychosis, foaming at the mouth, crazies. We are talking about trouble with sleep, nightmares, jumps a little. And the only way, the only way to tell whether or not the defendant has this flashback problem is from the defendant's own version of what happened." He added, "I would submit to you the way the defendant told the story, he fought the whole Vietnam war by himself. And we are grateful for him doing it, but it's not a defense to this crime unless you make it one and license it."

Showing a photograph of Officer Tompkins' patrol car, Nesbitt asked the jury, "Does this look like a foxhole or a cave, or does that look like the ride back to the penitentiary? Does this look like a war scene at night or does that look like a police car with sirens on top on a four-lane highway in Shreveport, Louisiana? That's a ride back to the penitentiary. Does this look like anything you see in Vietnam? Or does that look like a ride back to the penitentiary? . . . You show me something that looks like Vietnam in this picture. You decide whether this looks like Vietnam or this looks like a ride back to the penitentiary, and you decide if that man did not intend to kill."

In his own final summation to the jurors, defense attorney Graves Thomas almost seemed to second the prosecution's plea for a verdict of guilty to first-degree murder. "Thomas Glen Tompkins . . . is dead," he told the jury, "and you have a decision to make as to whether or not something positive is going to come from his death or something negative. You put Wayne Felde in prison for manslaughter, which I don't think the state has proved by the evidence. There is no criminal intent in this case. There is no escape attempt. But if you put him in for manslaughter, that's negative . . . not accomplishing a thing. He's got a Maryland hanging over him, anyway, and he is going to be dead by his own hands or some of those 'dudes' who are down at Angola, and he'd go to Angola involving the death of a police officer, and he's crippled.

"Second-degree murder, the same thing . . . First-degree murder, the best thing you can do for him, if you don't go with insanity, is first degree-murder with the death penalty. That's the best thing you want to do for him because that is the easiest way out, because insanity is harder than first-degree murder with the death penalty, because he's facing Maryland. They will probably charge him with possession of a firearm after this is over. I don't know. But he's still got to be committed until the court determines, unless and until, the court determines that he is no longer a danger to himself or others, and we are not talking about Cabrini (Hospital) when we talk about hospitals. We are talking about a place with bars and locks and guards. We are talking about a mental institution for people who are, have gone through criminal trials and are found not guilty by reason of insanity, so, and don't let all this talk about getting out in a couple of years fool you, because it is not accurate."

However, Thomas added, the jury in this landmark case had the opportunity to make a real difference for other veterans suffering from PTSD, other "walking time bombs." He told jurors, "So we have quite a dilemma here. I grieve for the Tompkins family in this case. And I feel that something very positive can come out of this, if you decide that the evidence supports a not guilty by reason of insanity in this landmark case."

After deliberations, jury foreman Keith S. Oliver handed to the clerk the unanimous verdict, which was then read. "We, the jury, find the defendant guilty of first-degree murder." Informed by the judge during the sentence hearing which immediately followed that the two possible sentences would be capital sentence or life imprisonment, the jury was asked if it would care to retire for the evening, but decided to continue.

Graves Thomas, in his statement on behalf of the defendant, told jurors, "I'm placed in a difficult situation right now because I have an obligation to my client to do what I think is in his best interest in this case and . . . if the Post-Traumatic Stress Disorder that we have heard about exists and he is suffering from it, life in prison ain't going to do him any good. He's not going to get any treatment at Angola . . . I feel that he has gone through hell for a long time and I can't see him going down to Angola in his condition and being subjected to what he would be subjected to there. So I am not going to ask you to do what I think would probably be the merciful thing to do. I am not going to ask you to do that myself. He is going to have to do that because I don't think I can, but I believe when you all were elected as jurors you'd said you could apply the death penalty and I think . . . if you return the verdict that was returned, you probably have to impose the death penalty, I would think."

Thomas then called to the stand the defense's only witness in the sentence hearing, Wayne Felde. And after being duly sworn to tell the truth, the defendant commended the jury on its intelligence and told them, "All I can say to you all is, I would advise you to return the death penalty in this case . . . I consider all of you people intelligent so I hope you will take my advice, return the death penalty." Asked by his attorney what would happen if the death penalty were not returned and he received no treatment, Felde replied, "I think other deaths will result. Yes, Mr. Thomas, I do. And that's why I suggested it, to prevent it from happening. They would be on your conscience if you can't return it. Now, I'm not trying to put you all in a bad position but you all are taking other people's lives in your hands, along with mine, so I think you should return it. I don't think no more needs to be said, Mr. Thomas. They're upset."

Explained Thomas to the distraught jurors, "He was not threatening you all, of course, from the stand. What he means and he wants to clarify the fact is that at some future time, if he was not incarcerated or if he should get out, someone else might die, either himself or somebody else, that he does not think he can control himself. Now . . . I think the evidence shows that he is, in a sense, already dead to some extent and . . . a policeman is dead. And all I can say to you is that he has voiced his feelings from the stand and I believe those to be his true feelings and, therefore, I think it is obvious as to what he wants you to do."

Pointing out that the case at point was much bigger than Wayne Felde, to whom he had grown exceedingly close during the past year and a half, Thomas begged the jurors not to "cop out on him, don't take the easy way out and go home and rationalize . . . because when you go home he will still be here . . . There are a lot of thoughts going through my head right now and . . . I'm waiting for something to come in here and tell me, you know, there's some reason I should ask you to spare this man, but there's not. There, honestly, is not. There's not one reason that I can think of for him to continue to experience what he has been experiencing. I cannot think of one reason. There's only one thing that would benefit him and that's treatment. There's only one thing that would benefit people like him and that's treatment and they're not going to get it. And I agree with him, I think it would be one hell of a note for you to return a conviction like this and then just leave him sitting there."

Felde added a few last words, thanking Judge Humphries for a fair trial and the weeping jurors for their attentiveness. "All I have to say," he told the jurors in closing arguments, "is, whether you all believed what we'd said throughout this defense or not, it is true. There are two hundred thousand other veterans suffering with it and I'm sorry you didn't believe it but, however, I do pray that you will come back with the death penalty. I'm not coming out and threatening anybody because that's not where it is. A walking time bomb, that's where it is. Somebody else will die as a result of it if I'm not put to death, I am sure. It's happened twice in eight years. There's been ten years of proof shown to you. I don't know where it went so, please, return that. I think, as countrymen, you owe me that much. I did my part. Please do yours."

The jury began deliberations at 8:30 p.m. on Wednesday, August 20, 1980. The verdict was returned shortly after 11 p.m. and, following a sentencing hearing, the death penalty was recommended shortly after 1 a.m. on Thursday, August 21. Under Louisiana law, the jury which convicts in a capital case also decides, after a separate sentencing hearing, whether the penalty should be death or life imprisonment, a recommendation which the judge then rules on; if the judge accepts the jury's recommendation, appeal to the state supreme court is automatic.

Cleancut but crippled by his shattered ankle, Wayne Felde approaches the Rapides Parish courtroom with his young attorney, Graves Thomas, in August 1980. Photo courtesy of the *Shreveport Times*.

The sentence verdict of the jury was as follows: "Having found the below listed statutory aggravating circumstance or circumstances and, after consideration of the mitigating circumstances offered, the jury recommends that the defendant be sentenced to death. Aggravating circumstance or circumstances found: The victim was a peace officer engaged in his lawful duties."

The jury in an unprecedented move then asked to read a statement, which said, "We, the jury, recognize the contribution of our Vietnam veterans and those who lost their lives in Vietnam. We feel that the trial of Wayne Felde has brought to the forefront those extreme stress disorders prevalent among thousands of our veterans. We have attempted, through great emotional and mental strain, to serve and preserve the judicial branch of our government by serving on this jury. This trial will forever remain indelibly imprinted upon our minds, hearts, and consciences. Through long and careful deliberation, through exposure to all evidence, we felt that Mr. Felde was aware of right and wrong when Mr. Tompkins' life was taken. However, we pledge ourselves to contribute whatever we can to best meet the needs of our veterans."

A new trial was quickly requested by the defense, citing among many legal reasons the recent locating of several vets who had served with Felde in Company D, 2nd Battalion, 35th Infantry, 4th Infantry Division, who could corroborate his nightmarish combat experiences; the supposition that sequestered trial jurors were pressured or coerced to reach an improper verdict as evidenced by the fact that each and every juror was crying or showed evidence of having recently cried upon returning to the courtroom to render their verdict, as well as the jury's statement to the effect that the defendant was indeed suffering from PTSD; and the physical exhaustion of those same jurors, who were said to be unable to pay sufficient attention to evidence due to the seven-days-a-week, fourteen-hours-a-day schedule set by the judge.

After denial of the request for retrial, the hearing for imposition of sentence by His Honor, Guy E. Humphries, Jr., District Judge, presiding, in the matter of the State of Louisiana versus Wayne Robert Felde, Ninth Judicial District Court, Parish of Rapides, State of Louisiana, criminal docket number 196,240, was held on February 13, 1981, in Alexandria. Said the judge, "Wayne Robert Felde, you have been found guilty of the crime of first-degree murder by a jury of twelve citizens of this community. That same jury recommended that you be sentenced to death. Under the law, it is my mandatory duty to follow the recommendations of the jury and impose the death penalty. Therefore, it is the sentence of this court that you, Wayne Felde, for the first-degree murder of Thomas Glen Tompkins, be put to death in the manner prescribed by law on a date and hour to be specified in a warrant to be issued by this court after all appeals and delays provided by law."

The judge and jury had made their statements. Now Wayne Robert Felde made his, reading the following to the court: "Judge Humphries, I know that you are only doing what you are required by law in sentencing me to death. I have and hold nothing personal against you and want you to know this. I also want the record to reflect that I have and hold nothing against my jury as they returned the verdict of death which I asked them to. I know that I could not survive in prison as I told the jurors, as I could not receive the help I need to cure my mental and emotional disorder, and given the choice between life in prison or execution, I prefer execution, as either means death to me anyway. My crippled state adds to this also.

"As I have tried many times to piece together what all really happened, as from my testimony I told of all I know to be true, leaving many gaps unfilled which no one knows the answer, not even I. This also add to the many nightmares, as I must try and live with this too, however long. Of course, I would rather receive mental treatment to possibly cure my delayed stress disorder so that I too could possibly be of a free mind and life to live a normal life and have the family I've always wanted.

"I feel you did the best you could to be fair under the circumstances of the long hours and seven-day-a-week trial. I feel the guilty verdict was wrong, and that the jury was tricked by the prosecutor, Mr. Nesbitt. I feel these things, fatigue, etc., hurt much to the defense since our turn came at the end of the trial. I feel an eight-hour day would have made all the difference in the world as to the verdict and the alertness of the jury when our experts took the stand, as they would have been much more comprehensive. The fatigue was shown throughout the end of the trial, as you could see that all the jurors were crying or had cried. Because of the long hours, my attorney was also not at his best, as he had to spend most of each night preparing for the next day, where the prosecutor has many assistants. My attorney was alone. Then I too was not able to express and say all I wanted to, as I had no sleep for several reasons, as I know my attorney will bring up on appeal one of the reasons.

"The interview Mr. Nesbitt gave the *Shreveport Times,* as in evidence, will show his character, as I feel he was also not interested in the facts, truth and justice, but only to win any way he could. But I also realize that these issues along with many more are all questions the Supreme Court must decide. Regardless of what happens in my case from here on out, I will continue to publicize the bad mental and emotional problems thousands of Vietnam combat veterans still have, because maybe this will prevent some other Nam vets from having happen to them what has happend to me and so many others.

"One nightmare I wanted to express was of a guy I hardly knew that had his stomach ripped open by enemy fire. I tried to catch his guts as they poured through my fingers. Then he was dead. The fight carried on to a small village where all that ran through minds was revenge and survival. We were trained in such situations to kill anything that moved. Before it was over, in minutes it seemed, that whole little village was dead. We found old men, women, children and dogs that appeared to even have slanted eyes. I know this is not the time to go into this, but the stress and fatigue left me without a lot of things I wanted to say.

"America needs to remember Vietnam, but most of all remember the many mistakes and problems it brought with it. President Carter dedicated a U.S. postage stamp to those veterans I feel lost their lives over there, and that stamp lasted less than a year. Thank you, America. Those that did return to this country were on the streets within hours not prepared for the welcome we received. I read where the Iran hostages were greeted by psychiatrists for stress and many others for much more. I don't want to be misunderstood, as I am very, very glad of their safe return, but feel if the Nam veterans were at least greeted by psychiatrists, warned of the unexpected welcome, it would of made a world of difference, as many of us needed help but were afraid to ask for it right off, then screamed for it and (were) ignored. If it were there when we stepped off the plane, many vets would not be in prison today, but treated instead. I know the hostages went through many things they too will not forget, but at least they had that help.

"My record speaks for itself. I know the two charges I have had in the last ten years are very serious; this too I must live with for now. But I am not a criminal, but a troubled and wrecked man, like many other vets, as I know what Vietnam did to me. I could go on and on, since I feel it's time the people listened, but will stop with something I pray people will think of often: Critical wounds do not always pierce the skin, but enter the hearts and minds and dreams that are only begging for the help so badly needed. I submit this with respect, (signed) Wayne Robert Felde."

2009 Update:

Kay Smith, the childhood sweetheart of Wayne Felde, continued a correspondence with *Angolite* co-editor Ron Wikberg, begun during her attempts to recover Felde's personal effects and understand his story; the two would marry and live in Maryland after Wikberg's release from Angola, although he soon died of cancer.

V

"When Judgment Day Comes, I Don't Want to Come Up Out of the Ground and Still Be in Prison": Death by Despair

"I have no memory of my father at all," Corky Clifton would write his fiancee of his early years. "I was told by my mother that when they separated, he took my brother and sister to his parents. But they didn't want me, for some reason."

He continued, "My mother became an alcoholic, with many different men in her life. As a very little boy I can remember trying to protect her when one of them would be beating up on her. Finally when I was around six years old, the welfare took me away and put me in a foster home. For the next ten years off and on, I was moved so many times that I lost count. You see, I was called troublesome, even as young as that. Then too, I'd run off and sometimes I'd find my mother, and naturally she'd let me stay with her until the welfare people came and got me.

"Finally my mother met a good man. She quit drinking altogether. He couldn't read or write, but was a hard worker. She had three children by him. For some reason I couldn't go home to her. I was put in a juvenile place up around Columbus, Ohio, probably until I was about sixteen, if I am remembering right. It has been so long ago.

"When I got out, my mother put my age up so I could join the Air Force. I liked it fine as I seemed to belong there. I was only in about seven months until they found out how young I was.

"Then I met a girl. We thought we had fallen in love. 'Course we spent most of our time in the backseat of my old car. We were both the same age and thought our lust surely was true love. We ended up having to get married at the tender age of eighteen. By the time our first child was born, a boy, we rarely had more than a few words to say to each other. We fought constantly. We had nothing in common. I did want attention from her since she was my wife. But at that time I was just self-centered; I never gave her feelings any consideration at all. This is why when youngsters marry young it almost never works out. You just aren't mature enough to handle things.

"When she was expecting our third child, I lost my job. I thought I hated her. I couldn't handle all the responsibilities, so I just took off hitchhiking. I worked some in different places. I also stole when necessary. You wouldn't have liked what I was before I ended up here at Angola."

Born Francis Aubrey Clifton in Hamersville, Ohio, on May 19, 1938, diminutive Corky had brown hair, hazel eyes, a ruddy complexion and would eventually grow to be five feet eight inches tall, though he rarely weighed more than 117 pounds. Small for his age even as a child, he was shuffled from foster household to household, always longing to return to his alcoholic mother, Mae, who was clearly incapable of caring for him properly during his early childhood. Only when Mae met and married farmer William Johnson did some order come into her life, but by then it was too late for Corky.

He finished eighth grade at Manchester Junior High School and lied about his age to enlist in the U.S. Air Force, where he finally felt he belonged. But Corky would be able to stay in the service only from May through December 1956, when his real age was determined and he was given an honorable discharge. He soon married Donna Skinner and the struggling young couple had three children, Eddie, Johnny and Debbie Ann, born every two years during the course of their turbulent six-year marriage, which terminated when she divorced him in 1966 while he was on Death Row.

Marital discord was accompanied by troubles with the law, for by 1957 Clifton had been arrested in Chillicothe, Ohio, for breaking and entering; his one-year sentence was suspended and he was placed on probation, which he successfully completed. But in June 1958 he was sentenced to five years for the crime of forgery of a government check, given a suspended sentence and placed on a five-year probation which was revoked, the original sentence being re-instated in April 1959 when he was sent to the federal reformatory in Chillicothe and later transferred to the Federal Correctional Institute at Ashland, Kentucky, in 1960. He was paroled in March 1961, but less than a year later Corky Clifton's days of freedom were over.

It was on September 14, 1962, that Corky was hitchhiking near Beaumont, Texas, when he was picked up by Clifton Carl Wilson, Jr., a poultry inspector with the U.S. Department of Agriculture on assignment in Gonzales, Texas. Wilson was on his way home to Jonesville, Louisiana, in a new blue Oldsmobile Starfire coupe.

Driving through Alexandria, the pair came to the small town of Jena, Louisiana, some thirty miles short of Wilson's destination. There, Clifton drew a .25 caliber pistol and ordered Wilson to stop the car and hand over his billfold, which contained a single dollar bill and a check for $143. Clifton ordered Wilson back into the car. The pair drove on a short distance, then got out of the car and walked briefly in the woods. They then returned to the car, where Clifton, who seemed ambivalent about just what he was going to do with Wilson, ordered the driver to return along the route they had just travelled, back through Alexandria toward Glenmora.

Four miles south of Glenmora, Wilson was ordered to turn off the Alexandria-Lake Charles highway and proceed down a gravel road about four miles to an intersection, where he was told to turn right. After driving a mile up that gravel road, Wilson was again ordered to stop the car, then forced to walk into the woods in front of Clifton. After walking awhile, Wilson was shot once in the back of the head and fell to the ground, then was shot again, this time fatally, at close range just above the left ear.

Clifton drove off in the blue Oldsmobile, but was soon apprehended through vehicle identification. Indicted by a Rapides Parish grand jury, he was tried in June 1963 before ninth judicial district judge Guy Humphries, Jr. He was convicted and sentenced to death by electrocution.

The delay between crime and trial was at least partly explained by a difficulty with legal representation for the accused. Alexandria attorneys Edwin O. Ware and Kelly Hamm were initially appointed to represent Clifton, but in jail the defendant met a personable attorney who offered to represent him instead. Ware and Hamm moved to be relieved of the case. Unfortunately, it turned out that the jailed attorney was awaiting a civil sanity hearing, his own, for which he never appeared, nor did he appear for any of Clifton's hearings. It would later be determined that the lawyer was not competent to represent anyone. Ware and Hamm were then re-appointed and the trial proceeded.

On July 31, 1965, Clifton somehow escaped from a cell on the eighth floor of the Rapides Parish jail, kidnapped four hostages whom he forced to drive him toward freedom in Mexico, and was recaptured on August 3 in Brownsville, Texas, when the hostages overpowered him. Returned to Louisiana, he once again escaped, this time from the state police barracks where he was awaiting the outcome of an appeal. He caught a bus to Ohio and was captured and sentenced there for armed robbery, served his time and then was transferred to the Louisiana State Penitentary at Angola. He would be returned to court in Rapides in January 1970 and re-sentenced to natural life, after the United States Supreme Court decision temporarily halting application of the death penalty. After returning to Angola on January 20, 1970, he would not again leave for two decades.

By the time Clifton applied for clemency in 1984, twenty-two years after the murder of Wilson and not the first time he had appealed for help, even his own defense attorney had turned against him. Ed Ware, by then the parish district attorney, opposed any shortening of Clifton's life sentence, calling him a sociopath too dangerous to be released into society. Clifton, Ware told local newspapers covering the clemency appeal, suffered from what he described as an untreatable personality disorder "where you just cannot stand for anybody to cross you." Admitting that the inmate, to whom he referred as "an itty bitty skinny fellow," had become a born-again Christian and a reasonably good self-trained artist while in jail, Ware nonetheless said, "He was as nice a fellow as you ever want to meet, but don't cross him."

This unofficial diagnosis bothered Clifton so much that he would correspond in September 1964 with the assistant director of the Johns Hopkins University School of Medicine about Ware's designation of his old client as a sociopath. Replied Dr. Fred S. Berlin, M.D., Ph.D., from Baltimore, "The definition of sociopath is someone who is lacking in conscience and who repeatedly acts in antisocial ways. A person's conscience is not something that can be changed by medical means, so therefore it is considered untreatable. However, that does not mean that people are unable to change. For certainly, one's life experiences do change all of us."

That Corky Clifton changed during his several decades behind the gates at Angola was evidenced by his status as a prisoner, working his way upward and eventually gaining sufficient administrative trust that he was rewarded with one of the facility's most coveted

Tiny and slim, Francis A. Clifton (5' 8" tall, 114 pounds) is shown in
a mug shot taken at Angola on January 21, 1970. Photo courtesy of
The Angolite.

inmate jobs, working at the dog pens where the prison's tracking bloodhounds and attack dogs are housed and trained, living and eating not in a cell but in a separate ranch house with other trusties. His main job there was to tend the many beds of colorful flowers and blossoming shrubs lining the steep driveway and picturesque hilltop site.

Prison is never easy for an inmate of small stature like Corky, but he somehow made it through more than twenty-five years at Angola. Other longtime inmates recall him as quiet and reserved, spending most of his time painting. His boss at the dog pens, personable Bobby Oliveaux, valued his affinity for animals, saying, "Corky liked all animals; he was always finding a bird out on the ground, and would take care of it and then let it go. If we had a sick puppy, he'd be a good candidate to nurse it back to health, 'cause he'd spend the necessary time with it. He had a lot of patience." Oliveaux adds, "Corky was a very intelligent person. If somebody could have gotten him on the right road when he was young, he could have been one of the best watch repairmen or artists. Anything he set his mind to, he could have done it."

In his cell or at the dog pens, chain-smoking Clifton did detailed pen-and-ink or pencil sketches, and painted fine wildlife and nature scenes, many of which he traded for cigarettes or gave to friends to send home as Christmas gifts. He did a number of portraits of favorite bloodhounds and shepherds, and also painted several highly realistic portraits of then-governor Edwin Edwards, which were apparently so well liked that not all of them reached the proud politician himself.

Corky took quiet pride in the fact that he once won second place in the watercolor category at the highly competitive annual Angola art show. Perhaps his most unusual pieces of art, however, were the intricately detailed miniatures, no larger than postage stamps, which he completed with the aid of several magnifying lenses of different strengths, tiny likenesses of squirrels or raccoons, ducks or egrets or brightly colored gamecocks, a still life of golden pears highlighted by the sun, an old abandoned water pump so carefully recreated the dew still glistened on the cobwebs. His earlier hobbycraft training in watch repair had uniquely qualified him for this demanding and minutely detailed work, in spite of such poor eyesight that Bobby Oliveaux says he was considered legally blind.

Clifton was not unaware of the transformation taking place within him over the years, especially while he was under sentence of death. He would later write his fiancee, "When I was first put on Death Row, I really did want to die. Then after a couple of years I started to really look into myself and decided to get rid of all the meanness and try my best to develop into a decent human being. Before, I hadn't let myself get interested in anyone but myself. Now I can say at least I became a better man and person here at Angola than I ever was out in the free world. If they will only give me the chance to prove it. When I came off Death Row, the old Corky really and truly had died."

After a self-imposed hunger strike on Death Row which would have lasting effects on his poor health, Clifton had been returned to the main prison population at a time in the early seventies when life at Angola was hard and acute staffing shortages meant escalating violence. But even in the face of the constant threat of danger, the inmates had one thing to hold onto, and that was hope. Sentences during those days were consistent and seemed appropriate to the crime, and convicts were given the opportunity to prove they could change, with rewards accompanying the effort to stay out of trouble. If a man did his time quietly and without problems, he could reasonably expect to have his sentence shortened for good behavior. A life sentence usually translated into no more than ten and a half years hard time before prisoners who had stayed out of trouble were parolled.

In many ways, those hard years were preferable for Angola inmates, for they had something to work toward and look forward to; they knew where they stood, and they knew what they could do to better their situation. There was at least a glimmer of light at the end of the tunnel, and the hope which was so important to them gave them an incentive for good behavior. It was, in a sense, the most effective means of behavior control.

But times have changed, and public sentiment regarding early release has changed right along with escalating crime figures. The politics of crime would manage to insert the ghost of Willie Horton into every election, so that the convicted rapist released under a furlough program in Governor Michael Dukakis' Massachussetts only to attack again returns to haunt anyone electioneering without "getting tough on crime." In response, sentences have become longer and harsher, and a sentence of natural life means just that.

Public perception seems to be that such a situation suits them just fine, that lawbreakers should be punished and punished severely, with sentences so long as to make others think twice before committing the same crime, and certainly long enough to ensure that the one sentenced won't be out on the streets commiting crimes again in his lifetime. And for some crimes and some criminals, that is appropriate.

But nowhere in this scenario is there room for the concept of rehabilitation, of change, and even worse, it leaves inmates with no reason for good behavior, nothing to strive toward. Couple the removal of that hope with Louisiana corrections' constant budgetary woes, overcrowding, staffing shortages and the state's penchant for interminable sentences, and life in prison becomes even more unbearable, especially since the first programs to be cut are recreational, social and educational.

Throw in a non-responsive administration like that of Louisiana's governor Buddy Roemer, whose clemency record is the worst in modern times and who became the state's first governor since 1892 not to grant clemency to anyone during the traditional largesse of the Christmas season, and what you have left is a prison population of some 5,000 desperate men at Angola without hope. Such a population is a time bomb waiting to explode.

That it eventually detonated surprised no one. That it exploded in the person of small quiet Corky Clifton was what did astound everyone, and no one more so than Corky himself. It would start in 1988, not long after Angola's warden Hilton Butler had been honored by his peers as the country's warden of the year, the career correctional officer being commended for restoring to the prison some semblance of order and an accompanying lack of escape attempts.

What newspapers would describe as "a rash of escapes, suicides and killings" began in April 1988. Eleven inmates escaped, ten of whom were quickly captured; there were four inmate stabbing deaths, plus an additional sixty-four non-fatal stabbings and cuttings; there were also four inmate suicides and dozens of attempts, all in a little over a year, a time period during which Governor Buddy Roemer pardoned a grand total of one lone Angola inmate, despite favorable recommendations from his own pardon board to grant clemency to hundreds of other inmates. Between 1978 and 1987 at Angola, a period of ten years, there were only seven inmate suicides; in the years 1988 and 1989 alone, there were nine.

State officials might blame drugs for the escalation of violence and self-destructive behavior at Angola, but prisoners blamed despair and desperation. "The real problem at Angola," said inmate Floyd Webb, "is nobody's getting out. When more inmates wake up and realize that, it's gonna blow up." Added *Angolite* associate editor Ron Wikberg, "It's the hope of release that generates faith in the system. When an inmate loses faith, you have a ticking time bomb." Responded Governor Roemer flatly, "I think that is an excuse."

The escapes during this trying period would include several attempts by trusties, inmates who Warden Butler explained rarely attempted to run unless they had given up and lost all hope. Said Butler, "I think the prison would be more manageable if the governor signed one or two pardons. Anytime a man gives up hope of getting out, there's gonna be trouble." That there was trouble is verified by violence statistics for 1989 and 1990, during which time there were nineteen escapes and attempted escapes, two hundred self-mutilations, over twelve hundred fights without weapons and nearly nine hundred fights involving weapons, thirty-four stabbings, thirty-three cuttings, four hundred thirty-two assaults on staff members, seven suicide deaths and four other violent deaths.

Cautioning that Angola was turning into an expensive "old folks' home" for an aging inmate population with lengthy sentences and increasingly costly medical needs, Butler told *The Angolite* editors in an interview, "Somewhere down the line, when a man shows that he's been rehabilitated, or just gotten too old for his continuation of crime, something needs to be done for him somewhere. I feel that everybody should be reviewed and given some type of hope. You're not telling him you're going to turn him loose this time or any other. There are no guarantees. But the man's record should be reviewed by a bonafide board that, when it makes a recommendation, something will be done about it...If you're going to keep him locked up until he dies, then all he's going to be looking forward to is seeing how much trouble he can cause. That's because he doesn't have any incentive to do it differently. Now, if he knows that people are going to be watching his record and maybe, somewhere down the road, making a recommendation for a commutation of his sentence, then he's going to try to improve himself and try to do better."

One of the escapees who made his way off the 18,000 isolated acres of state penitentiary property during this period would be captured near St. Francisville after a very scary shootout with West Feliciana Parish sheriff Bill Daniel in the parking lot of the local high school, a situation which could have involved nearly a thousand students had it not occurred on a designated teacher in-service work day when only faculty members were present. Another of the escapees would be shot by guards at Camp A's Farmline 21 when he simply turned his back on officers, said he was tired and was going home, and walked away, drawing a volley of shots from correctional officers checking the farmhands out for work, including one guard on horseback brandishing two revolvers.

There's often a fine line in prison between an escape attempt and a suicide attempt, and this inmate was not unaware that one of the surest ways of crossing that line has to be ignoring a direct command and walking away from armed officers. His determination must have been just as strong as that of the state penitentiary's very first suicide in 1906, fifty-year-old Elphare Navarre of Iberville Parish, who at five feet, six inches tall was so distraught over charges of incest with his daughter that he hung himself from a four-foot-high iron window grating with a rope made of twisted strips of sheeting from his bed, drawing up his feet to keep them from touching the floor. "Melancholia" was listed as the official cause of Navarre's death by suicide.

Another of the inmate suicides was an obvious mental case whose refrigerator had been found packed with neatly wrapped human remains, presumably his missing roommate, while yet another was a twenty-six-year-old black inmate who had only seven months left to serve on a sentence for simple robbery when he reportedly attempted to summon guards to his Camp J cell throughout one morning to no avail, then was found hanging from his cell bars in mid-afternoon. Strangely, when his body reached his hometown funeral home, it would be said by the embalmer to have not only a broken neck but also a broken back and a deep fresh knife cut on the right leg. None of these injuries had been mentioned by West Feliciana's coroner, who at the time was an insurance agent filling the job in the absence of any professional medical applicants willing to qualify for election, nor had they been identified in the autopsy performed by pathologists at Earl K. Long Hospital in Baton Rouge. The parish coroner, who would soon resign his office in the face of criticism, reportedly told *The Times-Picayune*, "When you're dealing with convicts and colored folks, they're always wanting to make something of nothing."

And another of the escapees would be little Corky Clifton, who, despairing of ever gaining release, simply walked away from the dog pens and disappeared into the rugged Tunica Hills wilderness area surrounding the prison at Angola. He had served twenty-seven years in prison and felt he could serve no more. In deteriorating health though barely middle-aged, Corky Clifton had a horror of dying and being buried at Angola. Said he after his escape, "I realized I had a lot to lose. To think you're gonna die here; it just gets to you. It gets to working on your mind."

Says Bobby Oliveaux, "You get to know the inmates up here at the dog pens a lot better than in other areas of the prison; they have a lot of trust put in them here. Corky never did get any mail from his family the whole time he was here, and I could tell when something wasn't right with him or any of them. Usually he got up early every morning and would be out working, but sometimes he would get so down. The day before Corky run off, he was just happy as a lark and he had on a new pair of blue jeans that were really too big for him, he had on a long-sleeved shirt which was very unusual for him, and he had on a pair of combat boots two or three sizes too big for him that one of the other boys had given him. And he wanted to talk, but we had a canine seminar going on and were real busy. I could tell he wanted to talk; he walked up just as happy as a lark, smiling. And that told me. I knew, when I found out he was gone. He was wanting me to comment on him someway, just like one of these dogs, looking for a little praise and petting. He was wanting to show that he could run off."

Continues Oliveaux, "Right up to the time that he escaped from here, he would come up to me at different times and ask me, 'You reckon I could make it up to the top of that hill?' I said, 'You might make it up that one, but we'd probably find you dead of a heart attack on the next one.'"

Clifton in April watched a segment of ABC television's popular nighttime show *20/20* featuring Angola inmate Wilbert Rideau, self-educated, highly articulate spokesman for prison reform and longtime editor of the prison's award-winning newsmagazine, *The Angolite*. Called one of the most rehabilitated men in America even by the ex-governor whose political maneuverings were at least part of the reason he was still in Angola, Rideau had spent nearly thirty years incarcerated on a murder charge, garnering national outside recognition for his writings and exerting considerable quiet influence in defusing volatile situations inside.

When Governor Roemer told the national television audience of *20/20* that he didn't feel Rideau yet deserved freedom, that he had not yet done enough to earn it, a collective sigh of disbelieving disappointment echoed through the cellblocks and dormitories at Angola. If Wilbert Rideau in thirty years of gaining a national reputation and support from around the world had not done enough to earn clemency and a chance at release, who had? Who would *ever* be able to? The obvious answer, according to Roemer, was no one.

Corky Clifton was watching that television show, and that's what precipitated his decision to leave. Within two days he would pocket some cigarettes and five moon pies, and run from the Angola dog pens into the foreboding Tunica Hills, a thick tangle of nearly impenetrable underbrush punctuated by steep hills and deep hollows. For five interminable days Clifton fought and clawed his way through the deep dark woods of Wilkinson County, Mississippi, just to the north of Angola across the state line, eluding pursuing bloodhounds who were often so close he could have reached out and touched them.

Says Bobby Oliveaux, who would participate off and on in the search for Clifton, "When Corky left he stayed gone a week, and we were running him, and the dogs would find places where he had fallen down cliffs that I never did think he'd come out, and then he'd go straight up a small mountain. We lost his trail one time, and I told the boys on the chase team he had a bad habit of smoking and I was sure he had carried plenty of cigarettes with him. I said, 'When you find a cigarette butt so short that he will have burned his fingers, that'll be his cigarette butt,' and it was. We found it and that got us on the right track again."

Clifton had known he had little chance of making good his escape before he ever left prison grounds. "On the night of April 15th, when I finally made up my mind to escape," he said, "I knew the odds were against me. I was fifty-two years old and had already suffered two heart attacks. In those final few days before April 15th, I fought many emotional battles with myself. I had a lot to lose and I'd be letting down a lot of good people who'd put their trust in me. But desperation is pretty hard to win a rational argument from. My time was running out. Had run out, really, because I was certainly in no condition to run through that jungle in the Tunica Hills. But even against all odds, I went for it anyway."

Asked by his fiancee later to explain the reasons behind his hopeless escape attempt, Corky would write, "You ask did I plan my escape. Actually, I hadn't thought about being free in a long time. I had a nice little house and I kept myself busy. I had a great boss, Bobby (Oliveaux), who I also considered my friend. Then out of a sound sleep, it was as if something would pull me awake, and I'd lay there, remembering home and my children. Of course they were real little when I saw them last, and then too, my daughter was born when I was in jail, so I never saw her. *20/20* done a show on our editor of our prison magazine, and old Roemer let the prisoners know what they were going to get at Angola. He isn't a soft person at all. Prisoners are going to die here. They put you here with a life sentence, and that is exactly what they mean.

"Anyway, I decided I was not going to die, I was going to be free. Anything would be preferable than waiting just to die. I've had two heart attacks. I don't think my heart is all that bad; I think it is just all the stress that I have had to live under. You forget that I remember how to get along in the woods very well. Remember our woods at home? I don't need a lot of food and I know how to survive. But the Tunica Hills, let me tell you, they should be renamed, as it is the jungle. Several times the chase team came so close they could have reached out and grabbed me. Other times I was able to get in behind them. Dogs aren't as smart as man, you know. They might be good, but they aren't as smart as we are. Each day, I got a little weaker."

Sleeping on the ground, with no food and little water, dehydrated and steadily weakening, Corky had planned to steal some means of transportation and leave the area, but found he no longer had the stomach for violence. Near Woodville, Mississippi, not far from the firetower on the Pinckneyville Road, he sat in the bushes near a house trailer, watching the female occupant arrive, unlock the door, go in alone, then come outside and wash her car, easy prey. Said Corky, "I had hoped to steal someone's car or maybe knock someone in the head and get enough money to get myself a ticket, hopefully far enough away from there. When the opportunity presented itself, I got a rude awakening. I couldn't knock anyone in the head, and I couldn't kill anything. In prison there isn't a certain point when you realize you have been rehabilitated. When it hit me I couldn't do the things I'd planned, I really did wish I was dead."

So Corky Clifton, weak from hunger and exertion and poor health, made his way to the road and flagged down the warden's son, surrendering. "I discovered that in reality I could no longer commit the crimes that I once did," he said. "So here I stood in those bushes, watching that house trailer—that car—and that lady—my ticket to freedom—and discover I can't pay the price. I can't think of any words that could truly describe the dejection and hopelessness I felt at that moment. There was no way I could continue on as I had those five days past. There was just no strength left in my legs to go on."

The spirit was willing and the thirst for freedom unquenched, but the flesh was weak and the price too high if it meant resorting to violence. He would later write, "If I get the chance, which I doubt seriously now I ever will, would I ever try again? I will never quit trying to be free of this prison. This isn't a country club, noways near even. To someone who has never been in prison, I realize it is hard to relate to what I tell you. You could never in your wildest imagination begin to understand what we as prisoners have to contend with."

He would continue, referring to earlier bids for release, "Years ago, I came so very close to getting out, but my judge who sentenced me, who has since retired, put up a lot of opposition. In this state, it's who you know that gets you your freedom, and of course, money definitely talks. Over the years I've been here, I've known of many who left who should never have got out. They done far worse than me, yet they were given their freedom. And yet there are so many of us who are here who truly deserve another chance, yet we are still here. It all boils down to who you know and how much money you or your family can come up with. Of course the officials deny it. Louisiana law is the worst of all the states, yet it is so poor. They can always find money to build prisons, though."

He continued, "We have one thing here that gives some prisoners hope, a little bit of hope. It's called the medical release. See, if you catch AIDS or develop a medical problem that is going to kill you anyway in a very short time, sometimes they'll let you out. But first you have to be really staring death in the face. More than one doctor has to agree you're dying. Can you imagine to be given freedom, yet they'll tell you first, 'You're going to die in a few months, so you can go.' Well, I hope that don't happen to me."

Said Warden Butler, who called the escape of men like Clifton highly unusual, "He was a trusty, living in one of the best places you could live in prison and had the best job here. I talked to him, asked him why. He said that he just gave up hope. He told me there was no way he could ever get out of the penitentiary the way things were, that he would just die here. So he ran off."

Bobby Oliveaux grew up on Angola, going out after escapees when he was as young as fifteen; he's grown up with inmates and can read most of them like a book, invaluable hard-won insights for the head of the chase team. He visited Corky in the cellblock after his return to the prison, saw that he received his art supplies and books, and says, "He always told me he didn't want to die in the penitentiary. It wasn't like he was going to run off and go somewhere and be free. He realized he was going to be caught. I'll tell you one thing, if I was in the penitentiary and I had a life sentence or any long amount of time, I would run. I don't ever blame any inmate for escaping; I don't ever get mad unless they break in or harm somebody. It's not my place to get angry at them, but I go and do my job, what's got to be done. But there are inmates right here that don't need to be in the penitentiary, that could go out and have a productive life and be with their people. I think some might need some guidance when they got out, but they could make a good living for themselves and they realize what they've done. I've been here all my life, and I could show you ones that could go home and you never would hear nothing out of them. After awhile, all Angola's gonna be is an old folks' home."

Clifton would write to *The Angolite* after his surrender, "For twenty-seven years I have submitted to discipline, the rules, the harsh conditions, the torment of my children growing from babies into men, without ever seeing them. I've never had a visit from any of my family during these twenty-seven years...I once thought, as most people do, that all you had to do in order to get out of prison was just be good and they'll let you out some day. One does not have to be in the prison system very long to learn what a joke that is. If Jesus Christ himself was in here with a life sentence, he couldn't get out unless he had money to put in the right places."

Within three months, in June 1989, Corky Clifton's escape would help precipitate an angry U.S. district judge Frank Polozola's declaration of a state of emergency at Angola, the appointment of former iron-fisted Angola warden (1976-1977 and 1981-84) Ross Maggio as a court expert on prisons to investigate security and administrative problems at the prison, an investigation by the U.S. Attorney and U.S. Justice Department into possible civil and criminal wrongdoings there, and the ensuing replacement of forty-year veteran Hilton Butler as warden. An "Angola Strike Force" of state police investigators would be sent in, eventually uncovering evidence of drug dealing and various other criminal activities within the prison, including a massive and far-reaching multi-million-dollar inmate scam operation which bilked unsuspecting homosexuals answering ads in gay magazines. Several former prison officials were charged with an assortment of criminal actions, including an associate warden indicted for malfeasance and the related indictment of the prison food manager for smuggling marijuana.

Louisiana generally has somewhere around 13,000 prisoners incarcerated throughout the state, the highest number per capita of nearly any other state in the country and growing every day. The sheer numbers so clogged the system that it would not be long before Maggio's duties would be expanded to include the inspection not only of Angola, but of all other crowded state prisons, as well as the parish and local jails across Louisiana where many overflow state prisoners are temporarily housed, a move hardly welcomed by the state's powerful sheriffs.

Maggio's detailed reports would provide updated information for Judge Polozola, who was at the time charged with overseeing population limits and living conditions in Louisiana's correctional facilities under a federal consent decree that stemmed from a 1971 prison lawsuit. It was an Angola inmate, Hayes Williams, who with a few other prisoners filed the original suit against the state complaining of undeniably poor conditions in the prison, though the suit would eventually be given class-action status, making every prisoner in state custody a plaintiff. In June of 1975, U.S. district judge E. Gordon West, since retired, ordered sweeping improvements in the state prison system, an order welcomed by struggling Angola administrators and the governor since it would mandate making desperately needed funding available to implement reforms, and Polozola would follow his lead in vigorously enforcing consent decrees entered into by state prisons and parish jails limiting inmate populations.

In 1989, when Polozola by court decree declared the state of emergency at Angola, Governor Roemer's secretary of the Department of Corrections admitted to the judge that he did not feel the state could correct its extensive prison problems without federal court intervention. By the end of January 1991, however, state officials were asking the judge to lift his emergency declaration, citing efforts under new Angola warden John Whitley to comply with court-ordered reforms in the areas of increased security, improved mental health treatment and suicide prevention for inmates, and enhanced employee morale. After twenty months and a massive infusion of state funds into the corrections system, U.S. district judge Frank Polozola lifted the state of emergency at Angola on February 21, 1991.

Before resigning under pressure, then withdrawing the resignation and being fired, Warden Hilton Butler insisted he was being made a scapegoat and held responsible for problems beyond his control. He said a court-appointed prison expert wasn't what was needed at the prison; instead, he said, Angola, where the remote and isolated location has always made it difficult to attract qualified staff, needed more guards and a bigger budget to offer better pay for them.

Added a fuming Butler, a veteran security officer who worked his way up through the ranks in a lifetime career in corrections at Angola, "Well, I forgot more about prison life than Maggio will ever know, but the judge is doing everything Maggio tells him to. You learn about prisoners in cells down in the ranks. The administrative angle is fine, but I mean learning about a prisoner in the cells, getting close to him and knowing what he's gonna do, when he's gonna do it, this kind of stuff you learn down the ranks. And Maggio has never been an officer, he's never been nothing but a warden." Besides, Butler commented, there had only been three murders at Angola the year the state of emergency was declared, and "there were three murders in one night under Maggio. When everything is dug out, you'll find out my record is better than the man who's investigating me."

He would appeal his dismissal to the civil service commission and in state courts. The dismissal would be based on the following allegations: failure to report prison escapes to the parish district attorney; failure to maintain shakedown equipment; failure to conduct searches of visitors and employees; using an electric generator assigned to Camp A for personal use; raising gamecocks on prison grounds; allowing unqualified inmates to visit at the prison picnic park; failure to train and certify employees in the use of firearms. There would also be complaints of hiring practices discriminatory against minorities and women. Butler argued that he had no control over the manpower or equipment shortages nor the effects of budget reductions of more than $7 million dollars in a two-year period. When his top two security wardens were also demoted, they too yelled politics, calling the action an extension of Butler's firing caused by their loyalty to him, and they would eventually be re-instated.

While the storm of controversy raged around Angola, Corky Clifton had been returned to the cellblocks as discipline for his escape attempt. But besides its impact on state corrections and the federal courts, and the undeniable effect of speeding the deterioration of his declining health, Corky Clifton's escape would have other far-reaching consequences, at least one of which would be beneficial. The escape, oddly enough, would also serve to introduce him to a fellow Ohioan by the name of Betty Lung, a felicitous meeting Corky described as destined by fate to bring into his lonely life the only unconditional and fully reciprocated love he had ever known.

Betty Lung first heard of Corky when an article covering his escape attempt ran in the little newspaper in her hometown in Ohio, where Clifton had lived as a little boy. "I'm just not the pen pal type, I never have been," she would attempt to explain. "I'm a people person. But there was just something about the article. It was headlined, "Destined to Die at Angola." There was just something about it, he was just so down and out, that I thought, 'Well, he's many hundreds of miles away, no way that he's gonna come knocking on this door, so I think I'm gonna write him.'"

After writing and then discarding the letter time and again, Lung finally went ahead and mailed it, thinking that would be the last of it, expecting no reply. "It was probably about a week," she says, "and here come a great big letter. He said my letter caught his eye, naturally, because it was from the town he was born in. He said if I didn't believe him, to go get his birth certificate, and he told me what I needed to know, his mother's and father's names. And I did, and sure enough. I thought, 'Well, that's something for this dinky little town; we have nothing in our town but a filling station and a pizza parlor and a post office and a grocery store.'"

A correspondence began. "He started to tell me things he liked to do," Betty says, "and I thought it was unusual, because it was my own interests. I started to write him, and then the letters started flying back and forth, really, really long letters. Before Corky had ever went to Angola, it was just truly a miracle that we had never met. We should have; we had lived so close around."

Continues Lung, "I had written and asked if there was anything I could do, since he had said he had nothing, what cigarettes he got he had to borrow from friends. The letter that come back, I was very shocked over it, because he said, 'You do not mention whether you have a husband or not.' I had forgot that I had not told him that I was a widow. So he said, 'How does your husband feel about your writing to me?' And he said, 'You ask could you do anything for me, but if you have children and you work, you probably can't do very much, so what I would like more than anything, even though I need so much, I would rather have your friendship and you write me. It feels wonderful to know that there is someone at home who is taking a little time with me.' Well, when I wrote Corky back that I had been a widow since I was thirty-two years old, the letters were just a little bit warmer."

Lung began trying to send a few necessities to Corky, as he had no one to help him, his family having severed all ties. She continues, "Corky would call at first once a week, always apologizing, saying he knew it was the man who was supposed to take care of the woman. It always made me feel so terrible that anyone could be so grateful for just a pair of levis or something. We don't really think about it when we go to the store and shop, we just get whatever we want if we've got the money."

She also began delving into the heartbreaking circumstances of his early life. "I happened to be working at a convalescent home where Corky's aunt was," she says. "He was so shocked after he told me her name and asked would I maybe know her, if she was still living. She is one hundred years old and her mind is still very good, so I asked her about Corky's early days and she just cried. She said, 'Oh, honey, he's been gone so long, they told me he had done something so bad and I was just to consider him dead'...She said, 'You tell him his Aunt Sally has never forgotten him.'

"I had asked why, out of all of his mother's children, Corky was the one just plain thrown away into the system. And she said his mother before she remarried just lay drunk, that she loved Corky but she had a lot of men around and the welfare didn't think she was fit. She said they would place Corky in the same county usually, but he would always take off, go into his foster mother's purse, like when he was a little boy he had never been taught right from wrong. I could not get over in letters when he would talk about how much he loved his mother. It was very plain for me to see that she simply did not want him, for whatever reason.

"I asked Sally about Corky's grandparents, who had his full brother and sister, and she said, 'Honey, Corky would try to see his brother and sister, and they would actually run him away, they wanted nothing to do with him.' She said, 'I tried to get him myself, but they would not let me have him because I was a relative.' She said he was just pushed aside by everyone. She said he was very small for his age and even as a little boy was already drawing pictures. When Corky's mother married for the second time she had children by her husband, the one Corky thought so much of, yet she still never had room for Corky. He was a person who was just starved for love, really. I always wondered that his own family could treat him like that as a small child. Sally said, 'Oh, honey, he just had it so rough, the homes that they put him in, a lot of times they would beat him for stuff and Corky would take off.' She said a few times she would give him money for shoes, clothes."

Learning that Corky had never had a visitor at Angola, Lung determined to make the difficult trip to see him in Louisiana. He hardly knew how to tell her how to recognize him in the visiting room for the first time, explaining that prison cells had no mirrors, only a bit of reflective stainless steel. "I'll have to ask someone if I'm goodlooking," he would write her, "since prisoners don't go around complimenting each other."

Says Betty, "He had sent me one picture of himself when he won second place for watercolor at the art show, and I was very surprised that he was so blond. He had told me on describing himself that he thought he had green eyes and that he was blond but that he had some gray coming in. I thought he would really look like the picture. In my mind, I had this picture of him, like the picture he'd sent me." Friends driving her to the prison for the first visit had to warn her that ill health had taken its toll on Corky's appearance, that he was very fragile in spite of his relatively young age, even though he was only five years older than forty-seven-year-old Betty.

He had already proposed, the steady stream of letters binding the two closer and closer with each exchange. "You have no idea the happiness you have brought into my life," he would write her, "and the dreams I dream now of you. I am only a prisoner and have nothing to offer you, but all the love I held in my heart all these long years. I want you for my wife. I want so badly to have a woman love me, and maybe someday, if the Almighty will let it happen, I will be free.

"I realize I am asking you for an awful lot, but would you really consider me as a husband, even before you actually see me in the flesh? You can have all the time you want to make up your mind, and I know there are many things against me. I may never get out of here and you will have to still support yourself in addition to what you send me. You have no idea how much I appreciate all the things you do for me, and all I can do is send you pictures that I am drawing with a pencil. If I'm lucky you can get a pen and ink from me. Someday I hope to give you anything your heart desires. One advantage you would have in marrying me is you would always know where I was and also you wouldn't have to worry about whether I was with another woman.

"I hold my breath until you give me an answer to this letter. It never ceases to amaze me that even before I ended up at Angola, our paths kept crossing over the years, yet we didn't meet. Yet as you say, in small one-horse towns most everyone knows everybody. I find it so odd that you know my Aunt Sally. This was fate that led us to each other many years into our lives and hundreds and hundreds of miles apart. When I saw the postmark on your first letter, my hands actually shook. I hope you aren't too disappointed when you see me in person."

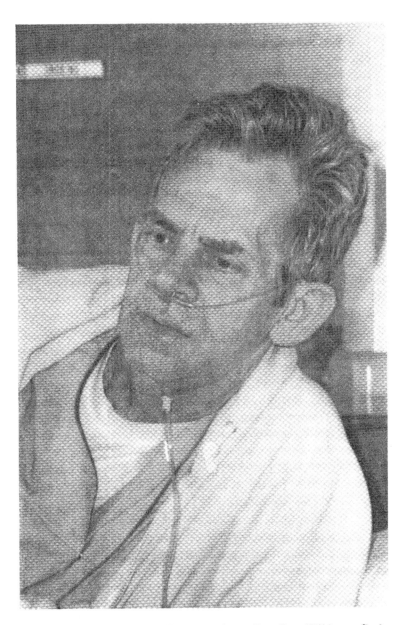

Photographed by *The Angolite*'s associate editor Ron Wikberg, Corky Clifton, on oxygen just before his death in 1990, not much more than a year after his escape, shows the ravages of time and existence at Louisiana State Penitentiary. Photo courtesy of Ron Wikberg.

Already a nervous wreck entering the sterile prison visiting room, the first time she'd ever been in such a facility, Betty Lung looked up and saw a very delicate looking man standing there. She waved and he hurried toward her table, asking how she knew him. She said, "Well, you looked just like your picture." But of course he didn't, she says now. He was nervous and shaking, perfumed by newly purchased aftershave mixed with powder, and when she hugged him, he burst into tears, explaining, "Oh, I was just so afraid you weren't going to like me. Do I look all right? I had my hair cut and shampooed twice, and I've been awake all night long. I thought the plane would crash." He had no self-confidence whatsoever, Betty says. Asked why he wouldn't take off his jacket in the hot crowded room, he told her, "I don't want you to see my skinny arms. I'm going to try to start building up my muscles."

"All of a sudden," Betty recalls, "he leaned over. He was going to kiss me, but he got my nose. I just laughed. He said, 'Well, I'm out of practice. I'll try to do better.' And at that time, I thought Corky looked really sick. But he said, 'You're not disappointed? Are you going to marry me?' And I said, 'Yes, yes.' And he said, 'Anytime that you change your mind, I will understand.' And I wanted to cry. Every time I would touch his hand, he would just shake. I've never had that effect on anybody. There was not any reserve, even that first time. It was like I had always known him, and he said I would not believe the change I had made in his life. He said it must have been a higher being that brought us together, and it appeared to be that way even to me."

When she looked around the visiting room and saw the many inmates closer in age to her sons than to her, Betty Lung says she wanted to cry. Corky told her, "Most everybody you see here in this room, they're gonna be here probably forever, 'cause hardly any of us ever get out. But if you got someone behind you, there are people that occasionally get out. And when Roemer goes out of office, even if (former three-term governor Edwin) Edwards doesn't come back in, no governor could be as bad as Roemer, so there'll be some of us coming out." He said to her, "There'll be a lot of things that you can do to help me now to try to really get out. I don't think I can stand it much more. But if you marry me, I want you to know that there is a strong possibility that I will be here until I die. Can you handle that?"

Betty replied that she could. And Corky added, "The thing that I fear the most, I know death comes to all of us at some point, but should I go first, I don't want to be buried here." Betty told him she had burial space in the Ohio town where his mother had been born, and that she would be buried there next to a deceased baby; her husband was also buried there. And he said, "If I go, can you put me on the other side? I want to make sure that I lay next to you. Would you promise me, because I do have nightmares of being buried in our cemetery." Betty asked him, "'Why, Corky? Because when you die, you go to live in another world, if you believe your religious faith.' I said that over the years, I had called on God so many times and He had never really let me down. And he said, 'Well, I believe that too, but you see, when Judgment Day comes, I don't want to come up out of the ground and still be in prison.' And I said, 'Ok, you've got it.'"

Corky's birthday was in May. Did she think, he asked Betty, they could be married by then? She made plans to at least visit again by then, purchasing a plane ticket from Ohio in advance. He mentioned after she returned home that he had been in the hospital and had had trouble breathing, saying that while he was confined in the cellblocks he would have smothered had it not been for the consideration of certain guards who put a fan close to his stuffy cell.

When Betty returned to Angola in May, his appearance shocked her greatly. "It had only been two months, but Corky was even thinner than he had been. I asked him how much he weighed, and he said he thought 117 pounds. He said the food didn't agree with him, but he didn't mean to be a crybaby. He was very short of breath."

The kindly Angola chaplain guiding Betty through the red tape attached to any request of marriage to an inmate had explained to her that the administration was not much in favor of allowing their wedding, but Betty persevered. She says, "I can see why they frown on young inmates being married. When you're very young, you don't know what is really ahead of you, or the people you're going to meet as you mature. In Corky's and my case, I felt we both were middle aged, and we did know our own minds. It was very hard for me to believe I had fallen in love with Corky, him being a prisoner. This was just not my way, nothing that I had thought would happen."

She knew what she wanted to do, though, and she also knew that time was limited. Says Betty, "Corky had called one night after I got home and he burst into tears, and said, 'You're gonna have to move out here.' And I said, 'What?' And he said, 'You're going to have to move out here. I can't stand it in prison much longer. And if you move out here and we get married right away, I'm pretty sure you can get me out.' And I said, 'I thought you told me your heart wasn't that bad.' And he said, 'Well, it is now. I'm over at the hospital again and they tell me I've got congestive heart failure.'"

Being in nursing, Betty knew what that meant. Her own husband had died of it at thirty-one, and she knew there was a possibility that Corky could die at any time. She began the moving process. "It was like something kept pushing me. Corky kept calling, and every time he would cry over the phone to me, 'I cannot stand it much more. You've got to do something.' I felt so helpless, because I didn't really understand how the prison system worked." By mid-July Betty had moved to a trailer park in Port Allen, across the Mississippi River from Baton Rouge, to be close to Corky.

It had only been two months since their last visit, but Corky had slipped noticeably downhill. "When the guard walked me back to the hospital and they wheeled Corky out," Betty recalls, "I just really could not believe he had gone down that fast. He could no longer walk more than a few steps. When he saw me, he asked me how he looked. I couldn't say anything. He said, 'Well, I probably look pretty bad.' And I told him he looked wonderful. I could see death, but I didn't think it was going to be that soon. I thought we would have a little time, I really did. I hoped so much. We had talked about when we married and when I got him out, the places we were going to. He wanted to look up his children, even if they slammed the door in his face. He still asked, 'You haven't changed your mind, have you?' Always he had this little doubt that if he said or did the wrong thing, I would quit caring for him. I tried to reassure him. He talked about his mother, and he got very tearful. And he was telling me how cold he was."

When their five-hour visit was over, Corky burst into tears. Betty told him, "Honey, please don't do that, you'll make yourself even sicker. And I'll be back in two weeks. And when I come the next time, we're going to be married." Corky replied, "You'd better hurry up. I know you've always told me to hang on, but it is so hard hanging on. I know I am very sick. I don't want to die in here. You've got to get me out, and it's got to be soon." Says Betty, "He just sobbed and he said he knew he was never going to see me again. And I tried to soothe him and said, 'Honey, don't talk that way, it upsets me.' And he said, 'I've just got this feeling I won't see you no more.'"

Said Betty, "The orderly came to push him away, and I gave him a kiss and told him to eat, because when we got married I wanted him to be standing, not in a wheelchair, even if I had to hold him up. When I went home, I was very upset, because I thought it would be soon; I knew he was dying, you could see it on him. But I prayed so hard that he would just hang on for a little while. One part of my mind knew that Corky would probably die soon, but I hoped with the other part that there would be a little time, a few memories. I felt so helpless. I really did not know what I could do. I had talked to the nurse that day when I first went in, and she had told me that Corky could go anytime, that it all depended on his will. She said that he was so very sick, and she said that it wouldn't take that long to get him out of there on a medical discharge. I was very hopeful for that."

On Tuesday, August 28, 1990, there was a knock on Betty's door. She had no telephone. When she saw the deputy sheriff and got the message to call the Angola chaplain, she says, "I knew that it had to be something terrible, or he would not have called me. The tears had already started by then. I just knew it." Betty called the chaplain and was gently given the news that Corky had died that morning at five o'clock in the prison hospital. "There was so much that went through my mind," she says, "so many 'If only's,' if we'd just had a little more time. We had both been married in our minds, we just wanted the piece of paper, and I never knew when our wedding date was to have been until I read it in the newspaper article about him the day after his death."

That same day, the day after Corky's death, Betty received a last letter from him, postmarked the day he died, joyously telling her that he had finally found a minister who had consented to marry them in the main prison chapel; they had previously been turned down by several. "The letter I got from Corky, he told me I had to come up soon, to hurry up before it was too late." The same day he wrote the letter, Corky was interviewed by Ron Wikberg, associate editor of *The Angolite,* and told Wikberg that he had finally found something to live for.

Says Betty, "I was so confused. When I was told he was dead, the first thing was that I had to get him back to Ohio. That was the promise I had to keep. It meant so much to him. It didn't matter how much it cost or anything."

More red tape followed, a multitude of phone calls to a funeral home in Ohio, and then the dreaded message that since the prison officials had not heard from the Ohio mortuary, they were planning to bury Corky at Point Lookout, the cemetery for unclaimed inmates at Angola, a grassy knoll at the foot of a hill punctuated by unadorned white crosses. Betty knew she had to stop that, for once he was buried, it would be impossible to have Corky moved. She made the long drive to Ohio in a state of shock, petrified of leaving Louisiana without Corky's body, and had the funeral home contact Angola again. The body was at Earl K. Long Hospital in Baton Rouge for the mandatory autopsy.

Corky would have been dead seven days before he arrived in Ohio, having been shipped in a flimsy container marked only with the name "Francis," no papers, no death certificate, the cardboard shipping box falling to pieces. Betty purchased a decent outfit for him to be buried in, then took the clothes to the funeral home.

"When I walked into the room and saw Corky dead for the first time, I suppose my mind was playing tricks on me. The funeral director had already told me that naturally, being a heart patient and being dead that long, there would be some swelling. But when I looked, my first thought was, 'Oh thank God, he's not dead. That's not him.' And I told the funeral director there had been a terrible mistake, that that was not Corky. And he said he'd never known Corky, though his mother had, but that body was the only one he was expecting from a funeral home from Louisiana. I just could not believe it. There was such heavy makeup on him, the only way I knew it was Corky was by his hair and his hands. He was probably about eighty pounds heavier than he had been."

The sons Corky had wanted so desperately to look up if he ever got out of prison would serve as pallbearers; his daughter would choose not to attend. Corky's sister and brother attended the funeral, as did the kindly elderly stepfather he had thought was dead. At the funeral, Betty says, "It was very hard for me to be civil. This was a family who had abandoned Corky. The children couldn't help it, naturally. They were very small when Corky went to prison, and they had no memory of him. They were his pallbearers. But his sister and his brother, I thought, 'You show up for his funeral, but you couldn't do nothing for him all those years, never a visit from anyone, nothing.' Sister and brother who never could find the time to write or visit over all those lonely years shed tears. Corky had believed his father and grandmother were dead, but in fact both were very much alive. Neither came to the funeral or sent flowers, though they had to have known about it."

Added Betty, "I decided not to be bitter or angry. I informed the entire gathering what Corky had told me concerning Angola. I told them he said, 'At least it made me a better man than when I entered.' How badly he wanted freedom to prove it."

He might have died there, unable to hang on any longer, but at least Corky Clifton was not buried at Angola. Betty visits his gravesite frequently and talks to him, secure in the belief that he hears. She even put up a Christmas tree for him during the holiday season, but says, "instead of feeling better, I felt worse for it."

"I miss him so much," she says, mentioning the constant flow of letters that had drawn them so close, some as long as thirty pages and not a few stained with heartfelt tears. "He is still very much alive in my heart. I go through his personal things real often, just touching and wishing with all of my heart. It makes me feel closer with him. Corky was like a book you can't stop reading."

It was on what she had thought would be her wedding day that she finally buried Corky Clifton in Ohio, some ten days after his death and a lot of miles from Angola. "My Corky is home now," Betty says, "and no fences, but what a long journey it was and what a terrible price he paid to reach freedom. "

2009 Update:

Bobby Oliveaux retired from Angola and ran unsuccessfully for parish sheriff.

VI

Conclusion:
The Warden Comments

If there's one thing I've learned in a lifetime career in corrections, it is that every criminal has a story which can teach us something, if we take the time to study it. The stories in this book are presented in a fascinating richness of detail just filled with clues from which we can learn a great deal. Of course when you are the victim of a violent crime, you or your loved ones, it is next to impossible to see the terrifying and tragic situation as a learning experience. But perhaps we give meaning to otherwise senseless deaths when we learn from them how to prevent recurrences, and who better to teach us how to halt the making of criminals than a flesh-and-blood offender. Let's look at each chapter and learn what we can.

The early seventies were a period of turmoil in Louisiana, as in many states, a period fraught with the conflict of opposing political ideas. During such a trying period, the problems wreaking havoc in the greater outside community inevitably seep into a prison, brought inside by public contact, the media, even some well-intentioned people desirous of bringing about needed reforms within the prison system without sufficient awareness of exactly what to change.

The murder of correctional officer Brent Miller came during such a period of turmoil, when some inmates at Angola insisted on thinking of themselves as political prisoners, although they had been convicted of crimes like rape, murder and armed robbery, hardly political actions. The tragedy of the death of young Miller, who was actually well liked and respected by prisoners and penitentiary staff members alike, was its complete uselessness. The position of correctional officer can be a very dangerous one requiring a great deal of courage and more than a little insight into inmate thought processes, as well as the ability to handle people while remaining alert and on guard at all times, particularly on the medium yard where there were some very dangerous people at the time. Brent Miller was a good officer from a fine family, and his killing was a deep shock to everyone at Angola.

Had we been adequately staffed, this whole tragedy might never have happened, though you can't ever completely stop unrest from seeping in from the outside. But opportunists will use almost any situation to advance themselves, even a tragic death, and this coupled with outside interests trying to involve themselves in internal prison affairs made this a situation which became nearly impossible to control.

This was a time between the gubernatorial administrations of John J. McKeithen, who had been an outstanding governor and very supportive of the administration at the Louisiana State Penitentiary, and Edwin W. Edwards, coming in for the first of four terms and already the kind of governor with the courage to be innovative and to try new approaches. We were at long last moving from a political spoils system toward professional leadership at Angola, employing staff on merit rather than the number of influential friends, but some members of the staff had not gotten the message and, considering themselves politicians of the first magnitude, were still vying for position with the new administration.

Looking back, I wonder how we got through this period without a full-scale riot, for Brent Miller's killing and its aftermath offer a prime and rather unsavory example of how politics can move in and complicate a situation, upsetting both staff and prisoners. Really what this chapter illustrates is how outside political forces can sometimes attempt to take advantage of a tragedy to promote their own political agenda. The administrative and security staff was split and official authority undermined, with one group getting encouragement from a local judge to look to him for leadership, the other group trying to do their jobs and hold the prison together.

Fortunately, it would be the latter group which eventually prevailed, but not until certain employees had used the incident to promote fear among employees and insinuate that the administration had little interest in their safety, although there was a training program going full blast that should have given the lie to this allegation. This was a highly dangerous trick to try, for any time there is dissension among administrative staff, it usually trickles down to the inmates and there is plenty of hell to pay. It's hard enough to operate a prison without having to fight on three fronts.

On top of the administrative changes and racial unrest inside, the tragic killing of an officer and a vaccum in the leadership in security resulted in a terrible period at Angola, and exploiting such a volative situation for personal advancement was unthinkable. We had no evidence to indicate that Gilbert Montegut had anything to do with the killing; quite the contrary. I think Montegut was deliberately inserted into the situation by Mr. Dees to embarrass Mr. Hoyle, and I've never been able to figure out why, because Hoyle supported Dees and did a lot to strengthen security. Maybe it was me, too, that he was trying to discredit, for certainly our philosophy of handling prisoners was different.

This first chapter includes several different types of deviant behavior, not all of which emanates from the so-called criminals. First we have the crime of murder, committed without justification or reason under the guise of racial retribution. Then we have the action of certain members of the administrative staff, who used the tragedy to try to advance their own political aims and in so doing very nearly caused a second murder of an outstanding prison administrator. And finally we have a judge who apparently wanted to discredit the top administration of the prison as well as the newly appointed secretary of the department of corrections, the first female to hold such a position and an appointment he had violently opposed. This sort of tragedy will happen whenever any system is politicized, and only through professional leadership, continual training and adequate financial support can it be avoided.

In the second chapter, we have Michael Burge, a classic example of someone rejected at home who spent years in institutions. It has traditionally proven extremely difficult to work with prisoners who are the products of childhood abuse, foster homes and the juvenile reformatories which today function merely as prep schools for the penitentiary. You can't isolate vulnerable children with the worst elements of society and expect them to come out the better for it; there must be some way for them to identify with positive adult figures, not take other criminals as role models.

Most experts agree that long-term institutionalization without professional help is disastrous and for the most part counterproductive, except perhaps for serial killers or those determined by psychiatric examination to be dangerous. In my opinion, had Michael Burge been given the professional help he so desperately needed as a child and teenager, he could have become a productive citizen instead of rotting away in a maximum-security institution. Mike is now forty years old, and I am not convinced that he could not adjust if released from lockdown, which in his case is a waste of human resources and further deteriorates an already damaged personality. In no way do I underestimate the seriousness of his offense, but prisoners deserve to have their cases reviewed periodically with a view toward allowing those capable of adjusting to be assigned to productive work inside the prison.

Robert Lee Willie of our third chapter was obviously of only borderline intelligence, though he was certainly streetwise. He never had a positive male figure to identify with, and as early as first grade was already assaulting young classmates in perhaps the only manner by which he had learned to settle differences. Here again, perhaps early intervention by well-qualified professionals could have headed him in a different direction. His father he hardly knew except by reputation, but even the father, though he too had killed, had never done so in cold blood or without provocation.

Though I think people are mainly shaped by their environment, certain sociopathic personalities seem to be lacking almost from birth the controlling influence of a conscience, and Robert Lee Willie never seemed to develop any warmth of feeling or respect for the sanctity of human life. He never expressed any remorse, regrets or misgivings about the road he had taken, and his final statements are very revealing, showing as they do his value system and what he considered important in life. He'd had it all, sex, dope, rock and roll, whiskey, he said, but there was nothing of any substance included in his list.

Having grown up myself in a family unconditionally opposed to capital punishment, I have had to wrestle with this problem all of my life, especially in light of my career in corrections. After a lifetime dealing with lawbreakers, I have come to the conclusion that there may be instances where the death penalty is justified, and perhaps it should be kept on the books, though I am convinced it should be used sparingly, only for those who have proven themselves incorrigible and beyond redemption.

I don't think capital punishment is a deterrent. It may assure that those who are executed will not commit additional crimes, but is of little value in controlling the actions of others. We Americans probably execute more criminals than any country in the world, and we just may have the highest crime rate in the world at the same time.

It is at the other end of this journey called life that we must concentrate our efforts at crime prevention. It's much more effective, not to mention cheaper in the long run, to intervene at an early age when a child first starts manifesting deviant behavior. Swift and certain intervention then can lead to behavior modification before patterns are learned and set, and in most cases will result in a change of direction. I have yet to see an adolescent who was not interested in something, anything that could give him a sense of achievement in accomplishing. This sense of achievement is the key ingredient which is so necessary for a person to feel good about any program and about himself, and the area of interest can easily be identified through proper testing, evaluation and counselling, accompanied by an appropriate adjustment in the curriculum to fill that child's particular needs. Examine these chapters with particular attention to the childhood of each person who eventually committed a crime, and ask where this early help and guidance was, and whether its presence might possibly have altered the course of history.

With the fourth chapter's Wayne Robert Felde, however, the environment didn't begin to press in on him until almost adulthood. In no way, of course, can the killing of a police officer in Shreveport or anywhere else be excused, but at the same time it is felt that the Veterans Administration bears a grave responsibility for not earlier recognizing and dealing with an illness now accepted in psychiatric circles as a legitimate and authentic mental disorder.   The Vietnam veteran is different from any other veteran. His service was not appreciated at the time by a large segment of the population; he was ridiculed, rejected and insulted. From the time of Caesar, conquering armies were welcomed home by cheering masses lining the roads leading to Rome, and this did much to give them the sense of approval and social acceptance so necessary for fighting men. When a soldier is welcomed back, this justifies his behavior. All wars have undeniably had their psychiatric casualties, but Vietnam was different, for to fight and kill in defense of one's country and then be rejected by a large segment of that country is bound to cause confusion, hostility and self-doubt, at the very least. At most, it creates a person who is a psychiatric casualty, one who without professional help can never work through his problems. The evidence would certainly indicate that Wayne Felde was such a casualty.

Had his trial been held today, when there is more understanding and acceptance of Post-traumatic Stress Disorder as a viable mental illness, the death penalty would almost surely not have been the result. Most likely he would have been institutionalized in a forensic hospital where he would have received longterm psychiatric help, which is all he was asking for in the first place. I would in no way downplay the grief of the family of the victim Officer Tompkins, but in this case Felde was also a victim, a victim of an unpopular war and a victim of government neglect and refusal to recognize a problem before there were hundreds and maybe even hundreds of thousands of casualties from PTSD.

The fifth chapter is a sad one. It has been my privilege to work for many governors in four different states and to be part of an occupation military government in Germany after World War II, yet I have never seen an administration with less concern or less social conscience than that of one-term governor Charles H. "Buddy" Roemer. His insensitivity extended not only to luckless longterm prisoners, but also to state employees, the poor, the handicapped and most unfortunate people, not to mention a disdain for the entire legislative process and the representatives of the very people of this state who voted him into office.

No one asked that he open the gates and let everyone out of prison. In Louisiana, understand, executive clemency is the only relief a prisoner can expect; the pardon board recommends, but it is the governor who must act upon that recommendation. There is not the flexibility in Louisiana as in other states, where boards of qualified professionals make decisions to release or retain after a reasonable length of time. What I can't understand is that this governor had a pardon board which he himself appointed and which appeared to have the confidence of the state bar association, all honorable and experienced people for whom I have a great deal of respect, but evidently he didn't share the same respect or he would have followed at least some of their recommendations.

In his own 1990 corrections plan, touted as "a balanced comprehensive approach to corrections," this very same governor proposed to provide the pardon board with several professional staff positions to review and make recommendations on cases, enhancing the board's efficiency and effectiveness with the stated objective of increasing "reintegration of offenders into society in a manner consistent with public safety" and to "ensure the expeditious hearing and objective determination of pardon cases." The same objectives were given for the proposal to increase coordination between pardon and parole boards by means of "executive action" in order to increase "outflow of existing inmate population." But it wasn't the *boards* whose actions needed to be expedited; it was the governor's.

Christmas in criminal justice systems everywhere is traditionally a time when some pardons are granted, a forgiving of sins in joyous reaffirmation of the deepest meanings of Christianity. To show a little mercy to deserving people during the holiday season gives hope to those who are left in prison and rewards those who are released. This age-old tradition is also a common-sense practice which doesn't require a genius to understand, and it's a heartless soul lacking in compassion who can remain unmoved by this season of hope and charity. And yet several Christmases came and went with no gesture of good will or mercy from Governor Roemer, which escaped no one at Angola.

Corky Clifton was a dying man, yet this feeble soul who had suffered two heart attacks and had nightmares about being buried at Angola preferred his chances tackling the wild Tunica Hills rather than trusting in the governor's mercy to let him die somewhere other than prison. I have never worked for a governor who would not have acted charitably on such a case. There are literally hundreds of such cases in Angola . . . old people, sick people and, yes, people who have been rehabilitated . . . who could be released without endangering the public. The evidence is that Corky Clifton was not only terminally ill, but so thoroughly rehabilitated that when he had a chance to steal a car and make good his escape, he couldn't go through with it because his whole value system had so drastically changed.

It doesn't take a lot of imagination to keep building more prisons and shelling out more hard-earned taxpayer dollars to operate them. It *would* take a little gray matter, however, though not much, to come up with some alternatives to incarceration and to revise the criminal code in this state to bring it in line with those of other civilized societies. What we've been doing hasn't worked. Isn't it time we found the wisdom and the courage to try something new?

It is difficult to understand what's happening in our criminal justice system in this country. Statistics show that crime is pretty well static per capita, rising primarily with the population count, yet the prison populations continue to escalate, at least partly because stiffer sentences lessen the turnover and keep inmates incarcerated long after any useful purpose has been served. All criminologists agree that it's not the length of sentence but the certainty of punishment that serves as a deterrent to crime. However, the prison population in this country has more than doubled in the last ten years, reaching an unprecedented figure of over one million inmates incarcerated in our jails and penitentiaries.

Andrew Rutherford, veteran of Great Britain's prison system and law professor at the University of Southampton, has commented on the doubling of America's inmate population in the 1980's while the crime rate here has certainly not dropped, as compared with European prison systems where prison populations have been decreasing with no discernible increase in criminality. What he explains has happened in European countries, even under highly conservative governments, is that prosecutors and courts have come to see imprisonment as less a solution than a part of the problem. Because imprisonment almost routinely makes offenders worse, he says, the best way to reduce criminality may be to keep them out of the criminal-justice system whenever possible. This is done by using for carefully selected lawbreakers certain alternative punishments like fines, victim restitution, community service, therapy, drug treatment. As one commentator assessed this situation recently, "It isn't so much that they believe alternative treatment will make criminals better (though preliminary evidence suggests it might) as their certainty that incarceration will make them worse."

So our favored solution is in reality part of the problem, and we would do well to look to other countries for inspiration on how to improve the situation. I think one difference between the system of justice in most parts of Europe and that in America, where you've got fifty different systems in fifty different states, is that overseas the systems are highly professionalized, with well-trained and highly qualified prosecutors and judges left relatively free to handle offenders as they see fit, without being bogged down by stiff sentences for minor offenses mandated by the legislative branch of government.

Sometimes I feel I sound like a broken record, pointing out the same problems year after year. But the same problems exist; they *persist*. Not long ago, I read a speech given in 1871 at the American Prison Association's annual meeting in Cincinnati. That same speech could be made today with hardly a sentence changed, except that things seem to have gotten steadily worse. It always sounds good to the public when politicans say they're going to get the criminals off the street. I don't know of anyone who's been able to do it, but the public still buys this worn-out record without challenging lawmakers and legislators to come up with the new ideas and new approaches required to handle a problem worsening year by year.

I have always felt that the criminal justice system in this country would not change because of high ideals, nor because the public wanted to do something just because it happened to be right, but rather when it became such a heavy financial burden that taxpayers will rise up in revolt and insist that there must be a more intelligent way of handling the problem. We can't be far from that breaking point now. The average cost of incarcerating a juvenile in America is $29,600 a year, and much higher than average in some areas, $42,600 in Washington, D.C., and $55,300 in New York City. Compare this with the estimated annual cost for room, board and tuition at Harvard University, just over $18,000. After comparing costs, compare results.

Surely there are more innovative ways of handling the crime problem than locking young lawbreakers up and throwing away the key. We need to experiment. Why not put up seed money for a hundred different experimental juvenile programs and see which one gets results, as is being tried in the educational system? We're always preaching competition, so why not establish some competition in this area to see which programs can most effectively deter crime and facilitate the youthful offender's adjustment as a productive citizen.

And as we learn from the educational system, we must work hand in hand with it. We must join with pre-school and elementary programs to give some attention to those youngsters beginning to exhibit problems, and give it early enough to make a difference, for early intervention is extremely important; it is difficult to change behavior patterns once set. Remember the apt old adage, *as the twig is bent, the tree will grow.* A comprehensive approach is needed, for it is not possible to attack the child's problem without working with the family, too, to prevent confusing conflicting signals. Our schools certainly can't be a cure-all or make up for all the deficiencies in the home, but with adequate professional staff they can make a difference for at-risk students and their families. Educators are beginning to see the need for almost lifelong intervention, training teens and adults in parenting skills while at the same time drawing at-risk children into the system as early as infancy in some cases, while there is time to combat the inequities life invariably hands out and remediate sufficiently to get everyone to the starting gate of pre-K or kindergarten functioning at roughly the same level. Equal opportunity, and where possible, no unfair handicaps.

In passing, it should be noted that the Louisiana corrections system has been under court order since 1971, the state first *unwilling* to provide the funding and support to allow professionals to handle its own problems and then later perhaps *incapable* of doing so regardless of budgets, yet not once have the court-appointed experts or the judiciary given birth to any idea other than building bigger and more prisons.

I consider myself no do-gooder in any sense of the word, yet I do consider myself a practical and reasonable individual who resents paying taxes to build bigger and better prisons to warehouse more and more prisoners unnecessarily, while other social needs of our communities are neglected to pay for them. This makes absolutely no sense. Somehow, some day, there has to be a new approach, though unfortunately I see nothing suggestive of change forthcoming in the near future. Eventually the whole system will fall under the sheer weight of the economic burden it poses for the taxpayers of this state, and at that point reform will come based on economics, if no other reason.

C. Murray Henderson
St. Francisville, Louisiana
October 1991

2009 Update:

Former Angola warden C. Murray Henderson would himself die in prison for the 1997 attempted murder of his estranged wife and co-author; she miraculously survived 5 bullets fired at point-blank range and lived to write their own story in the book Weep For The Living.

Bibliography

INTERVIEWS

7-12-90 Ron Wikberg and Wilbert Rideau, The Angolite office, Louisiana State Penitentiary at Angola (present: Anne Butler, C. Murray Henderson)

7-16-90 Mr. and Mrs. Huey Miller, parents of Brent Miller, D'John's Restaurant, Star Hill, LA (present: Anne Butler, C. Murray Henderson)

7-31-90 Sheriff W. M. "Bill" Daniel, West Feliciana Parish Courthouse, St. Francisville, LA (present: Anne Butler, C. Murray Henderson)

8-10-90 Hayden Dees, by telephone - declined to be interviewed on Brent Miller case (Anne Butler)

8-30-90 Col. Mike Gunnells, Louisiana State Penitentiary at Angola (present: Anne Butler, C. Murray Henderson)

8-30-90 Ron Wikberg and Wilbert Rideau, The Angolite office, LSP at Angola (present: Anne Butler, C. Murray Henderson)

9-5-90 former Angola warden Hilton Butler, his home in Pinckneyville, MS (present: Anne Butler, C. Murray Henderson)

9-9-90 and 9-13-90 former inmate Bob Colle, St. Francisville, LA (present: Anne Butler, C. Murray Henderson)

9-11-90 Ron Wikberg and Wilbert Rideau, The Angolite office, LSP at Angola (present: Anne Butler, C. Murray Henderson)

9-18-90 Jewel Miller (Mrs. Huey Miller), D'John's Restaurant, Star Hill, LA (present: Anne Butler, C. Murray Henderson)

9-28-90 Lloyd Hoyle Jr., St. Francisville, LA (present: Anne Butler, C. Murray Henderson)

10-19-90 Warden Richard Wall, Cottonport, LA, by telephone (C. Murray Henderson)

10-22-90 William J. W. Kerr, Sr., his home in St. Francisville, LA (present: Anne Butler)

11-1-90 Michael Burge, Camp J, Louisiana State Penitentiary, Angola, LA (present: Anne Butler, C. Murray Henderson)

11-8-90 Nell and Malcolm Holmes, St. Francisville, LA (present: Anne Butler, C. Murray Henderson)

11-11-90 Nell Holmes, Baton Rouge, LA, by telephone (Anne Butler)

11-13-90 Nell and Malcolm Holmes, St. Francisville, LA (present: Anne Butler, C. Murray Henderson)

11-21-90 Ron Wikberg and Wilbert Rideau, Louisiana State Penitentiary, by telephone (Anne Butler)

11-22-90 Betty Lung, Hamersville, Ohio, by tape (Anne Butler)

11-28-90 Robert Shriver, Main Prison Complex Visiting Room, Louisiana State Penitentiary, Angola, LA (present: Anne Butler, C. Murray Henderson)

11-28-90 Hilton Butler, his home, Pinckneyville, MS (present: Anne Butler, C. Murray Henderson)

12-5-90 Jesse Means, Civil Defense office, St. Francisville, LA (present: Anne Butler, C. Murray Henderson)

12-7-90 Charles Griffin, attorney, his office, St. Francisville, LA, by telephone (Anne Butler)

12-17-90 Nell and Malcolm Holmes, St. Francisville, LA (present: Anne Butler, C. Murray Henderson)

12-20-90 Michael Burge, Louisiana State Penitentiary, Camp J, Angola, LA (present: Anne Butler, C. Murray Henderson)

12-20-90 U.S. Marshall Bo Garrison, U.S. Marshall's Office, Baton Rouge, LA, by telephone (C. Murray Henderson)

1-12-91 Chief Deputy Wallace Laird, St. Tammany Parish Sheriff's Department, his office by the courthouse in Covington, LA (present: Anne Butler, C. Murray Henderson)

1-12-91 Lt. Donald Sharp, St. Tammany Parish Sheriff's Department, courthouse, Covington, LA (present: Anne Butler, C. Murray Henderson)

1-12-91 Vernon and Elizabeth Harvey, Holiday Inn, Hammond, LA (present: Anne Butler, C. Murray Henderson)

1-13-91 John K. Willie, Holiday Inn, Hammond, LA (present: Anne Butler, C. Murray Henderson)

4-11/14-91 Kay Smith, St. Francisville, LA (present: Anne Butler, C. Murray Henderson)

4-12-91 Nick Trenticosta, Loyola Death Penalty Resource Center, New Orleans, LA, by telephone (Anne Butler)

4-12-91 National Coalition Against the Death Penalty, Washington, D.C., by telephone (Anne Butler)

4-12-91 Wellborn Jack, Jr. , Shreveport, LA, by telephone (Anne Butler)

4-25-91 Dr. Aris Cox, St. Francisville Inn, St. Francisville, LA (Anne Butler, C. Murray Henderson)

5-31-91 Bobby Oliveaux, dog pens, Louisiana State Penitentiary at Angola, LA (present: Anne Butler, C. Murray Henderson)

BOOKS

Politics and Punishment--The History of the Louisiana Penal System, Mark T. Carleton, LSU Press, Baton Rouge, 1971

Last Rights, Joseph B. Ingle, Abingdon Press, Nashville, 1990

The Crime of Punishment, Karl Menninger, MD, The Viking Press, New York, 1966

Corrections: Problems and Prospects, David M. Petersen and Charles W. Thomas, Prentice-Hall Inc., Englewood Cliffs, New Jersey, 1975

The Felicianian, St. Francisville High School, Volume XVIII, St. Francisville, Louisiana, 1968

The Wall Is Strong: Corrections In Louisiana, edited by Burk Foster, Wilbert Rideau and Ron Wikberg, The Center for Louisiana Studies, University of Southwestern Louisiana, Lafayette, Louisiana, 1991

Diagnostic and Statistical Manual of Mental Disorders, third edition-revised, American Psychiatric Association, Washington, D.C., 1987 (309.89 Post-traumatic Stress Disorder)

Post-Traumatic Stress Disorder--Diagnosis, Treatment and Legal Issues, C. B. Scrignar, MD, Bruno Press, New Orleans, Louisiana, second edition 1990.

MAGAZINES

THE ANGOLITE
November-December 1979 issue, "Prison: The Sexual Jungle" by Wilbert Rideau
May-June 1982 issue, "Vietnam: A Criminal Legacy"
July-August 1984 issue, "The Victims--The Tragedy of Faith"
January-February 1985 issue, "Death Watch-Louisiana"
May-June 1985 issue, News Briefs, "Iron-Mike Convicted"
May-June 1985 issue, Life or Death, "A Roll of the Dice" by Jason DeParle, Times-Picayune staffwriter, reprinted from the April 7, 1985, Times-Picayune (New Orleans)
March-April 1988 issue, "Death Watch: The Ides of March" by Ron Wikberg
January-February 1989 issue, "A Tale of Two Men" by Ron Wikberg
May-June 1989 issue, "The Omen" by Wilbert Rideau and Ron Wikberg
September-October 1989 issue, "Omen III" by Wilbert Rideau and Ron Wikberg
November-December 1898 issue, "Omen IV" by Floyd Webb
September-October 1990 issue, "Death Watch: The Horror Show" by Ron Wikberg
March-April 1991 issue, "Prison Crisis Ends" by James Minton, reprinted with permission

DETECTIVE
January 1972, "The Execution that Changed Your Life" by Webb Garrison

SPECTRUM
February 1973, Vol. 10, No. 2, "A Grand Success" by Theodore Bernstein

MEDICAL INSTRUMENTATION
November-December 1975, Vol. 9, No. 6, "Theories of the causes of death from electricity in the late nineteenth century" by Theodore Bernstein, Ph.D.

VANITY FAIR
November 1990, "Letter from San Quentin--Playing for Time" by Mark MacNamara

CORRECTIONS TODAY
August 1990, "Capital Punishment Gaining Favor As Public Seeks Retribution" by E.J. Dionne Jr.

PLAYBOY
January 1982, "The Unreturning Army" by Philip Caputo

THE NATION
January 2-9, 1982, "Viet-Vet Syndrome: The Long War of Wayne Felde" by Doug Magee
March 26, 1988, "Soldier's Home" by Doug Magee

TIME
February 11, 1991, "Behavior: Lost in America" by Paul A. Witteman
April 29, 1991, "Race and the Death Penalty" by Jill Smolowe

BOSTON: THE EDGE
June 16, 1986, "Death Row Vet" by Susan Benjamin

NEW ORLEANS MAGAZINE
March 1991, "PEN STATE, a Year in the Life of Angola" by Jason Berry

NEWSPAPER ARTICLES

MORNING ADVOCATE
4-2-72 "Angela Davis Tells of Love for Jackson"
4-5-72 miscellaneous articles giving flavor of the times
4-6-72 "Diggs Raps Rarick as Racist"
4-8-72 "Past, Present Back in Step in West Feliciana"
4-9-72 "Reds Extend Offensive to US Installation"; "Search For DB Cooper Continuing"
4-12-72 "Hearing for Eames Continues Thursday"; "Fired Prison Employee Claims
     Proper Discipline Neglected"
4-18-72 "Several Suspected in Killing at Angola"; Obituaries
4-19-72 "Guard Death Blame Pinned on Militants"
4-20-72 "Moon Landing Slated Today for Astronauts"; "Special Meeting to Probe Killing
     of Grand Jury (sic)"
4-21-72 "Spacemen Make Lunar Landing"
4-22-72 "Prison Guards Fail to Back up Threat" by Richard Munson
4-23-72 "Moon Mountain Tour Made in Lunar Rover"; "Angola Quiet After Threat of
     Walkout"
4-25-72 "Edwards Names Blacks to Posts"
4-26-72 "White House Reveals Peace Talks Resuming"; "Day Brings Walk"
4-27-72 "Number Quitting Posts at Angola is Exaggerated"; "Angola Receives New Fire
     Truck"; "Count Reveals Inmates Missing at Louisiana Prison"
4-28-72 "Representative Taylor Disowns Blame for Unrest at Angola Pen"
4-30-72 "Governor McKeithen Pauses to Take a Look"
5-2-72 "Guard Death Sees Four Face Charges" by Richard Munson
5-6-72 "Guard Death Sees Jurors Indict Blacks" by Richard Munson
5-13-72 "Corrections Director Takes Walking Tour of Prison" by Richard Munson
5-14-72 "The Penal System: A Tough Task Ahead" (editorial)
5-16-72 "Wallace Is Seriously Wounded"
5-24-72 "Representative Taylor, Mrs. Hunt--A Penal Reform Coalition Acknowledged"
     by Candace Lee
5-31-72 photo of Angola electric chair "Still Operational"
6-1-72 "To the Citizens of West Feliciana Parish" (paid advertisement)

6-3-72 "Kilbourne, West Feliciana Jury Agree on Pen Security Probe" by Richard Munson

6-17-72 "Trial of 4 Inmates in Guard Slaying Set"

7-16-72 "Pen Officials Remain Silent on Request"

7-25-72 "Death Row Men's Status To Be Mulled" by Richard Munson

7-29-72 "Angola Security Suit Sent to Another Judge"

9-14-72 "Grand Jury Angola Report Gives Few Suggestions" by Richard Munson

9-16-72 "Murder Trial of Inmates Shifted to East Feliciana"

10-7-72 "La. Inmate Gets Change of Venue"

1-10-73 "Newsman Remains in Coma One Year After Baton Rouge Violence" by Ed Cullen

1-10-73 "Recusal Hearing Slated In Angola Murder Trial"

1-13-73 "Trials of 4 Inmates Set in Slaying Case" by Richard Munson

3-6-73 "Trial Starts in Killing at Angola" by Richard Munson

3-7-73 "Inmate Tells of Stabbing at Angola" by Richard Munson

3-8-73 "Black Angola Inmate Convicted of Murder" by Richard Munson

5-2-73 "Trial for Trio Set May 14 in Guard's Death"

5-15-73 "DA Plans to Appeal Indictment Quash"

6-13-73 "Inmates Reportedly Not Told of Charges" by Deidre Cruse

1-9-74 "Inmate Testified He Witnessed Fatal Stabbing at the Penitentiary" by Deidre Cruse

1-10-74 "Prison Inmate Gives Evidence on Slaying of Guard at Angola" by Gibbs Adams

1-11-74 "Convict Complains About Jury Makeup" by Gibbs Adams

2-18-74 "Court Affirms Conviction of Angola Inmate"

10-6-76 "Newsman Bob Johnson Gets Hospital Release"

undated 78 "Another Refusal"

2-3-78 "Civil Court" by Yvonne G. Foreman

undated 1978 "Angola Deputy Warden's Suit Dismissed"

6-4-80 "Arkansas Arrests Suspects in Louisiana Rape-Shooting Case"

6-5-80 "Louisiana Kidnap-Rape Suspects Held on $500,000 Bond"

6-6-80 "Girl's Body Found Near Franklinton"

6-7-80 "Two Suspects To Be Returned in Louisiana Crimes"

6-13-80 "Two Louisiana Men Indicted in Kidnap of Couple"

8-22-80 "Defendant Asks For and Gets Death Verdict" - AP

10-22-80 "Murder Trials Begin in Death of Woman"

10-25-80 "Murder Convicts Face New Trial in Kidnap-Rape"

8-9-83 "3 Killed, 1 Hurt in Angola Stabbings" by Karen Didier, Baker-Zachary Bureau

8-10-83 "Grand jury to probe Angola stabbing deaths" by Karen Didier, Baker-Zachary Bureau

undated 8-83 "Two Inmates Indicted in Angola Stabbings" by Karen Didier, Baker-Zachary Bureau

undated 83 "Inmate Involved in Killings Asked for Protection"

3-1-84 "New execution dates set for Knighton, Willie"

3-1-84 "Edwards speaks on executions" by Marsha Shuler, capitol news bureau

12-29-84 "Family Members Believe Justice Served at Last" by Allen Pursnell

5-22-85 "Inmate Receives 3 Life Sentences" by Steve Culpepper, Baker-Zachary Bureau

3-15-88 "Wayne Felde Execution Appeals Denied" by Marsha Shuler, Capital News Bureau

6-22-89 "State of emergency declared at Angola" by Mark Lambert and John Semien

9-21-89 "Embalmer's report of inmate's injuries to be investigated"
9-22-89 "FBI enters Angola suicide probe" by James Minton and Marsha Shuler
5-18-90 "Prejean put to death" by Bill McMahon, Capitol news bureau
8-29-90 "Inmate who triggered LSP shakeup dies" by James Minton, Baker-Zachary bureau
9-11-90 "Expert to inspect every parish jail" by Mark Lambert
9-14-90 "Executions moving out of the South" by The Associated Press
9-30-90 "Appeals from La. death row going before Supreme Court" by Joan McKinney, Advocate Washington bureau
10-1-90 "State wants inmate to take medicine to allow execution" by Malcolm Ritter
10-3-90 "Justices explore La. death penalty case" by Joan McKinney, Advocate Washington bureau
10-5-90 "Polozola erred in refugee case, court is told" by Joe Gyan, Jr., New Orleans bureau
10-7-90 "Old Gallows Hangs Around Courthouse" by Steve Culpepper
11-14-90 "Supreme Court returns Perry case to state" by The Associated Press
11-18-90 "People in Government" by Anne Price
12-21-90 "Study Says Abuse at Home Major Factor in Later Violence" by Paul Recer, AP Science Writer
1-5-91 "U.S. has world's highest imprisonment rate, report says" by John Flesher, AP writer
1-7-91 "Doctors uneasy about lethal injection" by Don Colburn, The Washington Post
1-7-91 "Perry case poses hard questions" by Advocate news services
1-7-91 "Ministers and doctors express opposition to lethal injection" by Shirley Benton
1-7-91 "Death penalty state by state"
1-26-91 "Federal court hears testimony on electric chair" by Joe Gyan Jr., New Orleans bureau
1-27-91 "Judge says La. executions not cruel" by Joe Gyan Jr., New Orleans bureau
1-29-91 "U.S. Supreme Court refuses to rehear inmate Perry's case"
1-29-91 "Judge gives class-action status to state prison lawsuit" by John Semien
1-31-91 "State seeks end to Angola order" by Mark Lambert
2-4-91 "U.S. troops tense awaiting ground war--Soldiers fight cold, battle anxiety" by Susan Sachs, Newsday
2-9-91 "Sailor convicted of double murders" by Ron Word, AP writer
2-18-91 "Child Abuse study" in News Briefs from Advocate news services
2-21-91 "Camp J reserved for inmates' 'attitudes'" by James Minton, Baker-Zachary bureau
2-22-91 "Polozola lifts 20-month state of emergency at Angola" by Mark Lambert
3-4-91 "Mental war scars certain to run long and deep" by Paul Recer, AP science writer
3-4-91 "Vietnam vets' shouts of 'welcome home' loudest of all" by Lisa Levitt Ryckman, AP national writer
3-7-91 "Officials want electric chair replaced with lethal injections" by the AP
3-9-91 "Sheriffs' lawyer wants Corrections' letters halted" by Mark Lambert
3-10-91 "Warden working to normalize Angola" by James Minton, Baker-Zachary bureau
3-13-91 "La. prisoners' lawyer asks for drug-treatment center"
3-16-91 "Judge West looks back at his career" by Dennis Hanover, State-Times writer
3-18-91 "La. ranks third in nation in police brutality probes" by the AP
3-23-91 "Perry's lawyers oppose medication"
4-4-91 Deaths--"Burge Sr., Alfred Louis"

4-5-91 "Prison officials to train security officers in suicide intervention" by James Minton
4-29-91 "FBI annual report shows violent crime is up 10%" by Harry F. Rosenthal, AP
5-2-91 "Blood money"
5-23-91 "Futility of imprisonment" by William Raspberry
5-28-91 "Powell says Vietnam vets 'need no redemption'" by W. Dale Nelson, AP
6-8-91 "Judge says press can watch, but can't film executions" by Bob Egelko, AP
9-13-91 "Angola removes electric chair, installs gurney" by James Minton, Baker-Zachary bureau

BATON ROUGE STATE TIMES
3-7-73 "Trial Over Guard Death Continuing"
5-6-75 "TV Newsman Remains Incapacitated"
10-13-83 "Shreveport Bar Association Says Public Misdirected Anger Over Execution Stays," UPI
5-31-89 "Commentary: Cuts may be closing prison's safety valve" by James Minton

NEW ORLEANS TIMES-PICAYUNE
9-23-83 "Supreme Court is asked to delay killer's execution" by Charles O. Bell
3-4-88 "Viet vet awaiting execution feels betrayed" by James Hodge, staff writer
3-15-88 "Felde executed for cop-killing in 1978" by Bill Grady, staff writer
6-25-89 "Despair chains inmates destined to die at Angola" by Keith Woods, staff writer
7-20-90 "Convict: Execution was of wrong man" by John Fahey and James Varney, St. Tammany bureau

ST. FRANCISVILLE DEMOCRAT
5-4-72 "Four State Prison Inmates Charged in Miller Case"; "Committee of Grand Jury Still Meeting"
5-18-72 "Aldermen Accept Bid Water Main Construction" (sic)
7-20-72 "Parish Files Mandamus Suit on Prison Security"; "Police Jury Authorizes Mandamus Suit"; "Hearing Continued on Death Row Restraining Order"; "Correctional Officers Silent on Judge's Request"
7-27-72 "Judge Bennett Issues Death Row Injunction"
7-27-89 "Prisoners lose hope due to clemency situation" by Wilbert Rideau and Ron Wikberg
8-3-89 "Prisoners' clemency records need to be reviewed" by Wilbert Rideau and Ron Wikberg

BATON ROUGE ENTERPRISE
10-13-76 "Bob Johnson Back Home in Texas" by Timothy Talley

ST. HELENA (LA) ECHO
4-19-72 Obituaries

ST. TAMMANY (LA) NEWS-BANNER
7-18-90 "Inmate says wrong man died for 1980 murder" by Lou Major, Jr., Pontchartrain Newspapers

THE BOGALUSA (LA) DAILY NEWS

7-15-90 "Innocent man died for murder, Vaccaro says" by Lou Major, Jr., Editor

7-16-90 "Lawyer: Vaccaro is lying" by Lou Major, Jr., Editor

7-17-90 "Former D.A. Farmer agrees that Vaccaro's claim is a lie" by Lou Major, Jr., Editor

THE BUFFALO (N.Y.) NEWS

5-2-82 "Execution That Jolted World" by Joel Stashenko

NEWPORT (TN.) PLAIN TALK

9-3-90 "It's The Law" by John A. Bell, Attorney at Law

THE TENNESSEAN (Nashville)

10-13-85 "'Hanging Judge' Wrote First Chapter in State Executions" by Frank Ritter, Staff Writer

10-14-85 "2 Hanged: A Fun Day for 15,000" by Frank Ritter, Staff Writer

10-15-85 "Past Records Lopsided Justice" by Frank Ritter, Staff Writer

10-16-85 "11-Year-Old Condemned To Hang" by Frank Ritter, Staff Writer

10-17-85 "Executions: A Legacy of Doubt" by Frank Ritter, Staff Writer

10-20-85 "Executions Require MD, Cleric" by Frank Ritter, Staff Writer

10-21-85 "Final Requests Often Gave Bizarre Twist" by Frank Ritter, Staff Writer

10-28-85 "Grim Scenario: An Execution In Slow Motion" by Joseph Sweat

THE DAILY STATE (Baton Rouge)

10-29-06 "First Suicide in Penitentiary"

THE SHREVEPORT (LA) TIMES

10-21-78 "Officer Slain Here; Suspect is Wounded" by the Times staff

10-21-78 "Policeman Shot to Death"

10-22-78 "Maryland Fugitive--Police Say Suspect is Escaped Convict" by Robert Moore

10-22-78 Deaths - "Slain Officer's Services Set For Monday"

10-24-78 "Final Tribute Given Slain Officer" by Bobby Lamb of the Times staff

10-24-78 "Sister of Suspect is Arrested" by Dawn Waitt of the Times staff

10-26-78 Forum of the Times-- "A Policeman is Dead, We are Less For It" (letter to the editor from Robert Woods, Police Officer)

10-26-78 "Memorial Fund Started for Slain Officer's Family"

10-28-78 "Homicide Charge Filed in Shooting"

8-11-80 "Felde Jury Selection To Begin" by Linda Farrar of the Times staff

8-12-80 "Five Felde Trial Jurors Seated" by Linda Farrar

8-13-80 "Felde Jury Seated" by Linda Farrar

8-14-80 "Judge Orders Independent Mental Exam for Felde" by Linda Farrar

8-14-80 "Defense Concedes Felde in Police Car" by Linda Farrar

8-15-80 "Felde Witness Contradicts Officer's Version of Firing" by Linda Farrar

8-16-80 "High Court Bars Testing of Felde" by Linda Farrar

8-17-80 "Witness Supports Police Version of Felde Capture" by Linda Farrar

8-18-80 "Mother's Affadavit Read at Felde Trial" by Linda Farrar

8-19-80 "Witness Says Felde Intended to Kill Self" by Linda Farrar

8-20-80 "'Save the Plot Next to Mother's For Me'" by Linda Farrar

8-21-80 "Wayne Felde Found Guilty, Jury Returns Death Penalty" by Linda Farrar

ALEXANDRIA (LA) DAILY TOWN TALK
8-11-80 "Caddo Man Accused of Killing Policeman Goes on Trial Here"
8-14-80 "Prosecution May Wind Up Case Against Vietnam Vet"
8-15-80 "Suspect Getting Sanity Hearing"
8-20-80 "Suspect Offers to Kill Self"
8-21-80 "Felde Seeks, Receives Death Penalty" - UPI
7-24-89 "Angola inmates fault Roemer" by Linda Ashton, AP

PITTSBURGH POST-GAZETTE
3-23-88 "Black on Black: From Vietnam to death row" by Lawrence Young

EVENING STAR AND DAILY NEWS (Washington, DC)
11-29-72 "Shots Keep Police at Bay In Slaying"

REVIEW ADVERTISER/RED RIVER JOURNAL (Alexandria, LA)
6-27-84 "Convicted Murderer Clifton Again Seeking Clemency" by Michael J. Burns,
    Town Talk Staff Writer

THE LOUISIANA WEEKLY (New Orleans)
8-12-89 "Angola Inmates Seek a Voice; Mom Wants a Brutality Probe" by Allen
    Johnson, Jr.
9-16-89 "Funeral Home: Hanged Inmate Had Broken Back; Kin Sickened" by Allen
    Johnson, Jr.
2-24-90 "Appeals Add Tensions at Camp 'J'" by Allen Johnson, Jr.

THE WASHINGTON POST NATIONAL WEEKLY EDITION
7-8/14-91 "Lessons of Vietnam Aid a New Generation of War Wounded" by Brent
    Mitchell

**LEGAL REFERENCE BOOKS, COURT RECORDS, MEDICAL
CORRESPONDENCE AND OTHER REFERENCES**
Mrs. Brent Miller versus Deputy Warden Lloyd W. Hoyle, Jr., Warden Murray
    Henderson, Louis M. Sowers, Director, The Department of Corrections of the State
    of Louisiana, et al; Number 5231, 20th Judicial District Court, Parish of Louisiana,
    State of Louisiana; filed April 16, 1973.

Answer to Petition: Mrs. Brent Miller versus Deputy Warden Lloyd W. Hoyle Jr.,
    Warden C. Murray Henderson, Louis M. Sowers, Director, The Department of
    Corrections of the State of Louisiana, et al; Number 5231, 20th Judicial District
    Court, Parish of West Feliciana, State of Louisiana; answer filed by C. Murray
    Henderson.

Lloyd W. Hoyle, Jr., versus State of Louisiana, through the Department of Corrections;
    Number 160,897, Division D, 19th Judicial District Court, Parish of East Baton
    Rouge, State of Louisiana; defense attorney Stacey Moak.

State of Louisiana versus Gilbert Montegut and Herman Wallace; Number 10-73-6820, 19th Judicial District Court, Parish of East Baton Rouge, State of Louisiana, Judge Elmo Lear presiding (January 7-10, 1974).

State of Louisiana versus Michael Burge; Number W-83-8-1097, Division A, 20th Judicial District Court, Parish of West Feliciana, State of Louisiana, Judge William F. Kline, Jr., presiding ((April 8-12, 1985); Stephen Laiche, DA ad hoc and Assistant Attorney General, for the state, Michael McDonald and David E. Stanley attorneys for the defendant; 538 pages.

Case W-83-8-1097, Criminal docket of 20th Judicial District Court in and for the parish of West Feliciana, State of Louisiana, Honorable William F. Kline presiding. State of Louisiana respondent versus Michael Burge relator. Application by defendant relator Michael Burge for writ of certiorari to Court of Appeal, 1st Circuit, Parish of East Baton Rouge, State of Louisiana, Docket Number KA-85-0899, Honorable Grover L. Covington, Honorable J. Louis Watkins, Honorable Melvin A. Shortess, presiding.

Statement of the District Attorney, First Judicial District Court, Parish of Caddo; Venue Changed to Ninth Judicial District Court, Parish of Rapides; Name of Offender: Wayne Robert Feld, a/k/a Harold "Harry" Hershey, WM, Docket No. 109,803 in Caddo, No. 196,240 in Rapides; signed Guy E. Humphries, Jr., District Judge, Ninth Judicial District, Rapides Parish, Louisiana; signed Dale G. Cox, Assistant District Attorney, Caddo Parish, Louisiana.

Correspondence from R. Fred Marceau, M.D., 827 Margaret Place, Shreveport, LA 71101, to Criminal Minute Clerk, First District Court, Caddo Parish Courthouse, Shreveport, LA 71102, Re: Wayne Robert Felde, No. 109,803, dated February 8, 1979, filed in courthouse February 12, 1979.

Correspondence from Andrew Young, Mayor, Atlanta, Georgia, to Mr. Lawrence Hand, Chairman, Louisiana Board of Pardons, 504 Mayflower Street, Baton Rouge, Louisiana, recommending clemency for Wayne Felde, dated March 2, 1988.

Correspondence from Mrs. Coretta Scott King, The Martin Luther King, Jr., Center for Nonviolent Social Change, Inc., 449 Auburn Avenue NE, Atlanta, Georgia 30312, to Mr. Lawrence Hand, Chairman, Louisiana Board of Pardons, 504 Mayflower St., Baton Rouge, Louisiana 70802, recommending clemency for Wayne Felde, dated March 2, 1988.

Opening Statement of Watt Espy, Capital Punishment Research Project, University of Alabama Law Center, Tuscaloosa, Alabama, at a Round Table Discussion of the Issues Raised for Press Coverage by Death Penalty Law and Executions, June 29, 1985.

Supreme Court of the State of Louisiana: State of Louisiana, plaintiff and appellee, versus Wayne Robert Felde, defendant and appellant; Appeal from Ninth Judicial District Court for the Parish of Rapides, State of Louisiana, Honorable Guy E. Humphries, Jr., trial judge, counsel for the state B. Woodrow Nesbitt, Jr., counsel for the defense N. Graves Thomas, Criminal Docket No. 196,240; 11 volumes, 2499 pages.

State of Maryland versus Wayne Robert Felde, Criminal Trials Number 12,865.

State of Louisiana versus Wayne Robert Felde aka Harold Hershey, Caddo Parish Docket No. 109,803.

State of Louisiana versus Florence Yvonne McDonald, First Judicial District Court, Parish of Caddo, State of Louisiana; Honorable Paul Lynch judge; counsel for the state Dale G. Cox, Assistant District Attorney; Don Minor, Indigent Defender's Office; Graves Thomas, counsel for Wayne Robert Felde; Criminal Number 109,636.

State of Louisiana versus Francis Aubrey Clifton, 172 So. 2d 657 (1965).

Louisiana State Penitentiary, Violence and Mortality Statistics, 1965 through 1990.

Parents of Murdered Children, Chapter Leader and Contact Person Training Manual, Compiled and Edited by Nancy K. Ruhe under a grant from the Office for Victims of Crime, Office of Justice Programs, U.S. Department of Justice; additional POMC materials including issues of newsletter "Survivors" and 1991 Calendar.

Letter to Francis A. Clifton from Fred S. Berlin, M.D., Ph.D., The Johns Hopkins University School of Medicine, 601 N. Broadway, Baltimore, Maryland 21205, dated September 4, 1984.

CORRESPONDENCE AND UNPUBLISHED WRITINGS

May, June, July, August, September, October, November 1990: almost daily letters from Michael Burge to Nell and Malcolm Holmes.

Voluminous correspondence and ARPs (Administrative Remedy Procedures) between Michael Burge and officials of the Louisiana State Penitentiary at Angola, the Louisiana Department of Public Safety and Corrections, various politicians and medical staff, attorneys and court officials.

"Looking Back," poem by Liz D. Harvey

"The Families Praise," poem left anonymously at Angola gate for the Harvey family after Robert Lee Willie's execution; Elizabeth Harvey attributes it to a member of the group there to support the victim's family.

Letter to Vernon and Elizabeth Harvey from inmate David E. Nicholson, Larned, Kansas, January 18, 1985.

Letter to Managing Editor Al Hansen, The Daily News, Bogalusa, LA, from Joseph Vaccaro, Leavenworth, Kansas, June 10, 1990.

Letter to Managing Editor Al Hansen, The Daily News, Bogalusa, LA, from Joseph Vaccaro, Leavenworth, Kansas, postmarked July 11, 1990.

Letter and case statement to Director Ira Glaser of the American Civil Liberties Union, New York, and Director Alvin J. Bronstein of The National Prison Project, Washington, D.C., from Joseph Vaccaro, Leavenworth, Kansas, June 2, 1990.

Letter to Ronald Reagan, President of the United States of America, White House, Washington, D.C., from Wayne Robert Felde, #100237, Death Row, Angola, Louisiana 70712, dated April 7, 1986 (unanswered).

Letters to Kay Smith, Maryland, from Wayne Robert Felde, Death Row, Louisiana State Penitentiary at Angola, LA, dated February 17, 1988, through March 14, 1988, the day before he was executed.

Letters to Anne Butler from Betty Lung, Hamersville, Ohio, concerning Francis A. Clifton, dated October 1990 through April 1991, quoting from letters written by Clifton to Lung.

Index

177

CPSIA information can be obtained
at www.ICGtesting.com
Printed in the USA
FFOW04n1804050118
44364261-44054FF

9 781935 754565